THE
HISTORY OF
IRELAND

THE HISTORY OF IRELAND

Daniel Webster Hollis III

The Greenwood Histories of the Modern Nations
Frank W. Thackeray and John E. Findling, Series Editors

GREENWOOD PRESS
Westport, Connecticut • London

Library of Congress Cataloging-in-Publication Data

Hollis, Daniel Webster, 1942–
    The history of Ireland / Daniel Webster Hollis III.
      p. cm.—(The Greenwood histories of the modern nations, ISSN 1096–2905)
    Includes bibliographical references (p.   ) and index.
    ISBN 0–313–31281–8 (alk. paper)
      1. Ireland—History. 2. Northern Ireland—History. I. Title. II. Series.
    DA910.H65   2001
    941.6—dc21   00–052136

British Library Cataloguing in Publication Data is available.

Library of Congress Catalog Card Number: 00–052136
ISBN: 0–313–31281–8
ISSN: 1096–2905

First published in 2001

Greenwood Press, 88 Post Road West, Westport, CT 06881
An imprint of Greenwood Publishing Group, Inc.
www.greenwood.com

Printed in the United States of America

The paper used in this book complies with the
Permanent Paper Standard issued by the National
Information Standards Organization (Z39.48–1984).

10 9 8 7 6 5 4 3 2 1

Contents

Series Foreword

The Greenwood Histories of the Modern Nations series is intended to provide students and interested laypeople with up-to-date, concise, and analytical histories of many of the nations of the contemporary world. Not since the 1960s has there been a systematic attempt to publish a series of national histories, and, as series editors, we believe that this series will prove to be a valuable contribution to our understanding of other countries in our increasingly interdependent world.

Over thirty years ago, at the end of the 1960s, the Cold War was an accepted reality of global politics, the process of decolonization was still in progress, the idea of a unified Europe with a single currency was unheard of, the United States was mired in a war in Vietnam, and the economic boom of Asia was still years in the future. Richard Nixon was president of the United States, Mao Tse-tung (not yet Mao Zedong) ruled China, Leonid Brezhnev guided the Soviet Union, and Harold Wilson was prime minister of the United Kingdom. Authoritarian dictators still ruled most of Latin America, the Middle East was reeling in the wake of the Six-Day War, and Shah Reza Pahlavi was at the height of his power in Iran. Clearly, the past thirty years have been witness to a great deal of historical change, and it is to this change that this series is primarily addressed.

With the help of a distinguished advisory board, we have selected nations whose political, economic, and social affairs mark them as among the most important in the waning years of the twentieth century, and for each nation we have found an author who is recognized as a specialist in the history of that nation. These authors have worked most cooperatively with us and with Greenwood Press to produce volumes that reflect current research on their nation and that are interesting and informative to their prospective readers.

The importance of a series such as this cannot be underestimated. As a superpower whose influence is felt all over the world, the United States can claim a "special" relationship with almost every other nation. Yet many Americans know very little about the histories of the nations with which the United States relates. How did they get to be the way they are? What kind of political systems have evolved there? What kind of influence do they have in their own region? What are the dominant political, religious, and cultural forces that move their leaders? These and many other questions are answered in the volumes of this series.

The authors who have contributed to this series have written comprehensive histories of their nations, dating back to prehistoric times in some cases. Each of them, however, has devoted a significant portion of the book to events of the past thirty years, because the modern era has contributed the most to contemporary issues that have an impact on U.S. policy. Authors have made an effort to be as up-to-date as possible so that readers can benefit from the most recent scholarship and a narrative that includes very recent events.

In addition to the historical narrative, each volume in this series contains an introductory overview of the country's geography, political institutions, economic structure, and cultural attributes. This is designed to give readers a picture of the nation as it exists in the contemporary world. Each volume also contains additional chapters that add interesting and useful detail to the historical narrative. One chapter is a thorough chronology of important historical events, making it easy for readers to follow the flow of a particular nation's history. Another chapter features biographical sketches of the nation's most important figures in order to humanize some of the individuals who have contributed to the historical development of their nation. Each volume also contains a comprehensive bibliography, so that those readers whose interest has been sparked may find out more about the nation and its history. Finally, there is a carefully prepared topic and person index.

Readers of these volumes will find them fascinating to read and useful in understanding the contemporary world and the nations that comprise it. As series editors, it is our hope that this series will contribute to a heightened sense of global understanding as we enter a new century.

Frank W. Thackeray and John E. Findling
Indiana University Southeast

Preface

This single-volume history of Ireland is part of the *Histories of the Modern Nations* series, published by Greenwood Press. The aim is to acquaint nonspecialists with the basic contours of modern states, emphasizing the twentieth century. The format includes a chronological timeline of major events from prehistory to 2000. It also provides brief biographical sketches of major figures in Irish history who are referred to in the text. Most of those listed have their own biographies for the reader who wishes to pursue in-depth reading.

I am grateful for the opportunity to participate in Greenwood's ambitious project. In particular, I appreciate the steady guidance and encouragement of Greenwood editors Barbara Rader and Heidi Straight and the series editor with whom I worked, Frank Thackeray, whose wisdom and experience I frequently tapped. Corrections by manuscript editor Beverly Miller enhanced the text. Two professional friends, who are experts on aspects of Irish history, read and critiqued various chapters of a draft version of the manuscript. My thanks to Tom Auffenberg and John D. Fair for their invaluable insights, suggestions, and corrections, which helped improve this book. I am also indebted to Fair's graduate students—Mauriel Joslyn, David Morgan, and Brian Veal—for reading a draft version and offering helpful comments. Donald Paxton gave valuable advice regarding economic issues. Thanks to Steven G. Ellis, National University, Galway, and Marie Bolger, University College, Dublin, for providing specific information. Jacksonville State University generously awarded me professional leave to complete the manuscript. As always, the staff of the Jacksonville State University library graciously assisted me in securing needed materials. I am especially grateful to Debra Thompson, Mary Bevis, and Jodi Poe. My wife, Lynda, remained patient and tolerated my preoccupation with the project throughout. I alone am responsible for whatever imperfections or errors remain.

Timeline of Historical Events

841	First Ostmen settlement in Ireland at Dublin
1014	Brian Boru, "king of Ireland," defeats Ostmen at Battle of Clontarf but is killed
1086	Death of Turlough O'Brien, high king of Leinster, Connacht, and Munster
1142	Malachy founds first Cistercian monastery at Mellifont; Latin liturgy replaces Gaelic
1152	Synod of Kells; Roman episcopal system displaces Celtic monastic church governance
1166	Diarmait MacMurrough, king of Leinster and Munster, expelled from Ireland
1169	Anglo-Norman invasion begins; Strongbow invades Ireland from Wales
1175	Treaty of Windsor; Irish chiefs recognize England's Henry II as king of Ireland
1210	King John lands in Ireland to reestablish royal authority over Anglo-Norman nobles
1299	First full Irish Parliament meets
1315	Edward Bruce of Scotland invades Ulster, followed by brother Robert in 1316
1317	Edward II sends English army to Ireland under Roger Mortimer to oust Scots
1366	Statutes of Kilkenny secure English rule within the Pale around Dublin
1394–1395	Richard II lands in Ireland to restore royal authority
1436	*Libel of English Policy* warns English monarchs of need to secure Ireland
1478	Earl of Kildare begins thirty-five-year tenure as deputy lieutenant of Ireland
1495	Poynings' Law prohibits independent Irish Parliament action
1519	Henry VIII begins Anglicization of Irish political rule
1536–1537	Protestant Church of Ireland established by Parliament; earl of Kildare executed

1567	Rebellion of Shane O'Neill, earl of Tyrone, ends with his death
1584	Elizabeth I authorizes Munster English colonization project
1591	Trinity College, Dublin, founded; became center of Anglo-Irish education and culture
1603	Lord Mountjoy defeats Hugh O'Neill, earl of Tyrone, in Ulster
1609	English colonization of Ulster begins
1625	Scholar-cleric James Ussher named archbishop of Armagh (Church of Ireland)
1641	Irish Catholic rebellion against English led by Owen Roe O'Neill
1649	Oliver Cromwell's army defeats and slaughters Catholic rebels at Drogheda
1654	Sir William Petty's "Down Survey" and confiscation of Irish Catholic lands
1662	Duke of Ormond becomes Charles II's lord lieutenant seeking justice for Catholics
1687	James II names a Catholic lord lieutenant, Richard Talbot, earl of Tyrconnell
1689	Deposed James II lands at Kinsale with French troops to reclaim his throne
1690	William of Orange defeats James's Catholic army at Battle of the Boyne
1691	Treaty of Limerick restores Protestant ascendancy; most Catholic lands confiscated
1720	Declaratory Act reasserts sovereignty of British Parliament over Ireland
1724	Jonathan Swift's *Drapier's Letters* attack crown's patent for Wood's halfpence
1735	George Berkeley begins journal the *Querist* seeking justice for Irish peasants
1742	First performance of Handel's *Messiah* at Dublin Music Hall

1761	Edmund Burke's *A Tract on the Popery Laws* criticizes treatment of Irish Catholics
1782	Irish self-government approved by Britain; Henry Flood and Henry Grattan lead Parliament
1791	Theobald Wolfe Tone and United Irishmen demand broader franchise
1793	Catholic Relief Act allows Catholics to vote but not to sit in Parliament
1795	Orange Order established by Protestants in Ulster to oppose Catholic threat
1798	United Irishmen rebellion crushed; Tone is arrested and commits suicide
1800	Act of Union ends Irish Parliament; representation in United Kingdom Parliament
1808	Thomas Moore's *Melodies* beginning of romantic Irish nationalism
1811	First Ribbon Society founded in Ulster to promote Irish nationalism
1823	Daniel O'Connell creates Catholic Association to lobby for Catholic emancipation
1829	O'Connell's election to Parliament forces passage of Catholic Emancipation Act
1842	Thomas Davis and Charles Gavan Duffy launch *Nation* magazine to promote "Young Ireland" nationalism
1845	Potato famine begins; 1 million deaths by 1851; 1.5 million emigrate by 1861
1848	Irish nationalist rising crushed; William Smith O'Brien and John Mitchel transported to Australia
1850	Duffy helps establish Irish Tenant League seeking agrarian reforms
1858	James Stephens creates Irish Republican Brotherhood to promote Irish independence
1859	John O'Mahoney founds Fenian Brotherhood in United States; allied with Irish Republican Brotherhood
	Irish Times begins publication as daily newspaper

1862	Harland and Wolff shipbuilding company started in Belfast
1866	Paul Cullen, archbishop of Dublin, named Ireland's first cardinal
1869	Irish Church Act disestablishes Church of Ireland
1870	Gladstone's Land Act grants several rights to Irish tenants
1873	Isaac Butt changes Home Government Association (1870) to Home Rule League
1879	Charles Stewart Parnell elected president of Davitt's Irish National Land League
1882	Kilmainham Treaty ends land war; Irish chief secretary murdered in Phoenix Park
1884	Michael Cusack forms Gaelic Athletic Association
1886	Gladstone's Irish home rule bill defeated in Commons
1890	Parnell divorce splits Irish party; John Redmond leads Parnellites; Justin McCarthy, antis
1893	Gladstone's second home rule bill passes House of Commons but is defeated in House of Lords
	Douglas Hyde organizes Gaelic League to promote Irish language
1894	Horace C. Plunkett founds Irish Agricultural Organization Society
	Irish Trade Union Congress holds first meeting
1895	Oscar Wilde's *The Importance of Being Earnest* published
1898	William O'Brien forms United Irish League to promote land reform
1899	George Moore and William Butler Yeats found Irish National Theater
1904	George Bernard Shaw's *John Bull's Other Island* reveals Anglo-Irish stereotypes
1905	William Murphy founds *Irish Independent* daily newspaper
	Ulster Unionist Council to oppose home rule; led by Sir Edward Carson
1907	John Myllington Synge's controversial *Playboy of the Western World* staged

	Sinn Féin League launched by Arthur Griffith to create a republic
1908	James Larkin and James Connolly found Irish Transport and General Workers Union
1914	Irish Labour party founded with help of Larkin and Irish Trade Union Congress
	Third home rule bill passed but suspended for duration of World War I
	James Joyce's *Dubliners* published
1916	Irish Republican Brotherhood declares Republic with Patrick Pearse as president
	Republican Easter Rebellion crushed in Dublin; leaders including Pearse executed
1917–1918	Irish Convention of Catholics and Protestants fails to find compromise solution
1919	Sinn Féin declares republic; Irish Republican Army begins war for independence
1920	Government of Ireland Act creates two Irish states
1921	Northern Ireland Parliament meets with Sir James Craig as prime minister
	War for independence ends; Anglo-Irish Treaty creates Irish Free State in south
1922	Dáil Éireann ratifies treaty; provisional government named; IRA insurgency begins
1923	Cumann na nGaedheal wins Dáil election; William Cosgrave president of council
	William Butler Yeats wins Nobel Prize for literature
1925	Boundary Commission report scrapped; no Free State–Northern Ireland changes
1926	Eamon de Valera creates Fianna Fáil party; G. B. Shaw wins Nobel Prize for literature
1929	Proportional representation abolished for Northern Ireland Parliament
1932	Fianna Fáil forms first Free State government headed by Eamon de Valera

1933	Fine Gael party created from Cumann na nGaedheal and two other parties
1937	New constitution approved for Éire as de facto republic; de Valera elected Taoiseach
1938	Anglo-Irish Agreement ends trade war between Éire and Britain
1939	World War II begins in Europe; Éire declares its neutrality
1940	John Andrews succeeds Sir James Craig as Unionist leader and Northern Ireland prime minister
1943	Basil Brooke named Northern Ireland prime minister
1946	Clann na Poblachta party created
1948	Fine Gael's John Costello elected Taoiseach; Republic of Ireland proclaimed
1951	Fianna Fáil and de Valera return to power
1955	Republic of Ireland joins United Nations
1958	T. K. Whitaker's economic development plan adopted in the Republic
1959	de Valera elected Republic president; Fianna Fáil's Sean Lemass becomes Taoiseach
1961	Radio Telefís Éireann begins television broadcasting in the Republic
1963	Terence O'Neill becomes prime minister of Northern Ireland
1965	Sean Lemass and Terence O'Neill exchange visits and begin dialogue of north-south relations
1966	Jack Lynch succeeds Lemass as Fianna Fáil leader and Taoiseach of Republic
1967	Northern Ireland Civil Rights Association founded; protests begin in 1968
1969	James Chichester-Clark replaces O'Neill as Northern Ireland prime minister
	Playwright Samuel Beckett wins Nobel Prize for literature
1970	Catholic moderate Social Democratic and Labour party organized in Northern Ireland

1971   Presbyterian Reverend Ian Paisley establishes Democratic Unionist party in Northern Ireland

1972   Bloody Sunday in Derry; British direct rule begins in Northern Ireland

1973   Anglo-Irish Sunningdale Conference; Republic joins European Economic Community

1979   Pope John Paul II visits Republic; Fianna Fáil's Charles Haughey elected Taoiseach

1981   Republican prisoners' hunger strike at Maze Prison in Northern Ireland

1982   Fine Gael-Labour government in Republic; Garret Fitz-Gerald Taoiseach

1985   Anglo-Irish Hillsborough Agreement on Northern Ireland

1987   Fianna Fáil government in Republic with Charles Haughey as Taoiseach

1990   Fianna Fáil's Mary Robinson becomes highest elected woman as president of Republic

1993   Fianna Fáil-Labour coalition with Albert Reynolds as Taoiseach

1994   Fine Gael's John Bruton elected Taoiseach

1995   David Trimble replaces James Molyneaux as leader of Ulster Unionist party

        Seamus Heaney wins Nobel Prize for literature

1997   Fianna Fáil-Progressive Democrat coalition; Bertie Ahern elected Taoiseach

1998   All-party signing of Good Friday Agreement for devolved Northern Ireland government

        Northern Ireland's John Hume and David Trimble awarded Nobel Peace Prize

2000   Northern Ireland multiparty executive and assembly elected; suspended February through May

1

Ireland Today

For a state with a relatively small territory and population, Ireland's influence in the English-speaking world is remarkable. Emigration from Ireland to Britain and America, which remained steady throughout most of the nineteenth and twentieth centuries, has produced Irish descendants abroad in much larger numbers than the population of Ireland itself. For example, it is estimated that 44 million descendants of Irish lineage lived in the United States in 2000. Hence, Irish popular cultural traditions such as St. Patrick's Day (March 17), the Irish shamrock, the Blarney stone, the Irish sweepstakes, mythical leprechauns, and other items remain large in the practices of millions outside of Ireland proper. Irish products such as Guinness beer and Waterford crystal have also become entrenched in Irish communities abroad. Irish culture is constantly exported to the English-speaking world. For example, Irish-American Michael Flatley's revival of traditional Celtic dancing, *Riverdance*, garnered huge audiences in tours outside Ireland in the late 1990s. Even Irish sports figures have secured international recognition such as two-time (1999 and 2000) British Senior Open golf champion Christy O'Connor of Galway.

GEOGRAPHY

Anciently known as Hibernia (Latin) or Erin (Celtic), Ireland is the smaller of the two large British isles covering 32,374 square miles, or about the size of Maine in the United States. The island's especially jagged coastline extends for 2,200 miles. The Republic of Ireland makes up 27,137 square miles, and the six counties of Ulster, which constitute Northern Ireland, contain 5,237 square miles. The heartland is a large, level area peppered with lakes and bogs. Ireland's rugged western coastline receives the brunt of the stormy westerly North Atlantic winds and rains (an average of sixty inches annually), so that few trees exist there. The west coast has never been an attractive site for ports and trade compared with the protected eastern shoreline along the Irish Sea. There are several modest mountain ranges, and the highest point, 3,414 feet, is in the southwestern mountains of Kerry at Carrantuohill. Most woodlands composed largely of oak trees have been deforested; only 3 percent of surface land in Ireland is wooded today.

The Shannon River, flowing north to south across the western portion of Ireland, is the longest in the British Isles, emptying into the North Atlantic 224 miles from its origin. Other rivers include the Suir, Barrow, Slaney, Boyne, Liffey, Lee, and Nore. Ireland possesses several large interior lakes, called *loughs*, the largest being Lough Neagh in Ulster. Of the many small offshore islands, Aran, Achill, and Clare are the most populous. Ireland was able to transform its numerous peat bogs, otherwise a nuisance, into a fuel, and peat is now regarded as a valuable natural resource. The ample rainfall gives the island a verdant green appearance, which is the basis of the nickname "Emerald Isle." Despite Ireland's northerly location, the gulf stream ensures a mild climate, with an average winter temperature of 40 degrees Fahrenheit and an average of 60 degrees in the summer.

The island has traditionally been divided into four provinces, the boundaries of which have changed little over two millennia: Leinster in the east, Munster in the south, Connacht in the west, and Ulster in the north. There are thirty-two counties within the four provinces—twenty-six in the Republic and six in Northern Ireland. Until the second half of the twentieth century, Ireland's geographical isolation served to maintain a high degree of insularity from all areas except Britain.

DEMOGRAPHY

The population of Ireland has never been large, though its peak of just over 8 million before the 1840s famine has never been matched. The 1996

Ireland's Geography from *An Atlas of Irish History* by Ruth Dudley Edwards (London: Methuen, 1973), p. 22. Courtesy of Routledge (Methuen).

Provinces and Counties from *The Irish Experience* by Thomas E. Hachey and Joseph M. Hernon, Jr. © 1990. Reprinted by permission of Prentice-Hall, Inc., Upper Saddle River, NJ.

census put the total at 3.62 million in the Republic and another 1.65 million in Northern Ireland. About 21 percent of the population in the Republic is age 15 years or younger, 67 percent between the ages of fifteen and sixty-four, and those 65 years or older make up 12 percent of the total. Life expectancy in Ireland has risen to among the highest in the world, at 73.64 years for males and 79.32 years for females, an increase of 23 and 17 years, respectively, from the mid-1920s. The birthrate of 13.58 per 1,000 is notably higher than the death rate of 8.43 per 1,000. The World Health Organization ranks the Republic's health care system nineteenth out of 191 nations surveyed in 2000. Ireland spends 6.2% of gross domestic product (GDP, the total of all goods and services produced in Ireland, including foreign investments and industries) on health care compared with 5.8 percent in the United Kingdom and 13.7 percent in the United States.

Although the rural farming class typified the Irish population for centuries, by 2000 the number of farmers had declined to 146,000, and projections suggest losing another 4,000 over the next decade. A large urban middle class has replaced farmers as the more prominent population segment, with 58 percent of the Republic's population being urban. With a population of 481,000, Dublin's place in the nation resembles the London metropolis's premiere status in England. Cork is the second largest city in the Republic, with a population of 127,000. Belfast remains the major urban center of Northern Ireland, with a population of 300,000.

RELIGION

The religious makeup of the Republic has changed little throughout the twentieth century, with Catholics accounting for 93 percent of the total. The religious lines in Northern Ireland follow the mostly segregated residential communities, with Protestants making up about 57 percent of the population and Catholics the remaining 43 percent. More Catholics live in western Ulster, while Protestants retain majorities in the east.

EDUCATION

Schools in both the Republic and Northern Ireland retain a strong sectarian element with religious instruction. Compulsory attendance at school is required in the Republic and Northern Ireland for children ages six to fifteen. The dropout rate past the primary grades has remained high in the Republic. The Republic's National University has three campuses, in Dublin, Cork, and Galway, while Queen's University in Belfast is the main institution of higher learning in Northern Ireland. Although the purported literacy rate is 100 percent, a June 2000 survey by Europe's Organization for Economic Cooperation and Development (OECD) revealed that 25 percent of Irish adults were functionally illiterate and another 20 percent semiliterate. The OECD also reported in mid-2000 that Republic spending on public education had declined from 4.7 percent of GDP in 1990 to 4.5 percent in 2000, ranking Ireland in the lower third of world industrialized states. Although Gaelic instruction is mandatory in the schools of the Republic, an increasingly smaller percentage of residents use the language for daily discourse, preferring instead to rely on English.

ECONOMICS

The Republic's currency is the Irish pound (or Punt Éireannach), which is subject to regulation by the Central Bank. Ireland is participating in the European Monetary System (1979), which has created a European currency designed to supersede all national currencies in the European Union at some near future date. Republic debt in mid-2000 totaled £31 billion, less than 50 percent of GDP, the lowest debt ratio after Luxembourg in Europe. Northern Ireland's currency is the British pound sterling, which also will likely be subject to the European currency unification, although the British government has not given final approval to that merger. The Republic's GDP in 1996 was £42 billion, or £11,667 (U.S. $18,667) per person. The Republic has attained a favorable balance of trade. In 1997, exports totaled £41.3 billion compared with imports of £31.5 billion. The United Kingdom, Germany, the United States, and France were primary purchasers of Irish products, while Ireland's import purchases came mostly from the United Kingdom, the United States, Germany, and Japan.

Regarding the labor force, service industries comprise about 62 percent of the 1.52 million workers in the Republic. Industry employs 27 percent of the workforce, while only 10 percent labor in agricultural areas. Further, agriculture has changed from predominantly small farmers to larger commercial farming, which exports cattle products and wool. Only 13 percent of the land is for arable crop use compared to 68 percent for pasture and 5 percent forest lands. The Republic has over 7 million cattle, almost 6 million sheep, and just under 2 million pigs. Fisheries brought in almost 300,000 metric tons in 1997. Traditional Irish agricultural products and related industries such as textiles and brewing have given way to high-technology industries such as computer software. Indeed, Ireland has become the major European producer of software, second to the United States in the world. The major Irish software companies are Baltimore Technologies, Iona Technology, Trintech, and Smartforce. In addition, American firms such as Intel, Cisco Systems, and Lucent Technologies maintain large production facilities in the Irish Republic. Although the number of Internet users in 1998 was only 15 per 1,000 compared to the United States's 112, the Irish figure is rising steadily. Tourists, averaging 4.2 million annually in the late 1990s, also contribute a major share of the economy, totaling £1.11 billion in 1997. The decline of the shipbuilding and linen industries in Northern Ireland has created the need for innovative new industries.

TRANSPORTATION

Transportation facilities are led by coastal shipping and the ports, such as Dublin, Belfast, Cork, and Limerick. The national agency Iarnrod Éireann supervises the passenger rail system. The Republic has 1,947 kilometers of railroad track connecting all major regions and cities. Republic railroads operate through a state agency, Córas Iompair Éireann (CIE), and are connected with Northern Ireland's Great Northern Railway. In 1987, CIE was divided into Bus Éireann and Iarnrod Éireann (trains). The Republic has over 1 million passenger motor vehicles traveling the 92,500 kilometers of roads and highways. Nine airports in the Republic handle traffic internally, with facilities at Shannon, Dublin, and Cork offering connections for international routes. The state airline, Aer Lingus, faces domestic competition from private companies such as Ryanair, as well as international lines.

MEDIA

The Republic has a high ratio of newspaper readers, led by Dublin dailies such as the *Irish Times* (circulation 113,000 in 1999) and the *Irish Independent* (circulation 166,000 in 1999), and the Cork *Irish Examiner* (circulation 61,000 in 1999) which has recently decided to compete as a national paper. There are 900,000 telephones in the Republic. Although the state-owned Radio Telefís Éireann (RTE) operates fifty-four radio and ten television broadcast stations, they offer limited programming through Telecom Éireann, modeled after the British Broadcasting Corporation. Irish listeners and viewers can receive broadcasts easily from Britain and parts of Europe as well. The Irish must purchase a television license to receive broadcasts—£70 (U.S. $152) for color sets and £52 (U.S. $83) for black and white. The 1998 income from license sales totaled £63 (U.S. $100) million. Telecom Éireann became a publicly owned company (Éirecom) in July 1999 with the offering of individual shares.

ARTS

Additional state support of the arts comes through funding subsidies coordinated by the Ministry of Arts, Heritage, Gaeltacht, and the Islands (originally created in 1993 as Ministry of Arts, Culture and the Gaeltacht). The ministry supervises such state cultural institutions as the National Museum, National Library, National Gallery, National Archives, and National Concert Hall. One of the major recent projects was a £50 (U.S. $80) million appropriation for the restoration of Dublin's Abbey Theater, which will celebrate its centennial in 2004. The Abbey was destroyed by fire in 1951 and rebuilt in 1966.

GOVERNMENT AND POLITICS

The representative political system in the Republic of Ireland resembles most states of Europe and North America today. Since the creation of the Irish Free State in 1922, the Parliament and local councils are elected by the distinctive system of proportional representation, which involves the single-transferable vote in multi-member constituencies. Voters rank choices of candidates so that when no candidate wins a majority, votes for second and lower choices may be transferred to alternate candidates until a majority is achieved. The intent of proportional representation is to promote smaller, regional political parties and prevent domination by larger parties. Two attempts to amend the constitution in the second half of the twentieth century to create a direct vote system failed in the popular vote. The Republic's central government has its capital at Dublin and consists of a bicameral parliament (Oireachtas), with five-year terms for members. The lower house, the Dáil Éireann, comprising 166 seats, is elected by proportional voting with multiple constituencies. The upper house, the Seanad or senate, totaling 60 seats, is appointed and does not have equal constitutional authority over legislation. The Seanad may only delay or amend legislation passed by the

Dáil. The three major political parties are Fianna Fáil, Fine Gael, and Labour. The largely ceremonial constitutional office of president is elected by popular vote and serves a seven-year term. Judges in the highest judicial institution, the Supreme Court, are appointed by the president from nominations made by the cabinet. The Irish military has always been small compared to other states in Europe. The total defense force of 12,700 is dominated by the army. Republic spending on defense in 2000 was only 0.8 percent of the GNP compared to a European Union average of 1.7 percent. The flag of the Republic is made up of three equal vertical bands of green, white, and orange.

The Republic of Ireland is a member of the United Nations and thus its affiliates, such as the International Monetary Fund and the World Trade Organization. The Republic has been a member of the European Union since 1973 and its Parliament since 1979, as well as a participant in the OECD, which compiles statistical surveys for members states. Northern Ireland, as part of the United Kingdom, is also a member of the same organizations.

The Irish people at the dawn of the third millennium are markedly different from at any time in Ireland's history. The younger generation in particular is not hidebound in the past, prefers an inclusive rather than exclusive nationalism, and is more secular and materialistic than previous generations. In short, Ireland's historic peripheral isolation, which promoted a peculiar, if somewhat diverse, insular culture, has ended. Ireland is becoming an integral part of Europe and the West, embracing both positive and negative aspects. Like the West, socioeconomically Ireland has become a predominantly urban-industrial society, gradually modifying its ages-old agrarian perspective. Most workers are employed in service sectors, high-tech enterprises, and the government rather than on farms. The technologically advanced economy has made Ireland the seventh most competitive nation in the world, ahead of former industrial giants such as Great Britain and Japan. In 1999, the Irish Republic's economy grew at a rate of 7.6 percent, fastest among members of the European Union. Typically, rapid economic growth produces a worrisome problem, inflation. The Republic's 2000 inflation rate of 5.2 percent was three times the European Union average. Most troubling, between 1995 and 1999, housing inflation of 76 percent and commercial real estate inflation of 170 percent were the highest in the world.

Ireland is moving away from its traditional conservative culture by allowing contraceptives, abortions, and civil divorces in contravention to

Catholic church policies. For instance, there were 2,500 "legal" (i.e., recorded) abortions in 1998, an unthinkable statistic a generation earlier. The advent of a high-tech industrialized urban workforce may be largely to blame for creating a high suicide rate for Ireland, at eighteen per thousand. Even Irish nationalism has been altered in both the Republic and Ulster. No longer does the Republic insist—politically or constitutionally—on reunification, at least not unless there is majority support in Northern Ireland. Becoming part of the larger European community since 1973 has quite dramatically affected political, social, and economic calculations in Ireland by muting the nationalist sentiment. Both the Republic and Northern Ireland are partners in and subject to the policies of the European Union.

2

Prehistory to 1300

The human settlement of Ireland occurred later than most other parts of Europe due to its peripheral isolation. Although the extent of the glacial cap during the Ice Age did not cover the southern portion of the island, that is, Munster, there is as yet no indication of human habitation during the Paleolithic (Old Stone) era. Toward the end of the Ice Age about 15,000 years ago, Ireland had some grassy vegetation and some reindeer and bears. Five thousand years later, however, large Irish deer became more prevalent. Still, no human hunters resided in Ireland. As the ice melted, by 6000 B.C. (some scholars estimate an earlier date of 18,000 B.C.), sea levels rose enough to flood the land bridges that previously had connected Britain to France across the English Channel and Ireland to Scotland across the Irish Sea. Ireland's famous peat bogs also began to form in this era.

MESOLITHIC, NEOLITHIC, AND BRONZE ERAS

Before the flooding of the land bridge occurred, some human settlers had arrived in Ireland. Unfortunately, as Michael J. O'Kelly in *Early Ireland* (1989) puts it, "We do not know who they were, where they came from or what they looked like." The best estimates suggest the original settlers came across the North Sea from Scandinavia to Scotland and then over an isthmus that became the North Channel to Ireland, settling initially in Ulster at Mount Sandel in county Derry and county Antrim. Some archaeological artifacts suggest the possibility of human origins from places other than Scotland. The first humans who came to Ireland were part of the culture known as Mesolithic, or Middle Stone Age. These people had advanced from the more primitive Paleolithic epoch with a somewhat more sophisticated hunting-fishing technology using sharpened, but not polished, stone tools and weapons such as axes and arrowheads, as well as hooks made from bones on harpoons. A Mesolithic flint pit at Larne, county Antrim, dated about 5500 B.C., yielded 15,000 stone flints used as tools and weapons.

The early population spent almost all of their waking hours gathering enough food for tribal members to survive. Mesolithic cultures used fire for warmth and cooking, but their housing did not consist of man-made materials such as bricks or lumber but only tree limbs and straw for shelters. Irish Mesolithic settlements were scattered widely, along the coast as well as inland, in all regions of the island. There was no written language, and communication consisted of a pattern of verbal sounds and physical gestures. A tribal wise man or priest gradually gained leadership authority through an observational ability to interpret or explain various aspects of the natural world, which probably seemed magical to other tribe members.

The major lifestyle change for all ancient prehistoric peoples was the Neolithic revolution based on the discovery of agriculture, which began earliest (ca. 5000 B.C.) in the Near East and gradually spread. About 3000 B.C. new immigrants from Iberia introduced grain crops into Ireland. The detailed seventh-century A.D. five-volume first printed version of *Lebor Gabála* (Book of Conquests) was compiled by monks at Clonmacnoise Abbey along the Shannon River. It lists six waves of invaders beginning with a group, often called Ligurians, whom the *Lebor* suggests originated in Egypt as Seth (god of evil) worshipers. These settlers' swarthy complexion, dark hair, and dark eyes distinguished them not only from the previous Scandinavian immigrants but also from the later Celtic peoples. The beginnings of agriculture, with accompanying domestication of animals and forest clearance, created food surpluses and allowed the prehistoric population to change from food gathering to food production. It also permitted the diversification of economic activity by creating the three basic divisions that have existed since: agriculture, manufacturing, and trade. The Irish tribes became well known for the manufacture of polished stone axes that were more sophisticated than Mesolithic flints, which they exported to Europe. Irish Neolithic pottery was made in either a round or flat-bottom shape. Pottery remains from the archaeological site at Lough Gur in county Limerick resemble the spiral or thumb print style of the Windmill Hill people (as for 300 B.C.) in Britain.

Man-made housing became more prevalent, with timber and stones used for walls and hearths for cooking. Neolithic religious activities became more noticeable by the appearance of elaborate chambered burial tombs covered with cairns (piles of rocks), showing belief in an afterlife. The graves were commodious burial chambers that initially contained multiple cremated remains. The Neolithic revolution also involved the origin of written languages, though the stone and stick artifacts containing the earliest Irish writings, known as ogham cipher, date only from the fourth century A.D. The three hundred ogham stones that have been recovered contain a type of obituary, complete with genealogical data. The Neolithic Revolution in Ireland did not involve significant urbanization as it did in other global sites. Ireland remained characteristically rural with small settlements in places such as Knowth in Ulster and Newgrange in county Meath.

The introduction of metals to replace stone began in Ireland about 2000 B.C. with the Bronze Age, which extended about fifteen hundred years. Bronze was made from the raw materials copper and tin, and bronze smelting involved the use of charcoal fuel. The molten metal was poured into molds made of stone or clay. Commonly manufactured bronze and copper items included axeheads, blades for sickles and scythes, spearheads, swords, and shields, as well as bowls and jewelry. Musical instruments such as horns also were made from bronze. Gold jewelry from the period includes necklaces, earrings, finger rings, bracelets, a variety of pins, and jewelry boxes. The people of this era are often called Beaker people, after a group that lived across Europe from the Mediterranean to the Baltic. The distinctive Beaker pottery is flat bottomed, yet taller, more symmetrical, and more decorative than Neolithic era examples. The Bronze Age also is notable for the introduction of horses into Ireland and a sharp increase in the number of sheep.

Religious practices in the Bronze Age changed with the appearance of mostly individual grave sites, though remains usually were still cremated and placed in metal urns. More than a thousand megalithic tombs found from this period are grouped into four types: court, portal, passage, and wedge. Approximately 330 court-style tombs have been discovered. Some are oval and others U-shaped and are large enough to accommodate three or four galleries. Most of these tombs held only one person, probably royalty, buried along with pottery, jewelry, and tools. The portal style was less numerous; about 163 have been uncovered. They are rectangular with a large capstone roof and a floor covered with small stones. The average size is 30 meters in length and about 9 meters wide. About 300 passage tombs have been found. Most were built on a hilltop with multiple graves (one to two dozen) grouped in a cemetery design. The tomb opening leads into an oval chamber ranging from 8 meters to 85 meters in diameter. Many passage tombs have pottery and jewelry pieces, as well as stone relief carvings of various designs. The wedge-type tomb is most numerous; about 400 have been discovered. They are normally U-shaped with roof slabs and a portico entrance. A cremation pit sits at the far end of the gallery, which typically measures about 7 meters long and 3½ meters wide. Clearly all of these elaborate tombs were reserved for royalty or nobility.

Ireland had a few ceremonial religious stone temples with megaliths similar to those found at Stonehenge in England. The best preserved circular site, 46 meters in diameter, is at Lough Gur and dates from about 1800 B.C. The *Lebor* suggests that immigrants (Partholians, Nemedians, Firbolgs) to Ireland from the Near East and North Africa between 2000 and 1300 B.C. were sun or comet worshipers. Thus, Stonehenge-type megaliths may have been designed for the worship of heavenly bodies.

In the middle of the Bronze Era about 1200 B.C., another new group of immigrants descended on Ireland from Europe. The *Lebor* identifies these matriarchal people as Tuatha de Danaan, who supposedly migrated from the eastern Mediterranean, perhaps Crete, and worshiped a female trinity. These settlers reflected a greater warlike tendency in their large swords and shields. Warriors decorated their bodies with distinctive *torques*, necklaces of gold with elaborate carvings. Their housing also had become more substantial, with rock walls and timber roofs. Settlements called ringforts typically were surrounded by palisades or stockades, which offered both protection from potential attack and safekeeping of livestock. The *crannóg*, a round platform built on stilts with thatched roof houses at the edges of lakes (loughs), was another common noble residence found throughout the island after 1000 B.C. Because they were polyandrous (i.e., women had more than one male mate), these non-Indo-European settlers followed a matrilineal inheritance custom, which meant that they chose a new ruler from the mother's line rather than the father's. The annual saturnalia festival allowed tribal members to mock and demean their leaders in various humorous rituals.

Because Ireland's first recorded history came only after the introduction of Christianity in the fifth century, the earliest non-Indo-European peoples, lacking any written annals, have remained obscure. They may have been related to the group that the Romans called Picts in north Britain and assumed other names such as Cruithni or Priteni in the modern Ulster counties of Antrim and Down, and Ciarraige in Connacht. The Priteni, possibly Celtic in origin, came from western Scotland to Ulster before 500 B.C. and established several small kingdoms, including Dál Riata, whose last notable king, Aédán mac Gabráin, reigned in the sixth century A.D. These people were later known by the Irish word *Scotti*, meaning "bandits." The Scots returned to Scotland in the fifth century A.D. from their settlements in Antrim to contest power with the Picts.

THE CELTS AND CHRISTIANITY

Much more is known about the next migrants to Ireland, who arrived in several waves beginning about 500 B.C. These fair-haired, blue-eyed Indo-European people were called *Keltoi* by the Greeks, so that we know them by the name Celts. They apparently originated in central Europe around Switzerland and were perhaps the first Europeans to perfect iron smelting. Iron-smelting progenitors of the Celts, such as the Hittites, migrated southeast from Europe into the Near East, where they introduced the Iron Age before 1200 B.C. The sixth-century B.C. La Tene Iron Age culture of Celts has been traced from an expansion in several directions from central Europe.

Probably the first wave of Celts who emigrated to Ireland from Britain after 500 B.C. were called Builg (Belgae) or Érainn. A sixth-century B.C. Greek text referred to Ireland as *Insula sacra*, or holy island, and the people as the race of Érainn. They settled in Ulster and were known later as the Ulaid tribe, whose last great king, Baétán mac Cairill (reigned A.D. 572–581), was known as the most powerful in Ireland. The next Celtic people, called Laigin, migrated from Gaul to occupy Leinster and Connacht by the third-century B.C. The third Celtic group, known as Goidels or Gaels, led by their legendary chief Mil, crossed the Atlantic from either Brittany or Iberia and landed in Connacht about 150 B.C.; and another group of Gaels, who originally settled briefly in Scotland, appeared in Ulster about the same time. The *Lebor* calls the Goidels Milesians (after Mil) and states they defeated the Tuatha after landing in Leinster and later expelled their former allies the Picts (Cruithni). Mil's sons founded the clans Connachta (later Uí Néill) in the west and the Eóganachta in Munster.

Celts constructed some settlements, called hillforts, in imitation of the earlier ringforts. An extensive hillfort at Dún Ailenn, county Kildare, was the capital of the Laigin tribe. Another was at Emain Macha, county Armagh, capital of the Ulaid. Although each of the early Celtic groups came in relatively small numbers, they would become the dominant population in Ireland. By the mid-first century A.D., the population of Ireland remained small, at perhaps 500,000. Ireland seemed unaffected by the first century A.D. Roman conquest of Britain, though the Roman general Agricola recommended a penetration into Ireland. In fact, during the fifth century withdrawal of Rome from Britain, Leinster tribes (mainly the Érainn and Déisi) attacked and occupied portions of Wales.

The Irish Celtic culture featured a new language designated either P-Celtic or Q-Celtic. The P-Celtic dialect was spoken by groups such as the Builg and Laigin, while the Goidels (Gaels) were the only group who used Q-Celtic, soon the preferred version. The Gaelic language borrowed words from both the pre-Celts and Latin. For example, all Irish words that refer to reading or writing have a Latin root since writing was not a Celtic tradition. In addition to the popular bards (singing balladeers), the Celts revered their *filid* (seer) or poets (originally prophets in the pre-Christian era) who served as protectors of customs, including the Gaelic language. The more talented poets, called *ollamh*, produced literary epic poems, the most famous collection being *Táin Bó Cuailnge* (Cattle Raid at Cooley), originating in an oral tradition perhaps as early as the first century A.D. The *Táin* possesses many structural and thematic similarities to the Homerian classic, the *Iliad*. The story follows the adventures of an unhistorical hero named Cúchulain who is strong and brutal, an appealing model for modern Irish nationalists immortalized in the Dublin post office statue. However, the *Táin*'s historical importance is notable in revealing the division of Ulster from the rest of Ireland through Cúchalain's defense of Ulster against an allied force led by Queen Medb of Connacht.

Celtic sociopolitical traditions, like their predecessors in Ireland, were organized around the tribe or clan, called *fine*, which was tied to the male lines back through at least six generations. A larger social unit numbering about 150 called the *tuatha* (i.e., a people)—a kind of mini-kingdom headed by a *rí* or king, a noble class, and druids (priests, scribes, jurists)—became the characteristic political organization. There were usually about a dozen *fines* within the *tuatha*. However, archaeological evidence shows the existence of an even larger Ulster territorial kingdom of the Ulaid with their capital at Emain Macha as early as 100 B.C. The Hellenistic geographer Ptolemy identified Emain Macha on his second century A.D. map of Ireland. It seems that for the early Irish, as well as those in the modern colonial era, Ireland was defined less by a political state than through an imaginary dream.

The *fine* clan unit was based on kindred, which meant that collective actions took precedence over individual acts. For example, the entire *fine* was liable for criminal acts of one of its members. Each person had an "honor-price," or wergild, set as his or her value, and a murder would require the compensation of the "honor-price" by the whole *fine*. All members of the *fine* had to approve contracts and acquisition of lands, thereby limiting choices by an individual. Unlike the pre-Celtic Irish matrilineal tradition, Celtic inheritance was strictly male controlled. All sons (in the absence of sons, brothers or nephews) would receive an equal share of the father's possessions at his death. Women were subject to either their father or husband or sons (if widowed). According to the *Annals of Ulster*, the kingship itself was grounded in the kindred so that any male member of the *derbfine* (certain kin), or the male line back through four generations, was technically qualified as *rígdomna* (material of a king) to succeed to the kingship. Thus, an election was required to determine the choice of a successor or heir apparent (*tánaise ríg*), most often a son of the previous king, though struggles over the royal succession were not uncommon. A typical array of officials, including a jester, wine/ale taster, master of the hounds and horses, and a steward, populated Irish royal courts. The king's judicial authority in settling legal disputes superseded the traditional judges (*brithemain*).

The class structure featured an aristocracy whose wealth was measured more by the number of cattle owned than by acres of land and whose income derived primarily from rents. A distinguishing feature of Celtic nobles was the expectation of demonstrating honor by providing protection—legal, political, and economic—to classes beneath them. The noble culture cherished a reputation for honoring the obligations of an oath to ensure personal security. Nobles also swore oaths of allegiance to the king and served him in various capacities, mainly economic and military. Popular loyalty to the kings depended on certain tests, primarily linking the king with the productivity of the land. If the king was defeated in battle or a famine or plague occurred, it would be blamed on the failed trusteeship of the king rather than simple misfortune. Thus, popular belief held that the reign of a king possessed of *fír* (truth) would be peaceful and prosperous, whereas an unjust king invited calamities upon the tribe. The common classes existed largely as clients of the nobles, renting both land and livestock. The lower classes consisted of either tenants-at-will (i.e., without a lease) or servants, but they were not bound to the land like medieval serfs. The Irish law of social contracts embraced both rights and obligations but provided a degree of personal freedom unusual for lower classes in the ancient world. Slaves were not numerous, and probably most derived their status from military conquests or debts.

Pre-Christian religion in Ireland reflected fairly typical pagan practices such as sun, nature, and ancestor worship, rituals relating to the fertility of the soil, and numerous superstitions. A few carved stones reflecting Celtic pagan beliefs have been found, such as the round Turoe pillar stone. At Killychuggin, county Cavan, a reconstruction site suggests a stone depicting the chief god Crom Dubh, with twelve lesser gods represented by stones in a circular pattern. There were four major pagan festivals—Imbolc (February), Beltaine (May), Lugnasad (August), and Samain (November)—marking seasonal change, as well as others honoring particular gods and goddesses. Some of these pagan festival days were later adapted by the Christians to their rituals and thus survived. The harvest festival (Lugnasad) in early August was accompanied by a type of fair at Emain Macha where sporting games such as hurling and personal business were conducted. The formal coronation ceremony of the high kings (i.e., king of Ireland) involved the mating of the earthly king with a tribal deity such as Boand, goddess of the Boyne. The druid priests supervised the religious rituals and festivals, ensuring priestly prominence in pre-Christian society. Yet pagan religious traditions were less dogmatic and routine than their Christian counterpart. There was little scrutiny by the priests of lay habits or enforcement of rituals.

It could easily be argued that the advent of Christianity was the most significant event in Ireland's early history. Upon the adoption of Christianity by Roman emperors in the fourth century, the Roman church organization fanned out across the territorial empire, reaching Britain by the end of the fourth century. Saint Patrick's larger-than-life legend has obscured earlier mission efforts to Ireland from Gaul before the end of the fourth century. The most important predecessor of Patrick was Palladius, a Gallican bishop sent by Pope Celestine I to Ireland in 431 to further the Christian movement, which had only an embryonic existence. Little exists in the documentary record to tell of his effort, though it likely was more effective than the later Patrick legend suggests.

Patrick (c.415–c.493) was a Roman cleric who arrived from Britain in 432 to begin a concerted conversion program. Patrick's father, Calpurnius, was a landowner, Roman official, and deacon in the church. Patrick's first knowledge of Ireland, related in his autobiographical *Confession*, was an unhappy teenage experience of being held captive for six years by an Irish chieftain named Milchu, wherein he learned about pagan religious practices before escaping back to Britain. After ecclesiastical schooling, probably under the tutelage of Germanus of Auxerre in Gaul, Patrick returned about 450 on a personal mission (not, as in some accounts, as a bishop) to convert the Irish to Christianity, traveling to most regions of the island, though the churches he established were located mainly in Leinster, Connacht, and Ulster. He established a headquarters of the Irish church at Armagh, near the old capital of Emain Macha, which had been destroyed in about 450. Armagh has remained the primary ecclesiastical center of Ireland since Patrick's day. Patrick's death on March 17 has been marked in the modern era as a day of celebration of Irish heritage.

The Christianization of Ireland was not as easy or as rapid as portrayed by contemporary Christian chroniclers. Christian zealots showed no tolerance for the pagan traditions and even exhibited violence in destroying heathen symbols. Despite having only a casual connection with pre-Christian religious practices, kings and nobles were probably most resistant to the new religion. When kings realized that the church actually favored strong political authority, their attitude changed. Thus, like other places in the Roman Empire, Ireland soon reflected a pervasive Christian influence not only in religion but also in society, politics, and culture.

By the sixth century, the predominantly monastic (i.e., decentralized) character of the Irish church became apparent due to the efforts of other clerics, including Columba, or Collum Cille (c.543–615), who founded monasteries at Derry, Swords, Durrow, and Kells, as well as Iona. Born in Leinster and educated at Bangor Monastery in county Down, Columba led a mission to Scotland, where a Christian community that grew up at Dál Riata (Argyll) would maintain close connections with northeast Ireland for centuries. Columba also preached in France and Italy, where he established additional monasteries. Other leading clerics included Brendan, abbot of Clonfert, whose legend had him sailing to America; Kieran (Ciarán), founder of Clonmacnoise on the Shannon; and Finnian, founder of Clonard Abbey. Noteworthy in the rise of monasticism was that bishops had been dominant leaders of the church prior to the great plague of 549, but afterward the abbots quickly eclipsed the bishops. Effectively assuming the former role of druids, the bishops had held a status in the *tuatha* almost equal to the king. Part of the explanation for the shift from an episcopal (i.e., hierachical) to a local monastic system may have been the pre-Christian tradition among the early Irish of blaming leaders for catastrophes. Over sixty new monasteries were established between 550 and 600. Monasteries allowed the monks to attain asceticism by isolating them from worldly temptations while they engaged in work and study in a highly disciplined environment.

Equally important to their leadership role within the church, the monasteries also became the primary Irish cultural center of intellectual and literary activity by Latin scholars, as well as a social and economic institution of employment and cultivation of food. Composed in the second half of the eighth century, the *Book of Kells* (now displayed at Trinity College, Dublin) is an excellent example of monastic illuminated manuscripts. The *Book* is a magnificently illustrated copy of the four Gospels created by several scribes and artists. The original may have been produced at the island monastery of Iona but later found its way to Kells Monastery for safety from Scandinavian raids. Several of the monastic centers, such as Kildare, Cork, and Clonard, resembled cities, with their closely knit communities combining clerics and laypeople, often including political chiefs. The Irish church showed little evidence of traditional hierarchy, thereby allowing bishops and abbots to exert authority in separate realms. The chief ecclesiastical centers remained Armagh, established by Patrick, and the seat of Columba's monastic order (563–825) at Iona, a small island off the southwest Scottish coast. The early church became the center of Celtic artistic expression through jewels like the Tara brooch, metalwork such as the Ardagh and Derrynaflan chalices, and the distinctive high crosses, such as the eighteen-foot-tall Muiredech's Cross in county Louth.

CELTIC CLANS AND THE SCANDINAVIAN INVASION

The fifth- and sixth-century Celtic clan kingdoms were controlled by several groups. Perhaps the largest was the Uí Néill, the Goidel kings of Tara, who had a northern and a southern division in the province of Ulster. The legendary fifth century founder Niall, originally from Connacht, may have been the first high king (*ard rí*) in Ireland. Following a Uí Néill victory in 563 over several Cruithin kings of Ulaid, at the 575 Convention of Druim Cett (county Derry), Bishop Columba orchestrated an alliance of the Uí Néill king, Aéd mac Ainmerech, with the Dál Riata king, Áedán mac Gabráin, which led to the defeat of the Ulaid king, Báetán mac Cairill, and reduced the territory of the Ulaid to county

Down by the end of the sixth century. After Dál Riata's king, Congal Clóen, ended the alliance with the Uí Néill the next century, he was defeated with his Cruithin allies in 637 at the Battle of Mag Roth (county Down) by the Uí Néill's Domnall mac Áedo, thereafter styled by contemporary annals as the high king of Ireland (*Hibernia*).

The Airgialla were composed of about nine small kingdoms in south Ulster (Armagh, Monaghan, Louth), which ultimately gave allegiance to the Uí Néill. Legend suggests that three brothers named Colla, allied with the Connachta, overthrew the Ulaid and established the Airgialla capital at Emain Macha about 331. Another clan, the Eóganacht kings of Cashel in Munster, was founded in the early fifth century, according to legend, by three sons of Niall: Eógan, Conall Corc, and Énda. They displaced earlier groups such as the Érainn (also known as Iverni), Múscraige, and Ciarraige and created a traditional geographical competition for a provincial capital between Tipperary and Cork. Cathal mac Finguine (ruled 721–742) was the only Munster king in the eighth century to claim the title of high king of Ireland, but the Eóganachta soon followed other regions in coming under the dominance of the Uí Néill.

The Laigin clan controlled most of Leinster (centered in county Kildare) as far back as the late fifth century, having displaced the Coriondi and Brigantes (named for the goddess Brigit). Early Laigin kings were also connected to the Ulster Uí Néill by marriage, and the most powerful seventh century king, Cormac mac Diarmata of the Uí Bairrche, probably was the last to rule over all Leinster. By the eighth century, the province was divided between a northern kingdom governed by the Uí Dúnlainge and a southern domain ruled by the Uí Chennselaig. The history of the Connachta west of the Shannon River is the least documented. They were supposed to have been established by a native of Leinster, King Ailill mac Mata and Queen Medb, in the sixth century after ousting the Auteini, but until later there appears to have been less political unity in Connacht than in other provinces. By the second half of the seventh century, the Uí Briúin (O'Brien) secured the title of over-king (i.e, regional) of Connacht, ousting their primary rivals the Uí Fiachrach, and established a capital at Cruachain (county Roscommon).

The vulnerability of Ireland to invasion had been demonstrated by the Celtic infusion, so it is not surprising that a pattern of external invasion continued. Indeed, another Scandinavian movement affected all of the British isles in the ninth and tenth centuries. The migration from Northern Europe also extended to many lands far distant from Scandinavia. The Scandinavian invaders were known by a variety of labels depending on the places where they traveled. They were often called Norsemen or Northmen, but were also known as Varangians in Russia, Normans along the Atlantic coast of Europe, Danes in Britain, and Vikings across the North Atlantic. The Scandinavians who settled in Ireland during the era were labeled Ostmen, though they probably originated in Norway. Because they were pagan, the Scandinavians frequently targeted church properties, especially monasteries, which contained valuable booty and lacked defenses. The island monastery of Iona especially was vulnerable, suffering three raids, the third leading to the death of almost all residents. Scandinavians reached the monastery of Clonmacnoise in the west by 842. Ostmen raids were constant after 795, reached a peak in the 830s, and became more sporadic by the 880s. Following a few decades of destructive raiding and looting, the Ostmen began to settle in the 840s along the eastern coast and established several port towns, including Dublin, Waterford, Wexford, and Cork, as well as Limerick on the west coast. Indeed, Dublin owes its subsequent historical importance to the Scandinavian settlement of 841. The result for Ireland was a new and important economic element of regular external trade across the Irish Sea and St. George's Channel to Britain.

While some Ostmen chiefs such as Turgéis (d. 845) gained reputations for their success, most remain obscure. Though initially at the mercy of the more militarily advanced Ostmen, the Irish soon adopted Scandinavian fighting methods and challenged the Ostmen's aggression. As early as the ninth century, combined Irish forces occasionally defeated Ostmen raiders. The ninth century expatriate Irish poet, Sedulius Scottus of Leinster, referred to such an Irish victory in one of his poems written in France. The Irish even formed a brief alliance with the Ostmen's Scandinavian rivals, the Danes, in the late ninth century. The Danish incursion into Britain caused the strongest Ostmen king, Ivar (d. 873) of Dublin, to send forces from Ireland to Northumbria in northern England to challenge the Danes. The momentary weakening of Ostmen control in Ireland allowed the Irish to seize Dublin in 902. Yet an Ostmen counteroffensive against the king of Leinster was launched from Waterford by Ivar's grandson, Sitric, and led to the recapture of Dublin in 917. The second Scandinavian settlement at Dublin, a more detailed plan with ramparts, was located two miles closer to the coast to provide greater security from Irish raiders. Dublin's population thereafter was dominated by merchants and craftsmen, who supported a distinctively commercial economy.

The turning point in balance of power between Irish and Ostmen was the famous battle of Clontarf in 1014, a watershed event whose facts are clouded through considerable contemporary literary hyperbole by both Irish and Scandinavian annalists. The reputed leader of the Irish resistance to the Ostmen was Brian Boru or Bóruma (c.941–1014), born in county Clare, whose father, Cennétig mac Lorcáin, had been king of north Munster (Dál Cais). After Brian succeeded his assassinated older brother to the throne in 976, he defeated a rival at Belach Lechta (978) to become king of Munster. Quickly Brian asserted a claim to the title king of Ireland and benefited from an internal split of the Uí Néill, the pre-Scandinavian high kings of Ireland. By 983, Brian defeated the high king and gained the submission of Leinster. He allied with the Ostmen against the Uí Néill as he moved from Munster into Connacht. A 997 meeting at Clonfert with the Uí Néill king Máel Sechnaill II resulted in a division of Ireland, giving Brian authority in Leinster, Munster, and most of Connacht. Brian shrewdly cultivated alliances with the Ostmen and the church leaders in his quest to oust the Uí Néill in Ulster and become king of a unified Ireland. He captured Dublin in 1000, and King Máel recognized Brian as high king in 1002. Yet Brian's success created many jealous rivals. Led by the Ostmen king of Dublin, Sitric Silkbeard, and his allies, a rebellion against Brian resulted in the Battle of Clontarf in 1014. Brian's forces won, but Brian perished, allowing Máel to reclaim the high kingship. The result of Clontarf was not so much the end of Ostmen control in Ireland, since it never had been territorially extensive. Rather, Contarf signified raising the concept of high king from symbol to substance, making it a prize worth fighting for among the Irish chiefs after Brian.

Nonetheless, after Clontarf, Scandinavian power in Ireland declined precipitously. Despite the initial threat of becoming overlords in Ireland, the permanent imprint of the Scandinavian invaders on early Ireland was limited. Other than the establishment of important urban trading cities, the Ostmen had limited influence on native Irish cultural traditions. Some Norse nautical terms (e.g., *boat, anchor, harbor*) and the word for market came into the Gaelic language as a result of their seafaring-trading emphasis. Unfortunately, violence against Christian churches begun by the Ostmen was imitated by Irish chiefs (not all of whom were yet Christian) in the era, making the blow to religious institutions doubly destructive.

HIGH KINGSHIP RIVALRIES AND NORMAN INCURSION

The Scandinavian concept of a unified political system blended with the Irish theory of the high king that Brian Boru brought to near-reality.

Scholars refined and enshrined the concept. Thus, the high kingship, something much larger and more important than mere local control, consumed Irish chiefs in the era between the Ostmen decline and the Norman invasion in 1169. Yet the more traditional decentralized Irish system of governance, featuring balanced threefold checks, worked against unity and ultimately proved most enduring for Ireland's future. First, local petty kings held political and military authority in their regions since the *ard rí*, or high king, was viewed as a ceremonial title with no judicial or financial authority or sovereignty over local chiefs. Second, abbots of monasteries more than bishops wielded the principal religious authority in Ireland. Third, the strict and inflexible Irish *brehon* law (a detailed body of behavioral rules), administered by jurists called *brithemain*, maintained social control.

The Ostmen influence, combined with Brian Boru's temporary success, showed the feasibility of a centralized regime in contrast to the traditional decentralized Irish system. During a lull in the Uí Néill ascendancy caused by the Ostmen invasion, several Irish pretenders attempted to assert their aspirations to the *ard rí* in the eleventh and twelfth centuries. The heirs of Brian Boru, the O'Briens (Ó Briain) of Thomond, faced an initial challenge of mere survival in the aftermath of Clontarf, clinging to vestiges of power in Munster. Brian's grandnephew, Turlough O'Brien (1009–1086) led an O'Brien revival. Turlough imitated the techniques of the successful Uí Chennselaig king of Leinster, Diarmait mac Máel (1042–1072), who extended his influence into Munster and Connacht. Almost immediately after Diarmait's death, Turlough O'Brien assumed his mentor's titles. Turlough made his son Muirchertach (d. 1119) king of Leinster. In Connacht, Turlough tried to divide the three major families—the O'Connors (Ó Conchobair), O'Rourkes (Ó Ruairc), and O'Flahertys (Ó Flaithbertaig)—against each other. When Rory O'Connor defeated Áed O'Flaherty in 1078 and appeared to be gaining control in Connacht, Turlough moved to remove O'Connor, who claimed the title king of Connacht. Turlough also defeated the O'Rourkes in 1084 in Leinster, ending their threat. Most Irish outside Ulster recognized Turlough O'Brien as high king of Ireland by his death in 1086.

Muirchertach O'Brien moved quickly to step into his father's position as high king, but he met severe challenges. Muirchertach faced stiff opposition from the O'Connors in Connacht and the O'Loughlins in north Leinster. In 1103, after failing to secure aid from the abbot of Armagh, O'Brien's forces were beaten badly by Domnall O'Loughlin's army at Mag Coba (county Down). Illness allowed a temporary removal of

Muirchertach from his Munster throne, but even after recovering it, he never again could claim the title of high king. Thus, aside from his innovative use of ships on rivers to support his land forces and some skillful marriage alliances, Muirchertach O'Brien failed to achieve the measure of his ancestors' political stature. He was known later as a church reformer, but his insistence that the king have the right to appoint clerics was based on political motives.

The O'Connors staged the next attempt at centralization. Rory O'Connor's son, Turlough (1088–1156), gradually assumed the kingship of Connacht in the last years of Muirchertach O'Brien's rule, and after O'Brien's death, he campaigned to become the next high king. Turlough O'Connor built a series of fortifications along the eastern frontier of Connacht, which enabled him to project military power into Leinster and capture Dublin by 1126. He also maintained a large navy of just under 200 ships, an important military lesson learned from the Ostmen. For a decade after 1121, Turlough O'Connor's political power was unmatched in Ireland, but troubles ensued after 1131. Turlough tried to engineer the succession to his favored son, Conchobar, but his untimely death allowed another son, Rory O'Connor (?1116–1198) to succeed his father by the 1150s. At the Battle of Móin Mór (county Cork) in 1151, the O'Briens suffered 7,000 killed from a combined force led by the O'Connors, O'Rourkes, and MacMurroughs (mac Murchada), thereby ensuring that none of the aspirants to the high kingship would succeed. Thus, the resilience of local loyalties and decentralized traditions against political centralization proved more powerful than the abilities of aspiring high kings.

Although Norman kings of England, William I (1066–1087) and Henry I (1100–1135), had contemplated extending their power into Ireland, it was the intensity of the quest for high king that led to an invitation for Norman intervention. During the 1150s and 1160, another titanic struggle for control of Ireland ensued in the rivalry for the high kingship between Muirchertach MacLoughlin (d. 1166), the new challenger from Ulster, and Rory O'Connor of Connacht. Among their allies, another fierce contest emerged between MacLoughlin's lieutenant Diarmait MacMurrough (1110–1171), the brutal king of Leinster and Munster, and O'Connor's backer, the one-eyed Tigernan O'Rourke (d. 1172) of Meath (Bréifne). Diarmait's fortunes declined as he lost most of his territory except Wexford. After the sudden collapse of MacLoughlin's power due to desertion of former allies by 1166, a temporarily unrivaled high king, Rory O'Connor, was willing for MacMurrough to retain a petty kingdom, but

O'Rourke wanted to annihilate his enemy because of resentment over Diarmait's kidnapping of O'Rourke's wife several years earlier. Thus, O'Rourke drove MacMurrough from Ireland in 1166. Meanwhile, the papacy became convinced that Ireland's isolation contributed to its cultural backwardness and barbarity, and Pope Adrian IV (the only English pope) gave Henry II (1154–1189) the authority to govern Ireland in 1155. During the twelfth century, the papacy had sent candidates for Irish bishoprics to England for their education in an effort to undermine monastic influence in Ireland. With a European rather than a provincial perspective, MacMurrough sought aid from Henry II, confident of assistance because MacMurrough backed Henry's 1165 Welsh campaign. MacMurrough returned to Ireland prepared to launch an ambitious military campaign that aimed not only to recover his own lands in Leinster but also to make himself king of Ireland.

In Wales, Diarmait MacMurrough recruited a shrewd Norman warrior, Richard FitzGilbert, earl of Pembroke, known as Strongbow, to join the campaign. MacMurrough agreed that the tall, red-haired Strongbow could marry his daughter and become king of Leinster in return for assistance in recovering MacMurrough's position in Ireland. Rory O'Connor and other Irish chiefs failed to understand the significance of Norman engagement in Ireland. Strongbow's Welsh expedition landed at Waterford in 1169 with about 1,200 soldiers and soon captured Dublin. MacMurrough's death in 1171 cleared the way for Strongbow to expand his own power in Ireland. But he quarreled with sometime enemy Henry II, who landed with an English army at Waterford in 1171. Henry allied with the Irish kings of Cork, Limerick, Airgialla, Breifne, and Ulidia, and, perhaps most important, bishops against Strongbow and seized Dublin. The treacherous Irish king primarily responsible for instigating the Norman intervention, Tigernán O'Rourke, was killed by the invaders in 1172. In the Treaty of Windsor (1175), Rory O'Connor recognized Henry as his superior, while Henry granted O'Connor high king status in the areas unoccupied by the English, mainly Connacht. The O'Connor fortunes experienced further decline when Rory was deposed in 1183 and replaced by his son Cathal. The O'Rourke lands in Meath were taken by Henry's commander, Hugh de Lacy; John de Courcy conquered eastern portions of Ulster, formerly the Ulaid kingdom; and Henry granted the O'Brien lands in the kingdom of Limerick to Philip de Braose. Connacht came under Anglo-Norman rule in the early thirteenth century following the collapse of O'Connor authority. That Henry II did not entirely trust Anglo-Norman barons is evident in the appointment of royal officers in each of the conquered regions and his recall of all except de Courcy back to England.

The Norman military success was due not to greater numbers but to superior methods, including weapons—crossbows, long swords, iron helmets, and chain mail armor—and experience gained fighting the Welsh. With the invasion, English influence affected Ireland for centuries thereafter, but since the heartland or bogland in the midlands was never entirely subdued, Irish culture survived. Unfortunately, Ireland's dynastic (as contrasted to the earlier tribal) wars for control of the high kingship had not produced a centralized monarchy before the Anglo-Norman intervention. Strongbow made his peace with Henry and later returned as the king's governor in Ireland until his death in 1176. He was buried at Christ Church, Dublin.

The incomplete Norman conquest of Ireland could have led to a fusion with native Irish, but Norman officials alienated the local population. The Normans did introduce feudalism especially in the rural areas, with its unique social, political, and economic elements. Feudalism involved a social hierarchy with vassals agreeing to various services for their lords in exchange for use of land (fief). Manorialism or economic feudalism, with its primitive subsistence farming, existed on large estates worked by serf labor. The parallel manner in which feudalism began in England and Ireland is rather striking, although it remained less complete in Ireland than in England. The Normans had adopted the Frankish system of feudalism before the Norman conquest of England in 1066. Anglo-Saxon England in the eleventh century was essentially a conquered kingdom, where feudalism was imposed just as Celtic Ireland was an occupied territory forced to accept Norman feudalism in the twelfth century.

In feudal theory, the king owned all the land of the kingdom, although in practice the church possessed much of the best land. The establishment of loyalty to the king was based on the subdivision of crown lands, the fief, through verbal contracts that detailed specific obligations of the vassal to the lord. Land tenures therefore were at the heart of the system; the primary obligation of the vassal to the lord was military or knight service, which gave the lord a private army. For example, Henry II granted the county of Meath in 1172 to his justiciar (chief royal minister) Hugh de Lacy, who agreed to provide fifty knights. The Norman assertion of authority over Ireland offered vast new lands for the king and his nobles to claim and divide to create additional vassals. Less interested in keeping the land for themselves (there were only five royal manors by the mid-thirteenth century), the kings of England sought to distribute their lands to noble vassals, who would contribute soldiers to secure and extend royal political authority in Ireland. The prospective vassals would be offered Irish lands in exchange. Scutage, a monetary equivalent and thus a substitute for knight service, seemed to be even more popular in Ireland than in England by the early thirteenth century. Forced to use the military to protect their own properties, the Anglo-Norman land-holders often ignored their obligation to secure the authority of the king.

Due largely to Norman influence, the Irish church was increasingly dominated by Roman methods of governance by the twelfth century. Upon being ousted as archbishop of Armagh, Malachy, or Máel Máedoc (1094–1148), visited the Continent in 1139 and came under the influence of Bernard of Clairvaux, the founder of a new monastic order, the Cistercians. Fearing the church was being corrupted by worldly influences, Bernard prescribed an order that would virtually isolate itself from the secular world. Upon his return to Ireland as papal legate, Malachy established the first Cistercian monastery in 1142 at Mellifont, and eight others were founded on the island. Malachy was also instrumental in changing the clerical liturgy from Gaelic to Latin and renewing regular use of the sacraments. In 1190, he became the first Irish cleric to be canonized. There were also nine new Benedictine monasteries, sixteen Augustinian houses, and various other monastic institutions established during the twelfth century. Anglo-Norman nobles proved to be generous supporters of monastic endowments.

Even with the new monastic entry, the authority of episcopal rule was being restored in Ireland. Bishop Cellach of Armagh, at the synod of Ráith Bressail in 1111, authorized an episcopal system of twenty-four dioceses, but very little of the plan was implemented. A more successful effort occurred in 1152 at the synod of Kells, presided over by Cardinal Papero, a papal legate, where the Irish church was divided into four archdioceses (Armagh, Cashel, Dublin, and Tuam) and thirty-six dioceses. Progress in establishing a parish system was much slower than the episcopal organization. The crown gradually exerted its right to fill vacancies in the clergy, which tended to entrench the Roman system further. The archbishop of Armagh, Gelasius (1137–1174), energetically asserted episcopal authority through regular visitations and cooperation with political officials. By the time of the Fourth Lateran Council in 1215, twenty Irish clergy attended the papal assembly. Church ownership of land in Ireland was greater than in other parts of Europe. The archbishop of Dublin, for example, owned about one-fourth of the land in county

Dublin, as well as additional estates in Leinster. The most visible symbol of episcopal power was St. Patrick's cathedral in Dublin, completed by archbishop of Dublin Henry (1213–1228).

ANGLO-NORMAN RULE

By the end of the twelfth century, Irish society consisted of three ethnic groups: the Gaelic Irish, the Normans (most were landowners in Wales), and the Anglo-Irish created by the intermarriage of English and Irish families. Henry II made his younger son, Prince John, governor of Ireland in 1177, and John visited the island in 1185. During an eight-month sojourn in Ireland, John managed to create deep-seated hostility to the Norman rule because of his demeaning attitude toward the Irish (e.g., pulling the beards of the chiefs who welcomed him) and the incompetence of John's officials. Following the typical pattern of subinfeudation (i.e., division of royal lands), the English rulers arbitrarily claimed and granted Irish lands to nobles, thus alienating Irish landed chiefs. For example, the crown ceded considerable property in Munster to two historically important Anglo-Irish families: Theobald Walter, brother of the archbishop of Canterbury who founded the Butler family, and William de Burgh, whose heirs were the Burke family. The Airgialla kingdom of Louth was given to another baron, Bertram de Verdon. The kings of Connacht and Munster had intended to submit to John, but quickly withdrew their backing on witnessing the ill treatment and arbitrary measures of the Normans.

In 1205, after the de Lacys defeated another Anglo-Norman baron, former justiciar John de Courcy, King John granted all of Ulster to them. One-time justiciar for Henry II and patriarch of the family, Hugh de Lacy, was assassinated in 1186, but his three sons carried on the family role in Ireland. William (d. 1233), Walter (d. 1241), and Hugh the Younger (d. 1243) aligned themselves with other Anglo-Norman barons seeking to gain independence from royal authority. John made Hugh the Younger earl of Ulster in 1205. One of the de Lacy recruits, William Marshal (d. 1219), the most prominent baron in England, inherited the Irish lands of Strongbow by marrying Strongbow's daughter, Isabel de Clare. To curb the growing independence of the Anglo-Norman barons, King John landed at Waterford in 1210, easily occupied Dublin, and marched up the east coast to Dundalk, causing Hugh de Lacy to abandon his castles and retreat farther north to Carrickfergus. After a brief siege, John captured Carrickfergus, forcing the de Lacys to escape to Scotland.

In addition to defeating his rebellious barons, John cemented the allegiance of about twenty Irish chiefs. Cathal O'Connor (d. 1224) agreed to pay the crown tribute in exchange for returning his lordship in Connacht. Despite John's successes in Ireland, much of the country remained turbulent and unpacified after the king's return to England. Given the existing troubles in Ireland, it may have seemed odd that the Irish did not participate in the baronial rebellion in England that forced John to sign the Magna Charta in 1215. The explanation in part is that it served the interest of the Anglo-Norman landholders to side with the king against the native Irish chiefs. In the end, the landlords had more in common with the English than the Irish tradition.

The relative peace of the thirteenth century was due in large part to an effective administration by the Anglo-Norman government. Royal councillors were salaried professionals, and the justiciar created a separate royal seal for Ireland. A separate chancery for Ireland began operating in 1232. County government under the sheriffs and royal justice also became more regularized. Yet the peace proved to be more of a temporary truce than any emerging unity. Neither Kings Henry III (1216–1272) nor Edward I (1272–1307) visited Ireland. The tradition of the high king waned, although Brian O'Neill of Ulster claimed the title in 1260—with the backing of Tadgh O'Brien, king of Thomond, and Áed O'Connor, king of Connacht—only to be killed at the Battle of Downpatrick trying to assert his lordship. The Irish kings even offered the high kingship to the king of Norway in 1262 in an effort to expel the English. The O'Donnells of Ulster were the most independent clan of the thirteenth century, but the clans continued to struggle against each other as well as against the Anglo-Irish overlords. Fierce rivalries among the Anglo-Irish revealed that little cooperation existed among the ruling order. Early thirteenth-century justiciars in Ireland such as Geoffrey de Marisco (1215–1228) and Richard de Burgh (1228–1232) found maintaining peace and protecting royal territory a daunting task. William and Hugh de Lacy returned to Ireland by 1220 to reclaim their lands in Meath and also began moving into Ulster. The justiciar used alliances with native chiefs such as Áed O'Connor to restrain the ambitions of the de Lacys. Nonetheless, by 1234, many of the gains registered during John's 1210 campaign had been lost. Henry III planned a personal venture in Ireland to seek remedies to the situation, but instead remained in England to face a new baronial rebellion based on growing opposition to the king's favorites. Richard Marshal, the second son of William, retreated to his Irish estates in 1234 to avoid capture by Henry. Many former allies of the crown such as the O'Connors, O'Briens, and MacCarthys began attacking Anglo-Norman settlements. Yet Henry reconciled with Anglo-Irish leaders such as the de Lacys and regained the initiative by 1235, defeating the Irish rebels and securing half of Connacht and parts of Ulster. During the justiciarships of Maurice FitzGerald (1232–1245) and John FitzGeoffrey (1245–1255), royal control remained secure in Leinster and most parts of Ulster and Connacht.

Another important factor that undermined prospective unity for Ireland was that neither the English common law nor the statutes of the embryonic English Parliament applied to Ireland. Only the decrees of the English kings provided a legal basis for governing Ireland. The lack of integration of Ireland into the legal-administrative system of English government permitted local Irish traditions to retain significance for the native population. The Irish laws collected in the eighth-century *Senchas Már* ("great tradition") still applied in most local settlements, giving the *brithemain* jurists continued influence. Edward I tried to extend the English common law to Ireland in 1277 by giving the Irish the option of being covered by the common law (based on English custom) instead of the ancient Irish law (based on codes), yet few commoners opted for the English system even though Irish bishops encouraged the shift.

The Norman conquest led to the establishment for the first time of towns in the interior with their related economic stimulation. Royal charters giving local self-government in exchange for a fixed tax payment were granted to older Norse port towns such as Dublin (1172), Cork (1189), Limerick (1197), and Waterford (1205). New coastal towns started by the Anglo-Normans included Carrickfergus, Coleraine, Newry, Dundalk, and Drogheda established in northeastern Ulster as a result of the de Courcy conquests of the 1170s. Interior towns grew up around noble castles such as at Kilkenny, Kildare, and Athlone. Smaller settlements sometimes obtained royal permission to hold fairs or markets. The towns contained the typical medieval craft guilds—goldsmiths, tailors, mercers (dealers in expensive fabrics), carpenters, bakers, and butchers. Still, the Irish chiefs maintained considerable independence of political control in the interior regions. The O'Connors controlled much of Connacht, the O'Donnells held west Ulster, and the MacCarthys dominated county Cork, while divided power existed in Thomond between the Clares and the O'Briens. The local Irish chiefs frequently used mercenaries (mostly Scots) called *galloglasses* (from Gaelic *gallaclach*) to bolster their private armies. A combined Irish force led by Fingen MacCarthy defeated an Anglo-Norman force under justiciar William de Dene at the Battle of

Callann (1261) in southwest Munster, ensuring the independent rule of the MacCarthys and O'Sullivans. In Connacht, a similar combination of native Irish forces led by Áed O'Connor complemented by *galloglasses* defeated an Anglo-Norman army headed by Walter de Burgh at the Battle of Athankip (1270). O'Connor proceeded to destroy numerous Anglo-Irish castles, including Roscommon, Sligo, and Athlone.

Even with Irish successes, the English controlled about three-fourths of the island. The government of Ireland was modeled after that in England, consisting of a justiciar assisted by a council. The justiciar possessed full royal authority to govern and issue writs. Ireland's chancery extended English law, and the exchequer, headed by a treasurer, received and recorded tax collections and performed an annual audit. Ireland also eventually would have its own parliaments. Royal justices made circuits through the territory held by England to hold judicial inquiries and empanel juries, while the justiciar acted as chief justice. County government was also established in Ireland, with the sheriff being the royal agent who collected taxes and enforced royal law. There existed within some counties a special jurisdiction called "liberties," which were largely free from feudal obligations. Some of these included Wexford, Kilkenny, Kildare (to 1297), and Carlow.

The church in Ireland underwent some significant changes in the thirteenth century with the arrival of new monastic orders. The mendicant Franciscans, preaching among the people after the 1230s, tended to promote native Irish individualism and revive ancient monastic traditions. The older order of Cistercians supported the Franciscan efforts to a lesser degree. The Dominican order also came to Ireland in the thirteenth century, but it was more concerned with controlling clerical education in the Latin style. Church lands, known as "crosslands," remained some of the best agricultural land in the island. Although rivalries were natural, Anglo-Norman and Irish clerics demonstrated considerable cooperation in administering the Irish church. While all bishops in the archdiocese of Dublin were English, most of the bishops and all archbishops in the archdiocese of Cashel were Irish. Extension of the parish system was virtually complete by the end of the thirteenth century.

The economy of Ireland remained predominantly agricultural in the thirteenth century. Anglo-Norman lords of manors usually retained about 300 acres of demesne land for themselves, while leasing the bulk of their lands for rents, their primary source of income. The lessees included feudal vassals, tenants at will, farmers who held hereditary leases with a fixed rent, and simple villeins (former serbs) with quite limited rights, who worked for the landlord providing labor services. Farmers adopted the English-European three-field rotation of crops: winter wheat or rye, spring oats, and fallow. Ploughing was done with teams of eight oxen. Ireland frequently shipped grains to Britain and, like England, had significant sheep farming and wool exports. Thus, the volume of trade shifted from Northern Europe to England and Southern Europe through eastern ports such as Drogheda, Dublin, and Cork. Most shipments connected across the Irish Sea to Bristol and included products such as grains, meat, wine, fish, and textiles.

Unquestionably, the introduction of Norman governance in Ireland altered the warring rivalries of the various clans just as happened with the earlier invasions by the Scandinavians and the Scots. The difference was that English rule would last much longer than previous invasions. Yet because English occupation was incomplete and English rule thus haphazard, ancient Irish traditions continued to flourish even though England's presence forced the Irish nobles to engage the interlopers. The mixed results of the Norman conquest left both the political and cultural future of Ireland unclear.

3

Late Medieval and Tudor-Stuart Ireland

Despite the fact that virtually every Irish chief by 1300 was the tenant of an Anglo-Norman (and increasingly absentee) landlord, the resurgence of Gaelic sentiment combined with anti-English feelings was notable by the end of Edward I's reign in 1307. It was perhaps ironic that Edward's success in centralizing his English regime was not extended to the profound divisions in Ireland among the king's government, the Anglo-Norman earls, and the Irish chieftains. The renewed Gaelic outlook was encouraged by Welsh resistance to Edward I and the drive for Scottish independence under Edward II (1307–1327). The desire for Irish freedom from English authority became more important than any actual reconquest of territory.

SCOTTISH INVASION AND THE HUNDRED YEARS WAR

Scottish attention to Ireland dated from the use of Scottish *galloglass* mercenaries by Irish nobles in the thirteenth century. During the Anglo-Scottish wars (1295–1323), Donal O'Neill, king of Tyrone and claimant of Ulster, offered the title of high king to Edward Bruce, brother of Scotland's king, Robert Bruce. Robert's wife and mother were both Irish, so that he was an Irish landowner. Looking for a second front against England, Edward Bruce accepted the O'Neill invitation and landed with an army at Larne (county Antrim) in 1315. Since English troops were withdrawn to England to face the Scots, local Anglo-Irish lords had only their militia to confront the invaders. Thus, Bruce captured Dundalk and Antrim, followed by an invasion of Meath, where he allied with the de Lacys. Edward Bruce also defeated Robert's father-in-law, Richard de Burgh, the "Red Earl" of Ulster, at the Battle of Connor in 1315, which fomented revolts against the de Burghs in Connacht. Bruce vanquished Edward II's favorite, Roger Mortimer, lord of Wigmore, in Meath. Edward Bruce convened a parliament in Ulster and was crowned "king of Ireland" near Dundalk in 1316, promising to oust the English and restore native Irish chiefs to their historical prominence.

Inspired by his brother's success and fresh from a decisive victory at Bannockburn (1314) over Edward II, Robert Bruce landed at Carrickfergus, Ulster, in December 1316. Bruce marched south into Thomond, decided to avoid Dublin, and continued through Kildare and Kilkenny to Limerick. He was checked in 1317 by an Irish force led by the king of Thomond, Murtough O'Brien, and Richard de Clare. The Scottish incursion forced Edward II to dispatch an army, which landed at Youghal in April 1317. Robert Bruce promptly retreated north and fled to Scotland, the de Lacys evacuated Meath, and Edward Bruce withdrew to Ulster. The English army, led by John de Bermingham, defeated Edward Bruce at the Battle of Faughart near Dundalk in 1318, and Edward was killed in the engagement.

The Irish did not bemoan the departure, as the Scots had become more detestable than the English during their brief stay. It would be decades before Ireland recovered from the physical devastation of arable lands wrought by the Scottish wars and a serious famine (1315–1317). The onset of the bubonic plague in the late 1340s compounded the troubles by reducing the population and thus causing additional economic hardship. While hoping for a Gaelic national champion, local chieftains acquired more and more land from the English.

As justiciar after 1319, Mortimer created new allies for himself through a series of land grants. At Mortimer's request, Edward II made John Fitzgerald of Leinster earl of Kildare in 1316, John de Bermingham earl of Louth in 1319, James Butler earl of Ormond in 1328, and Maurice Fitzgerald of Munster earl of Desmond in 1329. These Anglo-Irish earls became the prevailing political powers outside the English-controlled Pale, a twenty-to forty-mile radius around Dublin, over the next two centuries. Mortimer tried to conciliate the Irish by inviting them to give up the ancient *brehon* law tradition and come under English law, but few embraced the opportunity. Following Mortimer's ouster in 1330 by Edward III (1327–1377), the king appointed Sir Anthony de Lucy justiciar, and restoration of order under English rule followed by 1332. Edward solicited allies loyal to him in Ireland. The most important was William de Burgh, grandson of the "Red Earl" of Ulster, and chief rival of the Geraldine (i.e., Fitzgerald) earls of Desmond and Kildare. De Burgh was murdered in 1333, and his estates and titles passed to his daughter, Elizabeth, who later married King Edward's third son, Lionel, duke of Clarence, who became earl of Ulster. The crown remained concerned chiefly to secure its income and maintain law and order.

The Gaelic revival created a genuine cultural uniformity outside the environs of Dublin. Support came from the Irish earls such as the O'Donnells and O'Neills in Ulster and the de Burghs in Connacht. It was not unusual for Anglo-Irish nobles to patronize Gaelic writers as well. The Gaelic output included compilations of literature used by Irish noble families to inculcate a sense of the past as well as to make contrasting distinctions with English culture. The library of the Fitzgerald earls of Kildare contained works in Gaelic, English, and Latin concentrated in religious subject matter. Among the Gaelic products combining poetry, short stories, and grammar were *Leabhar Breac* (1390–1410), a poem-book by Murchadh Ó Cuindlis that was part of a genre called *duanaire*, *Yellow Book of Lecan* (1392) by Giolla mac Fir Bhisigh, and *Book of Balymote* (1384–1406) by Solamh Ó Droma, Robert MacSítigh, and Magnus Ó Duibhgeannáin, which recounted legends of the early Celtic era and traced fourteenth-century family lines and territories back to the pre-Norman invasion. A great revival of bardic poetry occurred after feeble Anglo-Irish efforts to suppress the Gaelic tradition. Other Gaelic writings included commentaries on the ancient Irish law of the *brehons* and some scientific writings. Religious leadership in the cultural movement was also notable. The continuing influence of Franciscan monks, marked by many new foundations mostly in Ulster and Connacht, nurtured the ancient Gaelic traditions. In 1320, a one-time justiciar, Alexander Biknor, archbishop of Dublin, gained a parliamentary endorsement to begin a university in Dublin.

The onset of the Hundred Years War between England and France in 1337 required Ireland to pay its own expenses. Since Edward I, the crown had used Ireland as a source of provision—money, men, and supplies—for military campaigns in Britain and France. Only during periods of peace with France could England contemplate Irish affairs. After the

Treaty of Bretigny (1360), a concerted effort to regain lost authority was led by Edward III's son, Lionel, appointed lord lieutenant from 1361 to 1366. He brought 1,500 troops to aid in reestablishing control over Ulster and Connacht but met with little success. Efforts to force English absentee landlords back to Ireland after the economic hardships of midcentury led instead to the sale of impoverished lands to local Irish lords. Former Anglo-Irish castles, so essential to maintaining an English presence, fell into Gaelic Irish hands. For the English landlords who remained, their tenants became almost exclusively Irish as English colonists vacated areas outside the Pale. As a result of these social shifts, most Irish disorder by the late fourteenth century was among the Irish fighting each other and Anglo-Irish earls for control rather than resisting English landlords. The O'Donnells challenged the O'Neills for power in Ulster, while the O'Briens fought the O'Connors in Leinster and Munster. Irish chiefs imitated the Anglo-Irish lords by constructing stone-tower fortresses and centering their political and economic operations within provincial walled towns.

The development of the Irish Parliament was the only distinctive feature of English government in the fourteenth century. Full-fledged English parliaments had their beginnings in the reign of Edward I (1272–1307), but statutes of the Westminster Parliament did not ordinarily apply to Ireland. Thus, an independent Irish Parliament developed, modeled on the bicameral English institution. The idea of representative government was unknown in Irish politics, yet the earliest parliaments became comprehensive bodies representing not only the lay and ecclesiastical lords but also elected delegates from counties (1297) and the towns (1299). Irish parliamentary statutes required the assent of the English sovereign. Illustrative of the endemic upheavals in medieval Ireland, many of the early statutes dealt with a system of maintaining the peace and placing limits on local wars. An Irish parliament called by Lionel passed the Statutes of Kilkenny in 1366, attempting to salvage the few counties still under English rule around the Pale anchored by Dublin in Leinster. The statutes labeled the Irish outside the Pale as "enemies" and stipulated that they could not hold government or ecclesiastical office. Irish *brehon* law administered by the *brithemain* jurists was forbidden within the Pale. The Statutes of Kilkenny, which remained in effect until 1613, were an admission by the English that they could not bring all of Ireland under their administration. A further royal effort to extend English authority outside the Pale occurred during the lieutenantship of Lionel's successor, Sir William de Windsor (1369–1376). Although the lieutenant captured the king of Leinster, the campaign proved too expensive and was abandoned by 1372.

Another occasion for English attention to Ireland came in the 1390s during a lull in the French war. In October 1394, a youthful Richard II (1377–1399) backed by a strong army of 8,000, landed at Waterford, the first Irish venture by an English monarch since John's 1210 campaign. Richard hoped to make allies among the Irish chiefs and begin civilizing the Irish. After subduing Art MacMurrough (often styled "King Arthur") in Leinster, within a few months other Irish chieftains, including leaders of the O'Neill, MacCarthy and O'Brien clans, one by one did homage to Richard. Richard convened a parliament in Dublin to complete negotiations with the Irish chiefs and then returned to England in May 1395. Yet no sooner had Richard left, confident that Ireland was pacified, than conflict resumed. Because the king's lieutenant, Roger Mortimer, earl of March and Ulster, was killed in 1398 fighting in Leinster, a frustrated Richard returned to Ireland a second time in 1399. Arriving with a smaller force than in 1394–1395, Richard found the Irish, led by Art MacMurrough, more difficult to subdue. Meanwhile, Richard's cousin, Henry Bolingbroke of the House of Lancaster, returned to England from exile while Richard was in Ireland. Henry successfully wrested the throne from Richard and began the Lancastrian dynasty.

No English kings came to Ireland for hundreds of years after Richard. The native Irish chiefs were always fortunate that England's rulers made Irish affairs a low priority. Yet royal neglect permitted Ireland to became a natural breeding ground for discontented English political elements and a frequent battleground for dynastic rivalries over the next three hundred years. While the king's deputy lieutenant, James Butler, fourth earl of Ormond, was busy transforming the royal administration into one loyal to the earl, factional rivalry with the Talbot family—holding the offices of archbishop, treasurer, chancellor, and chief justice—prevented unity of effort. The Drogheda parliament of 1440 claimed an independent jurisdiction for Ireland, including more executive authority for the lord lieutenant and his deputy. Archbishop Richard Talbot became chancellor (1442) and justiciar (1445), and John Talbot, earl of Shrewsbury, was appointed lord lieutenant (1445). Sensing the consequences of factional rivalries and cross-channel English noble involvement in Ireland, the author of *Libel of English Policy* (1436) warned English kings to be certain of control in Ireland whenever they were engaged in defense of the realm.

The structure of English government for the lordship of Ireland became slightly altered by the early fifteenth century. Even more important than structure was the fact that English authority had shrunk to its smallest territorial extent around the Pale by the fifteenth century. Although the king's representative, the lord lieutenant, was often a member of the royal family, the effective governor was the lieutenant's deputy. In the three-quarters of a century before 1534—the next change in England's governance of Ireland—English-born deputies held office for only nine years, and for about half the period the office was held by one of the three great Anglo-Irish nobles, the earl of Kildare. The lieutenant or his deputy governed through a privy council, which included the chancellor, who served at the pleasure of the king, and the chief justice, who enjoyed a lifetime appointment. The council worked with other local judges (who administered the English common law), sheriffs, and magnates to ensure proper administration. Supervision of taxes remained in the hands of the exchequer, headed by the treasurer (a figurehead) and vice treasurer (the actual administrator). Income was derived from rents of crown lands (brought to the exchequer by the sheriffs), court fees, feudal incidents, customs duties, and a property tax on absentee landowners. Very little income derived from places outside the English Pale. In the vast majority of territory beyond the Pale, governance operated through the various lordships of the Gaelic and Anglo-Irish nobles whose household officers, known as *kern*, handled administrative and military matters. The nobles used stewards as tax collectors. Marshals supervised military forces with the assistance of a constable in each noble castle. The criminal law relied on the ancient custom of *brehon* law administered by *brithemain* judges.

Anglo-Irish lords outside the Pale became increasingly more Irish than English in seeking to maintain their hold over lands often threatened by Irish chiefs. Since the early fourteenth century, there had been three major Anglo-Irish territories belonging to the Butler earls of Ormond and the Fitzgerald earls of Desmond and Kildare. The process of Gaelicization among the Anglo-Irish was demonstrated by the one-time justiciar (1367–1369) Gerald Fitzgerald, third earl of Desmond, who in the 1390s composed some Irish poetry preserved in *Book of Fermoy*. The war in France diverted royal attention, allowing local alliances to foster struggles for petty kingships in Leinster, Ulster, Munster, and Connacht. The private armies of both the native Irish chiefs and the Anglo-Irish lords ravaged the countryside, destroying or seizing crops and livestock of peasants. A recurrence of the bubonic plague in 1398 added to Irish miseries. On top of the physical losses, the population also faced taxes and other measures, such as the infamous coign and livery, a billeting of the military on the civilian population.

IRELAND IN ENGLAND'S CIVIL WAR

Beginning in the mid-fifteenth century, the delicate political balance of English, Anglo-Irish, and Gaelic interests was permanently altered as a result of Ireland's becoming integral to English national interests for the first time. Toward the close of the Hundred Years War in 1449, King Henry VI (1422–1461) sent a veteran of the French wars, Richard, duke of York, to Ireland as lord lieutenant, the king's minister. As head of the Yorkist family, Richard already was contemplating a move to seize the throne he felt was rightfully his based on the Lancastrian deposition of Richard II in 1399. Possessing hereditary rights to the earldom of Ulster through the de Burgh and Mortimer families, the duke was received warmly by the Anglo-Irish earls and even by many Irish chiefs. In little more than a year, Richard of York established important ties in Ireland that would prove useful in his struggle with the Lancastrians during the English dynastic struggle, the Wars of the Roses, which began in 1455. When Richard fled England for Ireland in 1459, he called an Irish Parliament at Drogheda, which asserted independence from the English Parliament as a means of protecting Richard, a direct challenge to the Statutes of Kilkenny. However, on his return to England from Ireland in 1460, Richard died on the battlefield.

Meanwhile, some dynastic fighting occurred in Ireland as well as in England. A Lancastrian, Sir John Butler, sixth earl of Ormond, was defeated in 1462 at the Battle of Pilltown in northeast Ulster by Yorkist forces led by Thomas Fitzgerald, seventh earl of Desmond. In 1463, the Yorkist king, Edward IV (1461–1483), named Desmond deputy lieutenant of Ireland. For the next four years under Desmond, English royal authority in Ireland reached an apogee not realized in over a century. Desmond persuaded the Irish Parliament to soften the Statutes of Kilkenny to allow more legal relations between the Anglo-Irish and native Irish, which stimulated profitable economic exchanges. The few English-oriented urban centers needed commercial intercourse with the Irish countryside in order to thrive. Still, travel between towns, even in the Pale, was quite hazardous and avoided by most Anglo-Irish. The earl of Desmond wanted a university modeled after Oxford at Drogheda, but it did not take root, although a successful college was founded at Youghal, county Cork, in 1464.

After the earl proved unable to manage the Irish chiefs, Edward IV replaced him as lord deputy lieutenant in 1467 with a wealthy East Anglian, Sir John Tiptoft, earl of Worcester, a classically educated admirer of Roman law who had been Irish chancellor. Demonstrating an officious arrogance, Tiptoft ordered the arrest and prosecution for treason of the Geraldine leaders, the earls of Desmond and Kildare, based on their associations with Irish chiefs. Desmond appeared before Tiptoft to defend himself at Drogheda but was summarily executed in 1468, causing Irish and Anglo-Irish nobles to rebel against Tiptoft, who sought peace and retired to England in 1470. The failure of Tiptoft to extend royal authority in Ireland was due not only to his brazen, undiplomatic tactics but also to the crown's refusal again to provide the deputy lieutenant with sufficient resources to establish control in the country. A more practical and less expensive method of ruling Ireland was to allow the Anglo-Irish lords to assume the king's authority since they had a better chance of maintaining good relations with the Irish chiefs and would not drain resources from England. Yet the problem in yielding power to an Anglo-Irish governor was that he might become ambitious and claim the ancient high kingship of Ireland. This is what happened with the rise of the Geraldine earls of Kildare in the later years of the fifteenth century.

The new political force in Ireland, Gerald FitzMaurice Fitzgerald, eighth earl of Kildare (held the title 1478–1513), was rewarded for backing the Yorkists by being named deputy lieutenant in 1478. The earl's six daughters married into prominent Irish families, including the O'Neills of Tyrone. An astute cultural as well as political leader, the earl sought to maintain close ties to both Anglo-Irish and Gaelic elites, which uniquely positioned him to become a national leader of Ireland. Yet his loyalty to the Yorkists made him vulnerable after Henry Tudor seized the English throne in 1485. Kildare, with other Irish chiefs, raised forces to support Lambert Simnel's flimsy claim as Yorkist heir in 1487, an abortive move to unseat Henry VII (1485–1509). In 1488, Sir Richard Edgecombe landed at Kinsale as royal commissioner with 500 soldiers. The show of force and occupation of Dublin was sufficient to persuade Kildare and other Irish lords to recognize Henry VII as king. When another bogus Yorkist pretender, Perkin Warbeck, came to Cork in 1491, Kildare and the earl of Desmond gave Warbeck nominal support to the failed effort, which caused upheaval in Kilkenny and Tipperary.

Henry VII could not allow such treacherous Irish acts to continue, which meant that he could not trust Irish leaders such as Kildare, who was removed as deputy in 1492 in favor of Walter FitzSimons, archbishop of Dublin, a member of the rival Butler faction. The king sent to Ireland in 1494 a force of 700 troops under Sir Edward Poynings, accompanied by Kildare, to bring the Irish lords into line and prevent further Yorkist plots from being hatched. When deputy lieutenant Poynings arrested the earl of Kildare in 1495 for Yorkist sympathies, a widespread Irish rebellion ensued, led by Kildare's brother, James.

Thus, Poynings called a Parliament to meet at Drogheda during 1494–1495, which enacted forty-nine statutes designed to implement a new English order for Ireland. In addition to new taxes and resumption of crown lands, the parliamentary laws stressed again the separate status of the Pale, comprising portions of four counties (Louth, Meath, Dublin, Kildare), by authorizing construction of a six-foot ditch around the border of the Pale to block Gaelic incursions. The seven major castles in the Pale would be supervised by an English-born constable. Parliament also reasserted the Statutes of Kilkenny (1366) proscription of the Gaelic language in the Pale. The Irish Parliament itself was forbidden, in what became known as Poynings' Law, to meet or enact laws without royal consent through the lord lieutenant or his deputy in council. This provision, motivated by security concerns, remained in effect until an independent Irish Parliament was authorized in 1782. Another provision of the Drogheda Parliament made English parliamentary laws effective in Ireland for the first time. Most of the measures in the Poynings' statutes were symbolic and could not of themselves stem the tide of Gaelicization that had occurred during the previous century. By 1537, laws designed to suppress Gaelic customs had to be reissued because of their ineffectiveness. Throughout the sixteenth century, attempts by all elements to distinguish between the division of Gaelic and Old English bloodlines proved confusing, since few family lines were pure due to constant intermarriages.

After Poynings' departure in 1495, Henry VII needed the cooperation of the Geraldines to govern Ireland. Moreover, Henry's foremost goal in Ireland was to secure the Tudor dynasty against Yorkist challenges rather than to subdue the Irish. When Perkin Warbeck returned to Waterford in 1495, he failed to capture the city, despite receiving aid from the earl of Desmond, and he soon returned to Scotland. After the earl of Kildare swore allegiance to the Tudors, he was released in 1496, reappointed lord deputy, led the Parliament of 1498, suppressed a Galway rebellion (1505), and remained the dominant Irish leader until his death in 1513. When the Burkes (part of the de Burgh family) of county Mayo challenged his supremacy, Kildare sent an army to crush them at Knockdoe in 1504. The earl's son and successor, Gerald Og Fitzgerald, became the ninth earl of Kildare (1513–1534), as well as royal deputy.

ANGLICIZATION AND THE REFORMATION

Henry VIII (1509–1547) and his chancellor, Cardinal Thomas Wolsey, decided not to allow Anglo-Irish leaders to control Ireland and began the Anglicization of Irish political rule. Henry dispatched Thomas Howard (d. 1554), second earl of Surrey, in 1520 as lord lieutenant. Although the king hoped diplomacy alone would accomplish an Anglicization of Ireland, Surrey found it impossible to subdue the country without significant military forces (an army of 6,000 was suggested), which Henry could not afford. Surrey also may have been the first English official to suggest transplanting English colonists to Ireland to undergird the conquest. Clearly Henry VIII did not yet comprehend the complexities of Ireland and recalled Surrey in 1522. Surrey's frustration over lack of cooperation from both Irish and English governments became a pattern that most future deputies faced for decades to come. By 1524, the king had reappointed the earl of Kildare as lord deputy. Even with peace restored between the king and Irish earls, the Irish situation had changed little. Outside the Pale, Irish rule was once again largely in the hands of the three great earls of Kildare, Desmond, and Ormond.

Determined to have a male heir, Henry VIII sought a divorce from his wife, who had passed the child-bearing years, in order to marry a younger woman. When the Pope refused to grant the divorce, the king agreed to the creation of a Protestant church of England that would approve the divorce. The English Reformation introduced a remarkable new element into Anglo-Irish relations. Just as English political control had been fleeting in the previous two centuries, only two dioceses, Meath and Down-Conor, were Anglicized. Surrey had argued that the Irish church as well as its political affairs needed English direction. With little actual authority over Gaelic territories, the English archbishops of Armagh found their influence limited to the Pale. Henry VIII's archbishop, John Kite, informed the king's religious adviser, Cardinal Wolsey, that the Irish were too backward to comprehend proper instruction or respect guidance. English bishops operating in Gaelic areas found the language barriers alone enough to prevent practicable governance.

Moreover, the upper clergy were too often preoccupied with secular matters as they assisted the political authorities to devote much time to religious duties among the Irish. The Irish clergy's spiritual role had become further marginalized by the practice of hereditary succession to ecclesiastical benefices. Bishops and even abbots, the traditional spiritual leaders, were members of the local aristocracy in both Gaelic and Anglo-

Irish areas. Thus, many churches, cathedrals, and abbeys were in states of extreme disrepair and neglect. Spiritual inspiration in Ireland depended on the mendicant monastic orders—Franciscan, Dominican, Augustinian—which carried on most of the preaching and sacramental duties. The fact that the church hierarchy was out of touch with and lacked confidence among the laity on the eve of the Reformation made it even more difficult for a fresh construct, a Protestant church of England, to assume a position of respect and trust among the laity and lower clergy.

When Gerald Og Fitzgerald, earl of Kildare, left Ireland for England in 1534 in the midst of the English break with the Catholic church, his son Thomas was left in charge. Upon hearing the unfounded rumor that his father had been executed in England, Thomas Fitzgerald, Lord Offaly (1513–1537), rebelled against the king and attacked Dublin, starting a rebellion that lasted fourteen months. After his father died in England, Offaly, thereafter known as "Silken Thomas," became the tenth earl and ended the historic cooperation with the earls of Desmond and Ormond. The earl of Kildare used the Reformation issue as the excuse for rebellion, but his real motive was the prize that many others had sought for centuries: to be high king of Ireland.

Although reaction against Protestantism was not the true basis of Thomas's revolt, it quickly consumed Ireland in the wake of the establishment of the Church of Ireland. An Irish parliament met at Dublin in four sessions (1536–1537) to implement the Protestant Reformation in Ireland by establishing the Church of Ireland, with the monarch as head, to replace the Catholic church with a papal sovereign. From the perspective of the English crown, the last thing it needed was additional grounds for Irish opposition to English rule. Yet the religious issue may well have provided Henry VIII's Protestant principal secretary, Thomas Cromwell, the incentive to pour significant resources into Ireland for the first time in centuries. Cromwell assigned George Browne, archbishop of Dublin, the task of bringing about reform in Ireland. Irish policy now shifted from a defensive to an offensive posture in order to integrate Ireland into the larger British kingdom. Increasingly English deputies in Ireland rationalized violence by characterizing the natives as "wild Irish," equating them with uncivilized savages in America. The social bias was underscored by the Protestant interpretation of history, which likened the papacy to the Anti-Christ. Repression of Catholic Irish had already begun with the appointment of Sir William Skeffington as deputy lieutenant in 1534. He returned to Ireland for a second tour (he served from

1529 to 1532), aggressively leading 2,300 English soldiers to seize the Kildare stronghold at Maynooth Castle in 1535, and he brutally executed the survivors. Kildare was soon captured and held in the Tower of London until 1537, when he and five of his uncles were executed. Only Gerald Fitzgerald, a half-brother of Silken Thomas, survived, but after several years in hiding he was sent to Europe in exile. Skeffington's successor as deputy, Lord Leonard Grey (1536–1540), completed a successful English occupation of Ireland by 1540, signaling the end of the Kildare era.

Henry VIII asserted his own imperial ambitions, seeking to rival the great continental powers such as Spain. His view that ruling Ireland was a necessary complement to governing England became a regular feature of future English crown attitudes toward Ireland. The earl of Surrey's earlier scheme to make Ireland an English colony suddenly seemed credible and plausible. After 1534, English troops, beginning with a few hundred and increasing to several thousand by the 1550s, were stationed permanently in Dublin; future deputies of Ireland would be English. Renewed castle construction in the Gaelic areas, designed to support English garrisons beyond the Pale, had not been attempted since the original twelfth-century Norman invasion. Completing the transition, an Irish Parliament in 1541 named Henry VIII as "king of Ireland." The semiautonomous, feudal "lordship" of Ireland had been transformed into part of an autonomous, centralized kingdom of Britain.

Although the economy had recovered from its low point in the mid-fourteenth century, the agricultural practices of most Irish remained primitive. Only on the fertile English-owned lands was much modern technology used. Irish tenants thought of their residence on the land as temporary, relying on plentiful peat for heating and cooking. Since their housing was never substantial and most of their modest wealth was in portable livestock, they simply packed up and moved whenever conditions became intolerable. Oats remained the predominant grain crop and thus the staple of the Irish diet in the form of oatmeal or oatcakes. Though meat and dairy products were rather plentiful, the absence of vegetable cultivation on Irish farms in the sixteenth century meant that nutritional deficiencies contributed to poor health. The birthrate in the sixteenth century might have stimulated population increases, but recurring episodes of plague, famine, and political upheaval prevented real growth. While most of Europe experienced a doubling of population in the sixteenth century, Ireland's population of 750,000 to 1 million changed little from 1500 to 1600. Less than 10 percent of Irish lived in towns, which were small by European or British standards, since trade was not capable of expanding, given the political conditions and technological backwardness. Most exports to England and Flanders were raw materials, such as wool, animal hides, and tallow; almost all manufactured goods and other essentials such as wine and salt were imported.

Thomas Cromwell's fall from power in 1540, because he arranged Henry VIII's unhappy fourth marriage, did not change the tumult in Ireland led by the Gaelic League of the O'Neills and O'Donnells in Ulster. Grey was succeeded as lord deputy by Anthony St. Leger (1540–1548), who used the same martial methods as his predecessors in dealing with the Gaelic chiefs. By 1541, St. Leger had reconciled the major Gaelic dissidents to the crown—the O'Neills and O'Donnells in Ulster, the O'Briens in Munster, and the Burkes in Connacht. St. Leger visited many parts of the island to negotiate with and obtain the cooperation of Irish lords. He also followed the practice of Skeffington and Grey known as "surrender and regrant," which required Irish nobles to give up their title to land in order to make them tenants of the crown. Such a method worked to the advantage of the Irish leaders as well as the English king. For example, after surrendering rights to lands in Thomond, county Clare, in 1543, Murrough O'Brien received the lands back through a crown grant along with the title earl of Thomond. Similarly, MacWilliam Burke was made earl of Clanricard and Conn O'Neill earl of Tyrone.

Dynastic changes in England after the death of Henry VIII in 1547 produced some disruptions in his policies. Although St. Leger returned with his policy of restraint on two occasions, 1550–1551 and 1553–1556, in between the deputies were soldiers inexperienced with Irish affairs. The deputyships of Sir Edward Bellingham (1548–1550) and Sir James Croft (1551–1553) featured military actions against the Irish chiefs designed to thwart aid to England's wartime enemies, Scotland and France. Thomas Radcliffe, earl of Sussex, succeeded St. Leger as deputy in 1556 during the reign of Mary Tudor (1553–1558). Despite Mary's abolition of the church of Ireland and restoration of the Catholic church, which pleased most native Irish, the administration of Ireland was not much affected by the religious shift. Sussex hoped to use his Irish tenure as a political stepping-stone to higher posts in England. Nonetheless, his ambition required that he establish a successful record as Irish deputy. Thus, he sought to replace Gaelic legal and political customs with English law and administration, including establishing local councils across the island reporting to the deputy. The councils proved instrumental in allowing the Dublin government to maintain authority in the localities. The

English residents of the Pale and eastern coastal cities depended on protection to operate in their sanctuaries. Yet in order to trade with the native Irish, they had to be careful not to force English language and customs on those with whom they wished to buy and sell.

COLONIZATION UNDER ELIZABETH I AND JAMES I

After Elizabeth I came to the throne in England in 1558, following the death of her Catholic half-sister Mary, she authorized the reestablishment of the Church of Ireland, albeit along vague theological lines, hoping to entice widespread compliance including Catholics. Elizabeth was keenly aware of the role that religion now played in European diplomacy; England's security required vigilance against its Catholic enemies. In the case of Irish politics, the queen realized that pacification could not be achieved without adequate resources and manpower. Elizabeth's initial Irish Parliament in 1560 failed to approve the reestablishment of the Church of Ireland, although statutes of supremacy (monarch head of church) and uniformity (established a Protestant liturgy) were ordered written into the permanent record. Only five Irish bishops agreed to accept the new religion. Thus, although Ireland's official state church was Protestant and only very slowly gained even a foothold, the Catholic church continued to function in the hinterland.

Civilizing Ireland, probably more important to the queen than religious uniformity, proved just as daunting a task. Since Elizabeth promoted her Irish deputy Sussex to lord lieutenant in 1560, his policy for Ireland remained intact. Sussex's authority was challenged by Shane O'Neill (1530–1567) in Ulster, who claimed the title earl of Tyrone in 1559. Shane's claim was based on Gaelic traditions of succession, while the English crown recognized Brian O'Neill, grandson of the previous earl, Conn O'Neill. Despite receiving ample monies and troops, years of conflict failed to subdue Shane O'Neill. Sussex used every tactic possible to undercut O'Neill's ambitions, including bribing his rivals, the O'Donnells and O'Reillys.

Finally, at the end of 1561, Shane O'Neill agreed to negotiate with the queen, Sussex, and Sir William Cecil. Looking very much like an unkempt noble savage to the English court and speaking Gaelic, O'Neill recognized Elizabeth's overlordship in Ulster and in exchange received the appointed title captain, but not hereditary earl, of Tyrone. He also recovered some, though not nearly all, of the lands he claimed. Upon his return to Ulster, Shane O'Neill tried to expand his power but over-reached his resources. O'Neill's sovereignty was recognized by the pope, and he began negotiating with Charles IX of France to send Catholic forces to assist him. Ultimately, after being defeated by Hugh O'Donnell, O'Neill fled for safety to the Scots (MacDonnells) in Antrim. After a drunken quarrel in 1567, Shane O'Neill was killed by the Scots. The English obtained O'Neill's severed head and brought it to Dublin for display.

Meanwhile, Elizabeth's new deputy (appointed 1565), Sir Henry Sidney, made progress in extending English authority in Ireland. Sidney proposed to use force immediately to quell any Gaelic resistance, which included seizing property. Confiscated lands would be parceled to English Protestant colonists following a 1556–1567 experimental Leinster plantation in parts of Leix (renamed Queen's county) and Offaly (renamed King's county). The Leinster lands were seized from local Irish landlords and given to English settlers, but the settlement remained incomplete and the plantation was not a financial success. The intrusion of English interlopers invited by Sidney created native Irish animus and led to another rebellion. In 1569, James FitzMaurice Fitzgerald, a Catholic zealot and cousin of the earl of Desmond, launched a rebellion in Munster protesting Sidney's encroachment. Normally secure government bastions such as Cork, Kinsale, Waterford, and Limerick were besieged by the rebels. Fitzgerald also dispatched an envoy to the court of Philip II of Spain seeking aid. Yet Sidney prevailed. He sent an army of 600 headed by Humphrey Gilbert to Munster and gained the reluctant backing of Thomas Butler, tenth earl of Ormond, a favorite of Elizabeth. Fitzgerald surrendered in 1573 to Gilbert's successor, Sir John Perrot, and later fled to France in 1575. Fitzgerald's ally, the earl of Desmond, was imprisoned first in Dublin and later in London. Sidney recommended that the queen establish royal administrative councils in Munster and Connacht, similar to England's Councils of the North and Wales.

Trouble recurred in 1579 when James FitzMaurice Fitzgerald returned from his self-imposed exile with a papal legate and 700 soldiers to sponsor another Munster rebellion. Employing papal banners for the first time, the rising spread as other local Irish lords joined, including especially Fitzgerald's cousin, Gerald Fitzgerald, fourteenth earl of Desmond. Elizabeth hastily raised an army of 8,000 under the command of Arthur, Lord Grey de Wilton, to aid the queen's Munster president and Irish chief justice, Sir William Drury, and crush the rebels. Significantly, several major Irish leaders, such as the earl of Ormond, remained loyal to the queen. The show of English force paid dividends quickly, as

FitzMaurice was killed a month later; Drury persuaded Desmond to make peace. The rebellion had been confined to Munster, despite Fitzgerald's appeal to Gaelic chiefs in Connacht and Ulster.

The two Munster rebellions convinced Elizabeth to alter her attitude toward English colonization in Ireland. Though unsuccessful, individual English expropriations of Irish land in Leinster and Munster by Sir Peter Carew, Thomas Smith, and Walter Devereux, first earl of Essex, in the early 1570s had provided a model for formal colonization. In 1584, Elizabeth authorized the confiscation and survey of 500,000 acres in Munster—most from forfeited estates of the earl of Desmond, who died in 1583—to be settled by 20,000 English colonists. Unlike the government-sponsored colonial enterprise in the 1550s, Elizabeth opted for a less expensive private undertaking in Munster. If private commercial companies could produce an expansion of foreign trade, why could they not also operate colonial plantations as farming-for-profit? Although only 4,000 settlers emigrated over the next several years, among them were prominent English figures such as American colonizer Sir Walter Raleigh and the poet Edmund Spenser (Castle Kilcolman). The key promoter of the Munster plantation was Richard Boyle, who bought Raleigh's estate of 12,000 acres in 1588. Boyle built new towns and launched iron and linen industries. He was made earl of Cork in 1620, and one of his sons, the chemist Robert Boyle (1627–1691), who was the author of the law of gases, became a leader in the seventeenth-century scientific revolution. The new English challenged and ultimately eclipsed the old English in Ireland.

Elizabeth's deputy, Sir John Perrot (1584–1588), also launched an ambitious plantation project in Ulster. The succeeding lord deputy, Sir William FitzWilliam (1588–1594), supported limited, small-scale confiscation and settlement in Connacht and Ulster. The English government hoped to gain the cooperation of Hugh O'Neill in Ulster. O'Neill was educated in England and gained military experience serving under the earl of Essex. After securing support in Ulster, O'Neill laid claim to the vacant title of earl of Tyrone. Hoping to use him in their plans, the deputy recommended and Elizabeth granted the title in 1585. Yet O'Neill's emerging ambition to be king of Ireland as well as lord of Ulster caused him to distrust his English allies.

Recognizing England's manpower shortage in Ireland after 1588 because of a war against Spain, O'Neill began an insurrection in 1594. O'Neill was joined in rebellion by Hugh Roe O'Donnell, earl of Tyrconnell, but O'Neill knew that he could never succeed without aid from a

European power such as Catholic Spain. Thus, the pattern of Irish Catholic rebels' seeking aid from Spain continued as O'Neill negotiated for an alliance with Philip II (d. 1598). Though some Spanish money and supplies arrived during the early years of the fighting, in 1596 the English navy destroyed a Spanish fleet at Cadiz scheduled to bring troops to Ireland. When the Spanish finally dispatched a fleet of ninety-eight ships with over 10,000 soldiers, it was turned back by a storm, as were two others afterward. The failure of direct Spanish aid forced O'Neill to make a temporary peace with the English in 1598.

Although a soldier with a solid reputation, Elizabeth's Irish deputy during 1599, Robert Devereux, second earl of Essex, proved incapable of defeating O'Neill. In 1601 a formal Irish-Spanish agreement finally was sealed with Philip III (1598–1621). Soon a Spanish army of 3,000 under Don Juan del Aguila landed at Kinsale, Munster, far distant from O'Neill's forces in Ulster. Elizabeth's new deputy (1600–1603), Charles Blount, Lord Mountjoy, supplied from England through Waterford, amassed an army of 10,000 to besiege the Spanish forces at Kinsale. Following a three-month stalemate, despite the late appearance of O'Neill and O'Donnell, Mountjoy routed enemy forces, causing the Spanish to evacuate Kinsale. Irish resistance to Mountjoy quickly dissipated, and O'Neill surrendered unconditionally in 1603. There were only a few holdouts after Kinsale. The most colorful episode involved Cormack McCarthy, lord of Blarney Castle, county Cork, who skillfully delayed surrender through his ability to confound the English with his empty talk (hence the term *blarney* meaning the gift of gab). The castle foundation block also became a symbol of Irishness thereafter, with visitors performing the ritual of kissing the Blarney stone.

The Catholic Reformation accomplished what had been sorely lacking in the pre-Reformation Irish Catholic church. A revitalized Catholic church appealed to Irish chiefs such as the O'Neills. Thus, the crown became concerned not only to defeat Irish rebels but also to dispossess Catholic landowners in order to enhance security. When James I (1603–1625) succeeded Elizabeth as the first Stuart monarch in England, he favored continuation of the policy of confiscation and suppression of Catholic political interference. In 1605, James decreed that all Irish, as crown subjects, must conform to the Church of England, and he ordered Catholic priests expelled. Also, a new plantation project developed aimed at other parts of Ireland—Ulster, Connacht, and Leinster—as well as Munster. Stuart colonies were planted in six Ulster counties, three in Leinster, and in two additional counties in Munster. The terms of land grants—in 1,000- , 1,500- , or 2,000-acre portions—required undertakers to place at least ten Protestant families on each 1,000 acres. Local residents could also qualify, but it was expected that the bulk of the Protestant settlers would come from England or Scotland. There was a modest annual rent to the crown per 1,000 acres. The economic implications of the plantation policy derived from the fact that most colonists possessed skills as craftsmen or merchants. Cattle and timber exports increased, as well as an extension of arable lands in colonized areas.

The symbolic end of resistance to crown policy in Ireland came with the 1607 "flight of the earls." When attempts by Hugh O'Neill, earl of Tyrone, and others to challenge the seizure of land through legal channels failed, O'Neill and Rory O'Donnell, earl of Tyrconnell, left England. They never returned and their lands were confiscated. James I named Sir Arthur Chichester as lord deputy in 1605. Chichester personally embraced the crown aim of substantial occupation by constructing a lavish residence, Joymount, at Carrickfergus, Ulster. After the unsuccessful 1608 revolt of Sir Cahir O'Doherty, lord of Inishowen, Ulster, the crown unveiled another large-scale plantation scheme in six counties of Ulster. The process began in 1609 and was completed by 1613. New walled towns such as Londonderry were laid out in Ulster to facilitate the occupation. In the Ulster plantation, care was taken to segregate English or Scottish Protestant communities from neighboring Catholics. Thus, a pattern that remains central to present-day troubles in Northern Ireland began at the outset of the Ulster colony.

The English colonies of the late sixteenth and early seventeenth centuries did more than any previous occupation project to transform the Irish landscape into productive farmland. Not only did the new English settlers introduce improved methods of management and tillage, but native Irish landlords copied the modern techniques on their remaining lands. In addition to increased numbers of English landowners, there was a commensurate addition of English tenants on both English-and Irish-owned estates. Although landlords demanded payment of a large entry fine to commence the leases, the rents were rather low, making them affordable to many. Between the Munster colony in Elizabeth's reign up to the outbreak of war in 1641, at least 100,000 English immigrants arrived in Ireland. Increased usage of the English language, which had virtually died out in most of Ireland by the mid-sixteenth century, was a complementary social development caused by the English colonization. English law also undermined the *brehon* traditions of old Ireland. Other cultural changes to the aristocratic society included English-style homes, carriages, and even decorative tombs for burials.

Culturally, the New English rallied around Trinity College in Dublin, an Anglican establishment chartered in 1592, which quickly strengthened the weak Protestant cultural presence. Perhaps the most outstanding graduate of Trinity was James Ussher (1581–1656). Ussher joined a group of British antiquaries, including William Camden, John Selden, and Robert Cotton, who sought to preserve English cultural heritage. Ussher became a fellow, professor of divinity, and vice chancellor at Trinity and always regarded himself as an intellectual. Yet he was also staunchly anti-Catholic, which may have led James I to appoint him bishop of Meath (1621) and archbishop of Armagh (1625). Ussher wrote a number of books on theology and history, but was forced to leave Ireland on the eve of the 1641 rebellion, never to return. His collected works were published in seventeen volumes in the nineteenth century. Ussher's library of 10,000 volumes was donated to Trinity College after his death.

While social and economic Anglicization occurred on a broad front, the early Stuart kings made no comparable effort to extend the influence of the Church of Ireland. Indeed, the recovery and reform in the Catholic church during the late sixteenth century gave it renewed credibility with the Catholic population, which helped to retain their loyalty and prompted James I to label Catholic Irish as "half subjects." There was virtually no enforcement of fines for nonattendance at Protestant services. Church of Ireland clergy made little attempt to recruit local Irish into their churches and relied heavily on the state for protection and nurture. Tacitly, Catholic clergy were permitted to organize their own parochial system to maintain the essence of an ecclesiastical structure. Seminary training for Irish priests necessarily had to be located on the Continent, so Irish schools grew up in Spain, the Low Countries, France, and Italy as early as the 1590s. Seminaries in Spain were controlled by Jesuits with a political agenda, which was not altogether satisfactory to many apolitical Irish students. Thus, Douai College, founded in 1594 in the Netherlands, proved more popular, and Father Francis Nugent established several other schools there in the early seventeenth century. Dermot MacCarthy founded an Irish seminary at Bordeaux in 1603, and the Franciscan scholar Luke Wadding of Waterford founded St. Isidore's College at Rome in 1625. Wadding's *Annales Minorum* (1625–1654) on the Franciscans went through several editions. While the social and economic trends following colonization might suggest the possibility of a unified Ireland, the dual religious system ensured that the two Irelands—Catholic and Protestant—would remain isolated from each other.

REBELLION OF 1641 AND THE CROMWELLIAN REPRESSION

Perhaps the first English minister to view Ireland as a source of political patronage was the royal favorite, George Villiers, later duke of Buckingham. Between 1616 and his assassination in 1628, with the backing of both James I and Charles I, Buckingham created Irish titles and granted Irish estates to English and Scottish supporters. Although the practice had the potential of integrating the nobility of the three kingdoms, the new royal servants instead merely assumed a separate place alongside the existing native Irish, Old English, and New English elites. Among other consequences of Buckingham's exploitation was a huge treasury deficit, which most affected the military, soon badly in arrears.

Desperately seeking allies against parliamentary opposition, the secret Catholic King Charles I (1625–1649) granted numerous exceptions to restrictions on the Catholic Old English in Ireland. Then in 1632, Charles's policy changed when he appointed Sir Thomas Wentworth as lord deputy to alter the policies of Buckingham's associate, Sir Henry Cary, viscount Falkland (1622–1629). Although a competent administrator, as an ambitious politician Wentworth allowed his naiveté about Ireland to merge with arbitrary methods. Even articulate opponents such as Archbishop Ussher were no match for Wentworth's single-minded methods. The deputy introduced a policy known as "thorough," designed to extract revenues badly needed in England due to the king's decision to govern without parliamentary taxation. His agenda frustrated relations with the Old English, especially because Wentworth made it clear that Irish Catholic landowners must contribute or lose their estates. Indeed, Wentworth intended to use the tax demands as a vehicle for a new round of land confiscation and English plantations in Ireland. Irish Catholics identified as their enemies not only crown officials such as Wentworth but also Protestant property owners seen as the crown's allies. Since the Scots had resisted successfully Charles's efforts to replace the Presbyterian church with the Church of England, Irish Catholics believed they could obstruct the king and Wentworth.

As it happened, Wentworth was tried and executed in England in 1641 at the same time that an Irish Parliament boldly claimed legislative independence. Encouraged by these events, several Catholics concocted a plot against the crown. Rory O'More of Armagh, Sir Phelim O'Neill of Tyrone, and Conor Maguire of Dublin believed that a show of force would create a strong negotiating position to rectify the land depredations. The plan called for demonstrations, but not a general rebellion, in Ulster and Dublin. Yet when the Irish rebellion began in October 1641, it became one of the bloodiest episodes in Irish history. The rising in Dublin, which aimed to capture the government castle, failed; Maguire was arrested. But the outbreak in Ulster proved more serious and spread rapidly beyond the control of O'More and O'Neill. Protestant landowners became primary objects of frustrated Catholic attacks; perhaps 2,000 were killed, and thousands of others had their property looted or destroyed. Quickly the revolt spread to other parts of Ireland. In Munster, the rebels captured Waterford and Limerick in mid-1642, while royal forces were hard-pressed to defend Cork and Kinsale. Furthermore, some royal allies among the Catholic Old English, such as Ulick Burke, fifth earl of Clanricard in Connacht, began to waver. The Kilkenny Assembly (1642) established the "Irish Confederation," an ad hoc Catholic government made up of native Irish and Old English. Key to the success of the rebellion was sixty-year-old Owen Roe O'Neill, who had commanded an Irish regiment in the Spanish army after 1605 operating from Flanders. O'Neill landed at Donegal, Ulster, as promised in 1642 to take charge of the military effort.

Meanwhile, the royal government was in disarray. The English Parliament's claim of authority over Ireland was condemned in both England and Ireland. General Robert Monro led a royal army of 2,500 Scottish Presbyterians to Ireland in April 1642. In 1643, Charles I named James Butler, first duke of Ormond, as lord lieutenant. Ormond negotiated a truce in 1643, which left Protestant forces in control of the Pale and significant areas in Munster from Kinsale to Cork to Youghal. The ensuing events of the English Civil War and Charles's ultimate defeat diverted attention away from Ireland until 1649.

During the interim, the papacy attempted to rally Catholic forces in 1645 by dispatching to Ireland a papal nuncio, Giovanni Rinuccini, archbishop of Fermo. Rinuccini's plan was to restore a Catholic state church in Ireland through diplomatic negotiations with Charles I's government, mainly Ormond, and the Irish Confederation, led by Edward Somerset, earl of Glamorgan. Although the crown was willing to concede toleration to the Catholics, Rinuccini used Charles's failing military fortunes in England to press for formal recognition of the Catholic church. The confederation split between the Old English, who backed Charles's toleration offer, and the native Irish, who supported Rinuccini's full recognition. When parliamentary soldiers seized Dublin in 1647, Rinuccini realized that hopes for a deal with a weakened King Charles were dim. Ormond was forced to seek his own peace with Parliament by promising only religious toleration to Irish Catholics. Thus, he became useless to Rinuccini, who was also frustrated by the lack of support from the Irish chiefs. Rinuccini left Ireland in February 1649, having failed to achieve his objective and, in fact, having created divisions among Irish Catholics. Upon refusing to negotiate with the victorious parliamentary forces in England, Charles I was tried for treason and executed in January 1649. Parliament abolished the monarchy, the Church of England, and the Church of Ireland and erected a republican governmental structure called the Commonwealth.

The Commonwealth's primary political-military leader, Oliver Cromwell, devised a strategy for restoring control in Ireland. All Catholics, clergyman and layman alike, who supported the rebellion would be removed and their lands confiscated. Since religious loyalty was now equated with political loyalty, a concerted Protestant proselytizing campaign aimed to eliminate Catholicism from Ireland. Named lord lieutenant of Ireland by Parliament in 1649, Cromwell used 20,000 troops, experienced and well trained, to attack Catholic forces from Ulster to Munster. A September siege of Drogheda, where a force of 2,600 Catholics held the town, revealed the harshness of his strategy. Cromwell's army of 10,000 entered the city after a week's siege and slaughtered almost all Catholics. The few prisoners were transported to Barbados. A similar assault on Wexford a few weeks later resulted in the deaths of about 2,000 Catholic defenders. Shortly after Wexford, the Irish military leader O'Neill died in Ulster. Cromwell returned to England in May 1650, leaving his son-in-law, Henry Ireton, as his political deputy and military commander. Ireton continued to push the rebel forces west toward Connacht, but he died in November; Edmund Ludlow succeeded Ireton as army commander. Due to exaggerations of the Catholic slaughter of Protestants in 1641, the English forces retaliated with numerous atrocities against Catholics. Priests were prime targets, and Catholic property was seized at will.

A detailed Cromwellian plan called for removal of all nonimplicated Catholic landowners to Connacht so that English occupation would be paramount in Ulster, Leinster, and Munster. Soldiers manned a four-mile-wide buffer zone along the eastern Connacht boundary to contain the Irish. In 1654, Parliament employed a Protestant surveyor, Sir William Petty, to provide detailed land surveys to facilitate property redistribution. His accurate "Down [i.e., mapped] Survey" made possible a swift land dispossession and resale in twenty-two counties. Petty's 1672 work, *The Political Anatomy of Ireland*, included a widely accepted population estimate of 1.7 million. Petty blamed the Catholic church for preventing Irish economic progress. The religious transformation included establishment of Protestant schools endowed by the government. A major obstacle to achieving religious indoctrination was the language barrier, since most Protestant clergy did not speak Gaelic. Insufficient volunteers to serve as clergy in Ireland also frustrated the religious goals.

CHARLES II's REIGN, 1660–1685

After the execution of his father in 1649, Prince Charles assumed royal authority in Ireland. He named Ulick Burke, fifth earl of Clanricard, as lord deputy in 1650, replacing Ormond. There was little that Clanricard could do to stem the tide of military defeats, however. The main Irish army surrendered in 1652, though without terms. Since an Irish Parliament had ceased to operate after the 1641 rebellion, the Commonwealth government in England allowed Irish representatives to sit in the Westminster Parliament. Under the Instrument of Government (1653), England's only written constitution, Ireland elected thirty members to parliaments of 1654, 1656, and 1659. Ultimately the interesting Protestant experiment ended with the collapse of Cromwell's regime in the late 1650s and the accession of Charles II to the English throne in 1660. In early 1660, Sir Theophilus Jones, Sir Charles Coote, and Roger Boyle, Lord Broghill—leaders of the "Old Protestants"—secured control of Ireland on behalf of General George Monck, who had engineered the restoration of Charles II in England.

Prospects for progress in Restoration Ireland were overshadowed by bitter conflicts over religion and property rights that stemmed from two extreme events of the previous era: the Catholic rebellion of 1641, wherein Protestants were the main victims, and the Cromwellian repression of 1649–1651, which punished Catholics. Yet despite seemingly insoluble problems, Ireland in the reign of Charles II (1660–1685) was both peaceful and relatively prosperous. Governance of Ireland under Charles II was given in 1661 to the enthusiastic Anglican, the duke of Ormond, a former beleaguered deputy in Ireland and member of the Old English aristocracy. As lord lieutenant during 1662–1669 and 1672–1685, Ormond wanted to allow dispossessed Irish Catholic landowners, represented by Sir Nicholas Plunkett, the opportunity to recover their estates seized in the Cromwellian era, but the crown deferred to Protestant landlords such as Lord Broghill, so little was actually restored. An English parliamentary statute in 1672 excluded land claims of Catholics involved in the 1641 rebellion. Since the thirty-six-member court of claims included only Protestants, the amount of property returned to former Catholic landowners remained small and concentrated in Connacht after 1660. A reestablished Irish Parliament (1661–1666) adjudicated individual land disputes through designated commissions, and although some Protestants complained that Catholics got too much land, actual recovery was minimal.

About a thousand civilians and 33,000 Cromwellian soldiers had received Irish lands as compensation for their service in the 1650s. England's Parliament confirmed the right of possession to 500 civilian Protestant owners and 7,500 ex-soldiers. Thus, although many Commonwealth era interlopers retained lands, the bulk of Protestant ownership went to previous Protestant residents of Ireland. The 8,000 Catholic landowners in 1641 controlled about 60 percent of the land, but they held only 20 percent by 1670. Catholic losses in Connacht were less severe, dropping from 80 percent ownership in 1641 to 50 percent in 1670. The Protestant landed dominance of the 1650s changed only slightly after the Restoration.

Religious upheaval leading to the 1641 rebellion revealed as much discontent as political and property disputes. When the Protestant Church of Ireland was reestablished in 1660, Ormond took the initiative in nominating ten new bishops, attractive posts because they paid rather well. Some clerics were able and others inept. Among the best was Jeremy Taylor, a scholar who quarreled frequently with Presbyterians in Ulster. Perhaps the worst, Thomas Hackett, was removed for absenteeism and lack of diplomacy. Despite being the legal state church of Ireland, the Anglican establishment had little influence in either Presbyterian Ulster or Catholic Munster and Connacht. Of the seventy Presbyterian and Independent clergy holding benefices in Ulster at the Restoration, sixty-two were removed. The towns of Leinster offered Anglicans their only bastions of strength. Church of Ireland bishops also held the important power of nominating schoolmasters. A wealthy landowner, Erasmus Smith, received a royal charter (1669) to establish several free grammar schools in towns such as Drogheda and Galway. Other new religious groups that arrived in Ireland during this period included Quakers, mostly Civil War era soldiers, and French Huguenots exiled by Louis XIV.

The top Catholic cleric in Ireland, Edmond O'Reilly, archbishop of Armagh, lacked credible standing with the English officials to plead for Catholic concessions. The Franciscan Peter Walsh, a friend of Ormond, tried to negotiate a comprehensive settlement. Although O'Reilly got Catholic leaders to agree that the pope would have no authority in Irish temporal affairs, because Walsh opposed the compromise Ormond also rejected it. O'Reilly was deported, but Ormond also soon lost office in 1669; a policy of Catholic toleration became English policy. Catholic clergy, numbering about 1,600, were allowed to return and resume their normal duties. It was an important concession that prevented the Catholic church from capitulating to the Protestants. Neither Ormond nor the other deputies under Charles II were allowed much freedom to resolve Irish issues internally. Instead, Ireland once more became a political playground for rival English politicians seeking higher office. Furthermore, inadequate revenues hindered governance. Tax arrears were endemic, and deputies had little cooperation from Irish parliaments.

On the occasion of the so-called Popish Plot (1678) in England, anti-Catholic Whig leaders needed to implicate Irish Catholics to make the plot credible. The plot supposedly involved a Catholic plan to assassinate Charles II in order to elevate his Catholic brother and heir, James, duke of York, to the throne. The main target of Protestants in Ireland was Richard Power, earl of Tyrone, who with other alleged agents was charged with seeking French military intervention. Although an attempted impeachment of Tyrone failed in the English House of Lords, he was held prisoner for three years. Others charged in connection with the Popish Plot included the Catholic archbishops of Armagh and Dublin, Peter Talbot and Oliver Plunkett, and Sir John Fitzgerald of Limerick. Arrested and charged with plotting to assassinate Ormond, Talbot died in Dublin Castle in 1680. Plunkett and Fitzgerald were acquitted in their trials, but Plunkett later was brought before an English jury, found guilty, and executed in 1681.

The relative strength of the Irish economy in Charles II's reign occurred despite interference by the English government to protect English economic interests. Parliament prohibited the export of Irish wool (1662) and cattle (1667), thereby hampering the island's most important export commodities. When the 1667 cattle statute expired in 1679, exports resumed, but they ended again in 1681. Since England's export market was often unavailable to Irish farmers, a brisk trade with Europe and America ensued. English economic interests also enjoined by statute direct shipping from Ireland to the American colonies for the period 1671–1681 and again after 1685. Nonetheless, the hardships caused by English interference led Irish entrepreneurs to develop new methods of stimulating their economic production as well as to create greater diversity. A few iron-works were established on English lands. Restoration house construction included a few impressive structures. Notable among them was Charle-ville in Cork, the house of Roger Boyle, Lord Broghill, raised to the title earl of Orrery. The College of Physicians in Dublin was chartered in 1667 (and became Royal College in 1890).

4

The Eighteenth-Century Protestant Ascendancy

The quiet, peaceful ending of Charles II's reign was deceptive as a portent of the immediate future. Ireland in the late seventeenth century was still a predominantly agricultural society, for the moment in the grips of a Protestant landed elite. Although English subjects accepted the Catholic James II (1685–1688) as monarch, the new Stuart king rapidly alienated his own supporters and prepared the way for a dynastic-constitutional crisis. Thus, although Catholic elements in Ireland were pleased by the accession of James and saw in the new regime hope for undoing at least the injustices of the Restoration land settlement, James's tactics not only failed to achieve equity for Catholic landowners but also ensured an even longer era of Protestant domination—political, economic, and social—in the eighteenth century. The religious-cultural estrangement between Catholics and Protestants was compounded by the ever-present conqueror-conquered syndrome. Because of its proximity to Britain and its common racial makeup, all Irish rejected the view that Ireland was a colony. Ireland, they argued, was a kingdom possessing a common monarch with Britain. The principal institution used by the Protestant minority to ensure their control of Ireland in the eighteenth century was Parliament, though its unreformed colonial status dimmed the potential. Two questions remained prominently unresolved in the eighteenth century:

Would the structure of British governance in Ireland change from colony to common kingdom, and if Ireland gained a measure of independence, would participation include both Protestants and Catholics?

REVOLUTION AND TREATY OF LIMERICK

James II named his Anglican brother-in-law, Henry Hyde, second earl of Clarendon, as lord lieutenant of Ireland (1685–1687). Clarendon favored continuation of the policies of Charles II. Yet another key figure in the Jacobite rule was the military commander in chief, a Catholic, Richard Talbot, created earl of Tyrconnell by James II. Talbot's brother, Peter, was the deposed Catholic archbishop of Dublin. Tyrconnell's wife was the sister of the wife of John Churchill, soon to be a prominent political-military figure in England. The earl's pro-Catholic policy, which included disbanding the Protestant militia, was at odds with Clarendon's. Tyrconnell's Irish army was soon made up of two-thirds Catholics among the enlisted soldiers and almost half among the officers. As James II gradually began erecting a Catholic political establishment, he removed Clarendon in February 1687 as lieutenant and made Tyrconnell deputy lieutenant, who rapidly turned over all key offices in the Irish government to Catholics. The deputy also made plans to return as much as half of the Protestant confiscated lands to Catholic owners. Protestant control of courts, local government, and the central bureaucracy was also endangered.

Motivated by both revenge and self-interest, Irish Catholics seemed intent not just to achieve power sharing but to root out the Protestants, one-fourth of the population. Yet Catholics were trying to undo a decades-long trend of Protestantization in Ireland, manifested primarily in the transfer of political power and property, which had been largely completed by 1660. Catholics needed a free hand and many years to alter the recent course of Irish history. Instead, they got only a few years of control to accomplish their goals. By 1691 the pre–James II Protestant trends were resumed with vigor.

Following the Glorious Revolution of 1688 and the removal of James II in favor of Protestant monarchs William III and Mary II (1689–1702), the Catholic gains were jeopardized immediately. After James II fled England for France, William III tried to negotiate with Tyrconnell to recognize him as king but failed to secure the desired support when the king's Catholic envoy, Richard Hamilton, joined Tyrconnell. Three months after arriving in France, James sailed for Ireland with French troops and landed at Kinsale in March 1689, seeking to recover his lost throne. Combined French and Irish forces eventually numbered about 40,000, although many were not well trained or properly equipped to fight a major war. The Catholic army, led by an inexperienced Hamilton, marched toward the Protestant stronghold of Ulster, where defenders had fortified several major towns, such as Enniskillen and Londonderry. The turning point in the Catholic invasion of Ulster was the siege of Londonderry and blockade of the port, which began in April. Protestant commander Robert Lundy expected to surrender and thus dispatched two regiments of reinforcements back to England. This left 30,000 people inside the city, where leadership was assumed by Reverend George Walker, who kept spirits high. After the Catholic forces under Hamilton failed to take advantage of their opportunity, Protestant reinforcements under Major General Percy Kirk arrived in June. When the 105-day siege was lifted on July 31, the Jacobite threat to Ulster seemed also to shrink.

Meanwhile, James had left his army at Londonderry for Dublin to oversee an overwhelmingly Catholic Parliament (224 Catholics out of 230 members) organized by Tyrconnell. The Parliament voted the attainder (without trial or due process) of 2,000 Protestants with the confiscation of their property, underscoring the primary grievance of Catholics since the Restoration. Yet Catholics quickly became dismayed at James's attitude. Focusing on the main objective of regaining his throne in England, a circumspect James opposed Parliament's repeal of Poynings' Law and the Restoration land settlement. Catholic clergy were also disappointed that James did not favor confiscation of Church of England properties, but only a grant of religious toleration. On the other side, although Irish Protestants did not at first declare against James Stuart, they feared bloody reprisals by the Irish Catholic army and began to organize local defense associations. A future Anglican archbishop of Dublin, William King, penned a rationale for Protestant opposition to James Stuart in his *State of the Protestants in Ireland* (1691). King argued that because the Jacobites threatened to eliminate the Anglican church, resistance to James was justified.

England's war with France beginning in 1689, and the presence of French troops under James in Ireland, posed a serious threat to William's throne, as well as his war effort. William dispatched a veteran Dutch commander, the seventy-four-year-old duke of Schomberg, with about 20,000 troops. Schomberg landed in Ulster at Bangor, county Down, in August 1689 and quickly captured the port of Carrickfergus. Yet his movement bogged down in the failed attempt to seize Dundalk; most fighting subsided during the winter of 1689–1690. Jacobites seized Trinity College and Christ Church cathedral in Dublin.

Frustrated by the slow progress, William arrived in Ireland with his own army in June 1690 to take charge of the campaign. The Williamite forces, which included Dutch, Danish, and French Huguenot units, swept across most of Ulster, putting James on the defensive. French reinforcements arrived to strengthen James's position. William's army of 36,000 troops moved up the Boyne River near Drogheda, where James had established a defensive position with about 25,000 soldiers. The Battle of the Boyne (1690) was not a truly decisive military victory, but William forced James to retreat west toward Connacht. To James, the war had been lost even though he still possessed substantial forces. A couple of weeks after the Boyne defeat, James sailed from Kinsale for France, leaving his forces under a French general and Tyrconnell. Meanwhile, William occupied Dublin and Waterford; his commander, John Churchill, seized Cork and Kinsale. Yet the Catholic forces successfully held out at Limerick for months under the spirited leadership of Patrick Sarsfield, earl of Lucan. Finally, a Dutch general, baron von Ginkel, captured Galway and Athlone and subdued the main Catholic force at the Battle of Aughrim. Limerick surrendered, and Lucan and Ginkel signed a peace.

For an uneasy Protestant minority, which had survived two Catholic rebellions since 1641, the Treaty of Limerick (1691) was intended to be an expression of conquest over Catholics, not settlement. Thus, Irish Catholics regarded the treaty thereafter as harsh and unfair. Fourteen thousand Irish soldiers, soon known as the "wild geese," were allowed to leave Ireland and join the French army, which removed the prime security threat to English rule. The Spanish army also maintained five Irish regiments during the eighteenth century. Catholics, of course, tried to secure religious toleration and the return of confiscated lands, but they failed. Instead, the disabilities invoked by the treaty were severe. Catholics could not vote, sit in Parliament, or hold other state offices. They were not allowed to serve in the British military and were excluded from organized economic trades. Despite owning less than 15 percent of the land, Catholics could not buy property from Protestants. Later, the government forced all Catholic clergy (1,000 priests and 4,000 monks and nuns) to register so they could be monitored. One million acres of land was confiscated (much of it from James, Tyrconnell, and other Jacobites) and either granted to William's nobles or sold to Irish Protestants. During the eighteenth century, about 5,000 Protestant landed families controlled most of the political power. Although no Catholic insurrection occurred for more than a century after the Treaty of Limerick, their hope for integration into a more tolerant British system would remain problematic.

POLITICS UNDER PROTESTANT ASCENDANCY

The Irish Parliament under William III, though made up only of Protestants, sought to retain its freedoms by claiming the right to regulate Irish taxes; but the English government vigorously returned to the principle of Poynings' Law that Ireland's constitution was regulated by England. The Irish Parliament's subordination to Westminster was reasserted by the Declaratory Act in 1720, which in theory meant there was no need for an Irish Parliament. Indeed, the frequently absentee lord lieutenant was unable to control the biennial meetings of Parliament and dismissed it in 1692. Yet because Parliament was made up of Protestant landlords, the English authorities depended on it to assist in governance. During the reign of Queen Anne (1702–1714), more religious penal laws—the Popery Bills of 1703–1704—resolved ambiguities by limiting Catholic investment and lease rights. Only Anglicans were allowed to hold office, so that not only were Catholics excluded but also the 1704 sacramental test removed dissenting Protestants such as Presbyterians from office. Attempts to repeal the act failed in 1731 and 1733. The Toleration Act of 1719 freed dissenting Protestants from attending Anglican churches but retained the political disabilities.

Party politics, which originated in England during Charles II's reign, began to influence Irish policy in Anne's reign. Most Tories insisted on control of Irish church and state affairs by Anglicans, while Whigs favored toleration toward dissenting Protestants. Desiring Protestant unity, Whigs favored repression of Catholics, whereas Tories argued that dissenting Protestants were the real threat. Anglican policies proved unpopular with many non-Anglican Protestants and eventually stimulated a large emigration of Ulster Presbyterians to the American colonies. The queen preferred Tories as her lord lieutenants, including the former chancellor of Oxford University, James Butler, second duke of Ormond (1703–1707, 1710–1713), and Thomas Herbert, earl of Pembroke (1707–1708). The exception was the term of the extreme Whig, Thomas, first earl of Wharton (1708–1710), forced on the queen by political circumstances. Tory governors faced stiff Whig resistance. The Whig solicitor general, Alan Brodrick, was dismissed by Ormond in 1704 because of obstructionist tactics. Yet Brodrick also served as Speaker of the House of Commons (1703–1710, 1713–1714), where he upheld a Whig agenda.

As the Tory party fortunes declined under George I, due to their leader's backing of the Jacobites, the Whig dominance in Ireland allowed greater focus on the political profit motive. Patronage in eighteenth-century British politics was notoriously corrupt, and it was no less so in Ireland. Yet since there were more applicants for office than offices to fill, political leaders found that a large contingent of disappointed office seekers could prove a source of disaffection toward political authority. During the reign of George I (1714–1727), there were two Whig factions of note in Ireland—one led by Lord Chancellor Brodrick (1714–1725), and the other by the Speaker of the House of Commons, William Conolly (1715–1727). Because Conolly most often gained the favor of the lord lieutenant, Brodrick, with his thirty loyal members of the Irish Parliament, worked diligently in opposition to obstruct policy, especially money bills. Although Brodrick usually followed a predictable pattern of political self-interest, he also could demonstrate opposition to British policy. As a member of the British Parliament, Brodrick opposed the Peerage Bill of 1719, which his political allies backed.

An elaborate "undertaker" patronage system developed from the 1720s to the 1750s. Undertakers were political favorites allowed to secure lucrative offices for their associates in the government, military, and church. As much as 60 percent of the seats in the House of Commons was controlled by a handful of landlords. In return for upholding a government position in the house, the elites received lucrative pensions and offices in both state and church. Also, over sixty Irish politicians held seats in the British Parliament in the first half of the eighteenth century. Among them, John Perceval (1683–1748), member of Parliament (MP) for Harwich between 1727 and 1734, was typical of Irish influence. Perceval's family arrived in county Cork from England in the seventeenth century, the beneficiary of highly valued confiscated native lands in the eighteenth century. The Percevals were major patrons of the arts and the Cork music society. In a late seventeenth-century reconstruction of Burton House, Perceval's father employed the best portrait artist of the era, the English-born Thomas Pooley, and the Dutch sculptor Arnold Quellin. John Perceval, educated at Oxford University, was made fifth baronet in 1691, baron in 1715, and viscount in 1723 and raised to the peerage as first earl of Egmont in 1733. He became the primary financial partner with General James Oglethorpe in the founding of Georgia in 1732–1733.

Typical of most other eighteenth-century Anglo-Irish leaders, Perceval focused his attention more on events in England than in Ireland.

During the Whig dominance of the second quarter of the eighteenth century, political integrity was often measured by the ideal of "patriotism," that is, putting the needs of the people and nation ahead of self-interest. In the case of Ireland, such patriots always constituted a minority in institutions such as Parliament. Provincial elites, whose personal concerns may have more often coincided with popular Irish interests, dominated the Irish Parliament, while the executive in Dublin reflexively followed the London government's agenda. Because of infrequent elections, Parliament was rather easy to control; only one Parliament was elected in the thirty-three-year reign of George II (1727–1760). The leading Irish parliamentary figure in George II's reign was Henry Boyle, Speaker of the House of Commons (1733–1756), who opposed British governments when they allied with his enemies such as the Ponsonbys. John Ponsonby succeeded Boyle as Speaker (1756–1771) and worked closely with his brother-in-law, Lord Lieutenant William Cavendish, marquis of Hartington. The archbishop of Armagh (1724–1742), Hugh Boulter, remained the most dependable government ally of Robert Walpole's British government. Inept or out-of-favor politicians in Britain were often given posts in Ireland as a sop. Absentee executives were the rule. Lord lieutenants resided in Ireland in only sixteen of the forty-six-year reigns of George I and George II. Only two lieutenants before 1760 showed genuine interest in Ireland. John Carteret (1724–1730) demonstrated sympathy with the Irish in opposing Wood's halfpence, and he put Irish finances on a sound footing. Philip Stanhope, fourth earl of Chesterfield (1745–1746), kept order in the country and Parliament during the Jacobite rising of 1745.

Political dissent became associated largely with the Tory party after the failed Jacobite rising of 1715. The chief spokesman was Dublin-born Jonathan Swift (1667–1745), Anglo-Irish graduate of Trinity College and dean of St. Patrick's after 1713. Swift's political ambition was always tempered by his self-conscious status as an Anglican cleric. Thus, while he often joined others in criticizing British government policy toward Ireland, he would not countenance attacks on the Christian religion by skeptics or deists or on the established church's constitutionally privileged status. Swift withdrew his backing for the Whigs in 1708–1709 because he believed they were not sufficiently committed to protecting the church's position. His political shift to the Tories may explain Swift's failure to be named bishop of Waterford. Though unpublished until

1720, Swift's first political tract on Irish affairs, *Story of the Injured Lady* (1707), contained the essence of his political views: greater independence for the Irish government and Parliament, an end to English political patronage at Ireland's expense, and an end to trade discrimination.

Aligned with the politically astute literary elite of England, including Alexander Pope, Joseph Addison, and Richard Steele, Swift began work on the prototypical modern dystopia through his pointedly political satire, *Gulliver's Travels* (written between 1714 and 1726), which lampooned a corrupt and ignorant British bureaucracy. Swift rejected the anomaly of Ireland as a dependent colony subject to the authority of Britain. Without consulting the Irish government, George I's mistress, the duchess of Kendal, was given permission in 1722 to mint an Irish copper halfpenny and subsequently sold the rights for £10,000 to an English iron manufacturer, William Wood. The halfpence named for Wood immediately met a hostile Irish public. Swift responded with *Drapier's Letters* in 1724, which showed resentment at England's manipulation of Ireland for some petty interest, (a royal mistress). Resorting to his familiar satire, Swift ridiculed English justice and thereby brought at least momentary economic unity to an otherwise fitfully divided Ireland, which universally boycotted Wood's halfpence. Swift wondered why the Irish should not be as free as Englishmen, an issue that would soon haunt Anglo-American relations. Although the lord lieutenant posted a reward for the identification of the author of the letters, no one came forward to identify Swift. Lord Lieutenant Carteret recommended the recall of Wood's halfpence, which occurred in 1725.

Later in 1729, Swift showed his frustration with the continuation of Ireland's exploitation by England. In *A Modest Proposal for Preventing the Children of Ireland from Being a Burden on Their Parents or County*, Swift suggested an outrageous solution to the scarcity of food. The Irish could eat their children "whether stewed, roasted, baked or boiled." Such a solution would be especially good for landlords, who effectively already had consumed children's parents. Several Irish "problems" could be solved: the Catholic population would be reduced and thus please the English administration; tenants could pay their burdensome rents and fees with their children; mothers would feed their children well to enhance their value; and marital relations would improve since the offspring of mating would increase family wealth rather than being a financial burden.

ECONOMY, SOCIETY, AND RELIGION

Until the mid-eighteenth century, the Irish economy remained under-developed, largely agricultural, and marked by crises in a nation replete with poverty. The Irish poor lived in the worst housing in Europe, though they tended to be better clothed than some peasant populations. Poverty was a major cause of emigration from Ireland by small farmers. The agricultural economy suffered from a limited amount of cultivation due to a small population of about 2 million. Irish peasants were accustomed to a hierarchy of clientage, so that having Protestant landlords was little different from previous centuries. Absentee landlords became a greater problem after 1689 than during the Restoration era. A 1695 act allowed landlords to establish tenancies at will, which permitted owners to remove unwanted tenants and raise rents arbitrarily. Traditionally, pastureland outstripped arable fields, so that the numerous small farms, averaging ten acres or less on average, retarded overall productivity. Opposition to the growth of cattle pasturage at the expense of crop tillage explains the violence in Connacht during 1710–1713 led by a group called the Houghers who maimed cattle as a form of protest.

The causes of poverty in the early eighteenth century included technological backwardness in manufacturing as well as agriculture, a narrow range of exports, and an Ireland forced to live in the economic shadow of England's prosperous commercial economy. Bad harvests, which appeared with regularity after 1660, compounded the troubles caused by the antiquated agricultural system. In the 1674 famine, thousands of livestock and hundreds of poor Irish died. The 1708 European-wide famine hit Munster hardest, and the 1721–1722 bad harvests were complicated by a severe trade depression. In 1739–1740, the grain and potato crops failed, leading to bread riots in Dublin and the deaths of 13 percent of the population (20 percent in Munster). The 1744–1745 famine included crop failures and livestock and population declines; one estimate claimed that 400,000 poor Irish died of starvation. Obviously such disasters inhibited progress for most Irish, although a successful farming regime became entrenched in Munster and Leinster and parts of eastern Connacht. By midcentury, farm prices rose and interest rates declined, ushering in boom times for the 1750s and 1760s. Ireland's first major manufacturing facility, a flour mill, opened in county Meath in 1767. Many small Irish farmers came to depend on swine and the easily grown, nutritious potato for their livelihood. Prosperity among small farmers after 1750 (by comparison with the previous era) explains why grain and potato crop failures such as in 1765–1766 and 1782–1784 did not lead to famine. One important result was steady population growth comparable to the rest of Europe during the second half of the eighteenth century.

Trade held great potential for the eighteenth-century Irish economy, yet the Navigation Act of 1696 prohibited potentially valuable colonial imports from reaching Irish ports. Furthermore, Irish exports, overly dependent on cattle and wool, were subordinated to English interests, resulting in restrictions on trade in essentials such as salt, beer, and wool. Prohibitions on Irish cattle and meat by-product exports to England were erected in 1680 and remained in effect until 1758. The favorite trade of the Protestant settlers, wool, was especially important to the economy because it flourished in both urban and rural locales. Before the crisis with James II, woolen exports had reached a peak in 1687; thus, England's Parliament placed duties on Irish exports in 1698, followed quickly by the Woollen Act of 1699, which prohibited all exports. Therefore, when duty-free exports of linen were allowed to England in 1696 and America in 1705, linen easily replaced wool as the chief export from Ireland. French Huguenot immigrants such as Louis Crommelin had made the linen trade profitable. Linen production, most of which was exported, rose steadily from 300,000 yards in 1700 to 11 million in 1750, and reached a peak of 40 million in the last two decades of the century.

The prosperity of trading towns such as Cork, Waterford, and Limerick increased slowly after 1689, then grew quite dramatically during the early eighteenth century, even encompassing Catholic merchants. Belfast in Ulster emerged as the fourth major port early in the eighteenth century. The largest interior town, Kilkenny, had a modest coal mining and woolen manufacturing economy. The Irish House of Commons petitioned for relief from economic discrimination in 1703. When England formally merged with Scotland in the 1707 Act of Union, the Irish House of Lords begged the government to allow Ireland to join the new entity of Great Britain. Yet there was no political pressure for the crown to adhere to Irish wishes; England's economic interests opposed union with Ireland. Even without relief from trade restrictions, Irish exports doubled from 1700 to 1740 and increased sixfold between 1700 and 1815. Cattle and linen made up 80 percent of the exports in the eighteenth century. There were as many as 3,000 cattle fairs by 1800, which enhanced the prosperity of many smaller communities.

About the only distinction Ireland could claim in the early eighteenth century was the position of Dublin, the second largest city in the British isles after London with a population of over 100,000. As the commercial economy grew, Dublin benefited as a center of sugar refining as well as silk and wool production. Arthur Guinness launched an auspicious brewery in 1759 at St. James' Gate. Over half of all Irish trade went through the port of Dublin, despite the fact that it was a rather poor harbor. With the increased importance of Parliament, including a new Parliament house designed by the greatest Irish architect of the era, Sir Edward Lovett Pearce, Dublin's status as the political capital became more significant in the eighteenth century than before. Dublin had become the cultural center of Protestant Ireland mainly through the success of Trinity College with almost three thousand students. New campus construction in the early eighteenth century featured a medical center finished in 1711 and a library designed by Thomas Burgh, completed in 1732. Other building in the Georgian era featuring open squares and malls as well as stylish buildings made Dublin an aesthetic delight. Several new hospitals opened in Dublin during the first half of the century. The Smock Alley theater, operated by the father of Richard Brinsley Sheridan, featured the first Irish performances of John Gay's *Beggar's Opera* in 1748 and the first opera in Ireland in 1761. Shakespearean plays and notable actors such as David Garrick and Samuel Foote also graced the Smock's stage. William Viner held the first post as master of state music beginning in 1703. Georg Frederick Handel's *Messiah* was first performed in the Dublin Music Hall in 1742 along with six other Handel concerts, and Italian violinist Francesco Geminiani settled in Dublin.

Ireland followed Scotland, Wales, and America in the development of a more sophisticated and cultured aristocracy. Notable Palladian country houses of the nobility with their magnificent gardens and art collections gave the Irish countryside a remarkable aesthetic appearance. The county Kildare estate of political leader William Conolly, Castletown (1722), was perhaps the most striking example. The primary architect was an Italian designer, Alessandro Galilei. Castletown's exterior facade and wings were completed by Pearce, whose tour of Italy and instruction in the Palladian style was guided by Galilei in the mid-1720s. Estate owners relied on modern methods of agriculture and reforestation promoted by progressive institutions such as the Royal Dublin Society (1731). Such reform of manners, however, did not mean the disappearance of baser social habits of drinking or dueling, especially among the gentry.

In addition to Swift, several other Anglo-Irish intellectuals came into prominence between the 1690s and 1750s. William Molyneaux was a respected mathematician-philosopher as well as member of Parliament. Strongly influenced by his friend John Locke, Molyneaux's 1698 publication, *The Case of Ireland's Being Bound by Acts of Parliament in England*, questioned the subordination of the Irish Parliament to that at Westminster, calling it bad law as well as unfair. He argued that if the English Parliament was sovereign, then Ireland should be allowed to elect members to sit in that body. The Dublin Philosophical Society (founded 1684), led by Molyneaux and Sir William Petty, was modeled on the Royal Society in England. It promoted scientific knowledge and established a museum as well as publishing its proceedings. Many Anglo-Irish scholars participated in the Dublin Society including Swift, William Congreve, and George Berkeley. Congreve's comic play, *The Way of the World*, was presented on the London stage in 1700.

George Berkeley (1685–1753) continued to break away from religious tradition begun at Cambridge during the Restoration era, arguing that the mind is the source of creativity. Berkeley influenced better-known eighteenth-century philosophers such as David Hume and Immanuel Kant. During a residence in Rhode Island, Berkeley immersed himself in the colonial milieu, seeking, without success, to establish a college to serve as a training place for missionaries. Upon returning to Ireland, he penned two noteworthy philosophical treatises in 1709–1710: *New Theory of Vision* and *Treatise of Human Knowledge*. Berkeley resided in London between 1713 and 1720, where he replicated Swift's literary friendships. After 1734, as Anglican bishop of Cloyne, Berkeley paid greater attention to Irish issues. Between 1735 and 1737, Berkeley composed a journal, the *Querist*, which mirrored the ideas of Swift and Molyneaux, seeking amelioration of the economic plight of the Irish peasantry. The several hundred questions posed by the *Querist* covered all pertinent Irish concerns—economic, social, and political—though Berkeley's suggested solutions emphasized innovative self-reliance rather than political confrontation.

Ireland's 250 booksellers and printers demonstrated an impressive market for the printed word. Cultural elites also patronized a variety of popular amusements for the lower social classes, as well as symbolic political celebrations that featured processions, ringing of bells, and feasts of food and drink. Hierarchical relationships of patron and client occurred in all realms—political, social, economic, and cultural.

The established Church of Ireland's four archdioceses (Armagh, Dublin, Cashel, Tuam) and twelve dioceses provided respectable incomes. Moreover, given that the church was no longer exclusive, attendance at services in the parish churches was rather good. Anglicans such as Archbishop Boulter of Armagh viewed the church as more than merely a religious institution, hoping it could become the basis for a complete organization of Irish society. Following the grant of toleration by the British Parliament in 1689, Anglican clerics were especially sensitive to the church's vulnerable position. The Church of Ireland convocation (clerical assembly) of 1703 sought to discipline the population in matters ranging from church attendance to censorship of profanities and immoral speech and publications. The ecclesiastical courts served as the main instrument of discipline, with jurisdiction over tithes, nonattendance at church, Sabbath violations, heresy, and sexual immorality. Excommunication not only meant exclusion from the church but also placed a social stigma on the excommunicant. Day-to-day problems of the church included too few clergy, clerical nonresidence and plural office-holding, and the poor physical condition of many churches. Still, the 800 Church of Ireland clerics serving 250,000 parishioners was a better ratio than their Catholic counterpart. High-church clergy were particularly wary of the growing influence of the Presbyterians, notably their social influence. The Church of Ireland clung to tradition in an Ireland that was changing much faster than usual in the eighteenth century.

After the defeat of James II, Protestants had a sense of purpose in protecting the Protestant ascendancy. Thus, Protestants jealously guarded their economic and social advantage over the Catholic population in addition to opposing Catholic political aims. Indeed, Protestants saw danger from Catholicism not so much in its theology as from its politics. The best illustration is Jacobitism, grounded firmly in the divine right theory of kingship. Seeking to restore the royal line of James II, Jacobites never considered basing their campaigns from Ireland since it lacked any strategic position in recovering the English throne. Repression of Catholics after the 1715 Jacobite rising subsided, and within ten years of the last failed Jacobite rebellion in 1745, Irish Catholics, urged by their clergy, had no trouble recognizing the Protestant Hanoverians as legitimate monarchs. With about 2,300 Catholic clerics in the 1730s, the influence of Catholicism was effective, even though many places of worship for the 1.8 million Catholics were simple and crude. Catholic churches in Dublin and some other towns remained in good repair, well furnished and well decorated. About 550 Catholic schools continued to function in most places despite being illegal. Yet problems remained. Many bishops refused to reside in their dioceses, and priests often neglected their pastoral duties. Probably fewer than half of Catholic communicants attended mass on a regular basis. Moreover, belief in magic and superstition was rampant among the lower classes. The traditional pilgrimage to "St. Patrick's Purgatory," a holy site at Lough Derg, brought over 3,000 visitors each year.

Religious issues in eighteenth-century Ireland were by no means confined to Catholics. About half of the Protestant population would not conform with Anglicanism, so they had grievances against the Church of Ireland as well. Clearly, Scots Presbyterians, congregated largely in Ulster, remained the core of Protestant dissent. Towns, the traditional center of Protestant craftsmen and merchants, were much smaller and scattered in Ireland compared with either Scotland or England. Before the Hanoverian succession in 1714, the established church insisted on persecution of dissenting Protestants because their growing numbers were deemed a threat to the Church of Ireland. Presbyterians outnumbered Anglicans in Ulster by the 1690s, with immigration of additional Presbyterians from Scotland continuing. The establishment of a Presbyterian synod in 1691 gave the church local organization and control, further threatening the Church of Ireland's position. Therefore, the establishment clergy pushed through a measure in the British Parliament in 1704 requiring a sacramental test for Protestants to block dissenters from expanding their political power. Just as with the Catholics, the Church of Ireland feared the political motives of dissenters, especially because most were from Scotland, where unpopular Anglicanism had been effectively routed. Irish elites did not want Ireland to follow Scotland's example.

The possibility of conversion by one group of another was not given serious attention by either Catholics or Protestants. Evangelism was foreign to Catholics except the Jesuits, and Protestants did not believe any religious conversion of Catholics would be accompanied by an embracing of capitalist economics so important to the Presbyterians. During the eighteenth century, only about 4,000 Catholics were converted to Protestantism. John and Charles Wesley brought their Methodist evangelical crusade to Ireland in the late 1740s, but did not make a lasting impression. Instead of conversion efforts, the Protestants relied on immigration from Ulster to the other three provinces to affect expansion of influence. Even more influential were the dissenting Protestant "charity" schools (funded by contributions rather than tuition) first inaugurated in Dublin in 1717. By 1721, there were 130 such schools offering instruction to 3,000 students. In 1734, the Anglican Society for Promoting English Protestantism launched its "charter" schools (tax supported) modeled on the charity system. By midcentury, about thirty charter schools operated, with about 900 pupils learning a trade as well as reading and writing. Yet the charter schools were badly mismanaged and detested by Catholics, thereby failing to achieve their main goal of proselytizing Catholics. Protestants also established the first charitable hospital in the British Isles in Dublin in 1718, spurring several other hospital projects over the next several decades. Given all of the religious divisions in Ireland and the growth of secularism in eighteenth-century Europe, religious belief continued to be significant in the lives of the vast majority of the Irish population.

Irish problems of law and order in the eighteenth century were typical of most of Europe. The chief source of external and internal security for Ireland was 12,000 British troops, almost twice as many as the standing army in England. The army was supported in theory by a Protestant militia that could be mobilized in emergencies. When units of the Irish army were sent to Scotland during the Jacobite rising of 1745, a Protestant Association raised a militia of 65,000 to face any invasion threat in Ireland. Local law enforcement was handled largely by over 2,000 justices of the peace, though only about 400 actually performed regular duties. The justices of the peace were assisted by constables and watchmen in each parish.

Crime was not a major threat to the peace of Ireland. The existence of bandits, mainly in Connacht, south Ulster, and Munster, came closest to an epidemic of crime in the late seventeenth and early eighteenth centuries. Most bandit gangs were thought to have been political Tories from the late seventeenth century, many of whom came from respectable families. The bandits did not resemble Robin Hood since they preyed on targets of opportunity irregardless of income status. Neither did they distinguish between Protestants and Catholics among their victims. Gangs of bandits virtually disappeared by the middle of the eighteenth century. The decline of banditry coincided with a significant era of prosperity rare in Ireland's history. Despite incidents of organized crime, most crimes were categorized as misdemeanor rather than felonies during the century. Towns often faced riots brought on by economic protests of varying sorts. Authorities in port cities frequently dealt with attempts at smuggling. By comparison, transportation (shipment to overseas possessions) of serious criminals was at least three times greater in Britain than in Ireland. The percentage of convictions by juries was quite low in the eighteenth century, not only because juries of commoners were independent of the control of judges, but also because the rules of evidence in criminal trials had become more stringent. Even Catholics could feel secure about obtaining equal justice under the law in Irish courts.

BURKE, GRATTAN, AND LEGISLATIVE INDEPENDENCE

Edmund Burke (1729–1797) followed early-eighteenth-century Anglo-Irish advocates lobbying for Irish reforms during the reign of George III (1760–1820). His father, Richard, was an Anglican lawyer who wanted his son to follow in his occupation. Burke's mother, Mary Nagle, was a Catholic, and young Burke even attended a Catholic school in county Cork in his early years. He later transferred to a Quaker school in county Kildare and in 1744 matriculated at Trinity College, Dublin, where he founded a philosophy club. Following the wishes of his father, Edmund entered the Middle Temple in London in 1750 to study law, but he soon dropped out and began to pursue his first love of political philosophy. He edited the first volumes of the *Annual Register* from 1758 until 1761, when he returned to Dublin to work for the Irish chief secretary, W. G. Hamilton. Increasingly conscious of Ireland's stepchild status, Burke's first important publication, *A Tract on the Popery Laws* (1761), criticized Britain's treatment of Irish Catholics. Upon returning to England in 1765, Burke accepted the patronage of the Whig leader, the marquis of Rockingham, and won election to Parliament the next year, representing the borough of Wendover. Burke served as MP for Bristol from 1774 to 1780 and for the small borough of Malton after 1780.

The first systemic violence in many decades appeared in Ireland in the 1760s with the Catholic "Whiteboy" campaign in Munster. Grievances originated over involuntary Church of Ireland tithe collections and extended to high rents and arbitrary evictions brought on by famine and high prices during 1765–1766. When authorities began repressing the Whiteboys, Burke criticized the government for not responding to their legitimate complaints. Long before the outbreak of the American Revolution in 1775, Burke had championed colonial rights from the floor of the House of Commons and became a well-known figure in America. Ireland had always been a fertile ground for recruitment of soldiers for the British army. The British government's need for military forces in America gave Ireland political leverage that it had previously lacked.

When Lord Lieutenant George, first marquis Townshend, came to Ireland in 1767, he not only set a new precedent of residency but also proposed several reforms in exchange for an increase in the Irish army from

12,000 to 15,200. The reforms included a time limit on the duration of Irish parliaments comparable to the seven-year limit for the British Parliament; Irish judges were to serve terms of good behavior rather than at the will of the British executive; a habeas corpus act similar to that in Britain to prevent arbitrary arrest and imprisonment of Irish subjects; the elimination of Irish pensions for life granted by the British executive, which drained the Irish treasury; and a promise that the lord lieutenant would remain in Dublin instead of being an absentee ruler. The Irish Parliament enacted an octennial bill (Parliament limited to eight years), but the army increase failed to pass the British Parliament in 1768. Furthermore, the security of judges' proposal failed because of British restrictions on the policy, and the habeas corpus proposal was vetoed by the British executive. Disgruntled and disappointed, a narrow majority of the Irish Parliament favored dissolution in 1768. Thus, the reform hopes raised by Townshend's agenda remained largely unfulfilled.

The Irish Parliament represented 300,000 Anglicans but not 1.8 million Catholics and 200,000 dissenting Protestants. Still, an odd parliamentary combination of former "undertakers" and patriots such as Henry Flood (1732–91) challenged the privy council privilege of proposing money bills. A constitutional expert with a pronounced moral tone, Flood later accepted appointment as vice treasurer (1775), hoping to influence the administration from within. Feeling pressure from the British government to quell dissent, Townshend suspended Parliament for two years (1769–1771), and was soon replaced as lord lieutenant by Simon, earl of Harcourt (1772–1777). When the idea of a tax on Irish absentee landlords was advanced by patriots in Ireland, Burke joined Lord North in opposing the measure; the Irish Parliament, still under the control of the administration, rejected the tax.

The 1775 outbreak of the American Revolution had an immediate impact on Ireland, resulting in reduced trade, especially linen, and an embargo on provisions exported to America. The revolution also led to the eventual removal of 4,000 British troops from Ireland across the Atlantic. The Irish followed events in America with great interest, in part because of numerous family connections, especially with Ulster Protestants. Moreover, Irish grievances against Britain were more serious than American concerns. In 1778, Britain's Lord North favored opening Ireland to imperial trade (except the export of Irish wool), but English manufacturing interests pressured North to limit the changes to minor adjustments, allowing only the export of cotton textiles and ships built in Irish ports. Following the example of American patriots, Irish merchants in

1779 adopted a nonimportation agreement, refusing to buy British imports until their grievances were addressed. Despite its reduction of security forces, the British government would not allow Ireland to eliminate the gap with its own militia. Thus, fear of a French invasion in Ireland, combined with episodes of internal violence, spurred the organization of paramilitary organizations, starting in Belfast in 1778, called Volunteers. By 1780, Volunteers, which included Catholic and Protestant members, numbered about 40,000 under the command of James Caulfield, first earl of Charlemont.

Meanwhile, the British government felt compelled to offer some conciliation to the Irish. The Catholic Relief Act of 1779 allowed Catholic Irish to obtain leases of 999 years and to inherit land. The 1704 sacramental test was voided in 1780, allowing Protestant dissenters (non-Anglicans) civil rights such as voting and holding office. A delayed habeas corpus act passed in 1782. The British Parliament even opened Irish trade to the empire, including the export of woolen cloth. Because Poynings' Law and the Declaratory Act were still in force, Irish patriots began a push for legislative independence. Through a Dublin social club, the Society of Granby Row, patriot leaders including Charlemont and Henry Grattan (1746–1820) orchestrated their campaign with skill. Unlike American patriots, Grattan desired a reconciliation with Britain and continued participation in the empire on terms similar to what Lord North offered the Americans in 1778, that is, legislative independence. Fortunately for the Irish, the chief secretary, William Eden, an expert on commerce, agreed that legislative independence was the right approach.

The 25,000-strong Ulster Volunteers called a convention at Dungannon in February 1782, chaired by Charlemont. Following a well-rehearsed plan submitted by Flood, the convention approved several resolutions asserting the right of self-governance, free trade, and the creation of an Irish-controlled militia. A committee of the Ulster Volunteers began making contact with other Volunteer associations around Ireland to promote similar resolutions. In the Irish Parliament at Dublin, Grattan asked King George III for the right of legislative independence but failed to get a majority. Yet Lord Lieutenant Frederick Howard, earl of Carlisle (1780–1782), warned North's government that discontent in Ireland was rampant. Within weeks of North's March resignation, a new administration headed by the marquis of Rockingham, including Edmund Burke, agreed to grant legislative independence to Ireland.

In May 1782, the colonial secretary, Sir William Petty, second earl of Shelburne, proposed in the British House of Lords and Charles James

Fox moved in the House of Commons to create a new relationship with Ireland. The Irish "constitution" of 1782 contained several substantive modifications of Irish government. The Declaratory Act of 1720 was repealed, and Poynings' Law was modified to allow the Irish Parliament virtual home rule authority. The lord lieutenant was prohibited from proposing legislation, as he had done in the past. The British Parliament would regulate only foreign policy issues for Ireland. There would be no appeals to Britain from decisions by Irish courts. Yet the exact relationship between the two parliaments remained unclear. The Volunteers dissolved; though failing to secure Irish consensus, their achievement permanently altered the relationship between Ireland and Britain. Indeed, events in France beginning in 1789 introduced the ideal of democracy, which would threaten the 1782 solution.

Despite improvements such as the chartering of the Bank of Ireland (1782), economic problems in 1783, including a bad harvest and price increases, briefly produced an unstable environment to launch the embryonic constitution. However, the new lord lieutenant, Robert Henley, second earl of Northington (1783–1784), proposed lowering trade barriers to stimulate Ireland's commercial and manufacturing development; he could not convince the British cabinet to make more than superficial changes, such as allowing Ireland to operate its own post office. When angry Irish MPs began discussing retaliatory tariffs against Britain, chancellor of the exchequer John Foster's warning that the lucrative linen export trade to Britain might be endangered led to defeat of the punitive trade measures. Some rioting aimed at merchants trading with Britain occurred in Dublin following the parliamentary setback. A radical reform congress met during 1784–1785 to pressure the Irish and British parliaments. William Pitt's British government entered negotiations in 1784 with Foster for serious free-trade concessions to Ireland in exchange for a taxable (customs and excise) portion of the trade profits. Yet the idea of using Ireland to obtain a new source of British revenue smacked of direct taxation, which had caused the American colonists to rebel. Moreover, Pitt's plan was a two-edged economic sword. While Ireland's exports would benefit, it would harm Irish manufacturing, ill equipped to compete on equal terms with British manufactures. Pitt's lord lieutenant, Charles Manners, fourth duke of Rutland (1784–1787), criticized the economic plan, and the Irish Parliament, led by Grattan and Flood, opposed it in 1785. Several alternate plans ensued. Although Pitt favored provisions that would be agreeable to the Irish, British parliamentary opposition rallied a majority to reject them. When a package acceptable to the British Parliament was approved, it was rejected by the Irish Parliament. The Irish Parliament insisted on a balanced budget and an Irish contribution to a sinking fund (i.e., paying down Irish debt) instead of funding the British military.

In 1788 King George III was incapacitated by illness, and Pitt's Whig opponents, hoping to overthrow his administration, pressed him to pass a bill to make the prince of Wales regent. The issue affected Ireland because parliamentary leaders such as Grattan argued that any British regent bill would violate the 1782 constitution. Rather, Grattan argued that Ireland should craft its own regency bill without regard to one introduced in the British Parliament. A staunch advocate of parliamentary independence from the executive, Grattan pressed hard for parliamentary sovereignty. He rallied a parliamentary majority against the lord lieutenant, George Temple, marquis of Buckingham. Still hoping for a reformed Irish Parliament, Grattan chose to back the political ambitions of the British Whig leader, Charles James Fox, against Pitt's government. However, Grattan lost his gambit when King George recovered before a regency bill was passed, thereby securing Pitt's power.

Emboldened by his newfound parliamentary majority, Grattan introduced two reform bills in the House of Commons. A pension bill would have limited the payment of government pensions from the Irish treasury and prevented those receiving pensions from sitting in the Commons. A second bill called for an end to government use of police forces for patronage. Both bills met defeat since the very pensioners in the Commons who previously supported Grattan in the regency debate opposed the bills. In fact, with Pitt still angry over Irish defections during the regency debate, the British cabinet authorized even more patronage for Ireland than in the past.

REBELLION OF 1798 AND ACT OF UNION

The outbreak of the French Revolution in 1789 quickly radicalized the British reform movement and caused a constitutional reformer like Burke to warn against such tendencies in his *Reflections on the Revolution in France* (1790). The spirit of revolution also changed the shape of Irish reform. Henry Grattan faced a recalcitrant Irish Parliament, which refused to consider parliamentary reform even under pressure from a self-proclaimed Volunteer "congress" urging franchise and representation reform. Grattan favored pushing for a Catholic franchise immediately, but the revolutionary climate caused Burke and Flood to oppose the idea at the time. Therefore, the major political question remained unresolved: Would Catholics be allowed to vote and hold office?

Gentry composed the Catholic Committee, founded in 1760 by John Curry, Charles O'Conor, and Thomas Wyse. Richard Burke, Edmund's only son, who led the committee prior to 1791, became the primary lobbyist for the Catholic franchise. When pamphleteer Theobald Wolfe Tone (1763–1798)—educated at Trinity College and in the law at London's Middle Temple—took over leadership of the Catholic Committee in 1791, he began a concerted campaign to unite Catholics and dissenting Protestants behind the concept of a wider franchise. Yet despite his call for toleration in *Argument on Behalf of the Catholics* (1791), Tone was a deist who despised the Catholic clergy and viewed an alliance of Catholics and Protestants strictly as a political expedient. The enemy was always Britain, and religious commitments were an inconvenient obstacle to be overcome.

Also in 1791, the newly formed, radical Protestant Belfast Society of United Irishmen agreed to back Tone and the principle of universal parliamentary representation. Merchant James Napper Tandy established a Dublin branch of the United Irishmen. In 1792, the United Irishmen launched the *Northern Star* newspaper edited by Samuel Neilson to promote parliamentary reform. The *Star*, placing Irish reform in a wider context, featured stories about progressive political causes in America and France. Combined with United Irishmen pamphlets, the *Star* kept pressure on the Irish Parliament. Although dissenting Protestant clergy such as Reverend William Steel Dickson in *Three Sermons on the Subject of Scripture Politics* (1793) embraced radical political ideas, they might not have provided the ecumenical basis for a Protestant-Catholic détente, which some scholars have suggested. Tone's goal of uniting Irish of every cultural-religious stripe to create an Irish nation independent of Britain was merely a dream.

Drafted by the chief secretary, Robert Hobart, the Irish Parliament's Catholic Relief Act of 1793 gave the vote to all freeholders regardless of religious persuasion. It allowed Catholics to serve in many civil and military posts and attend the universities, but it did not allow them to sit in Parliament. Thus, Grattan proposed in 1795 that Catholics be permitted to serve in Parliament. This time he was backed by the Whigs, Burke, and even Pitt's lord lieutenant, William, earl Fitzwilliam. Opposed to the proposal was the wily former law-and-order attorney general (1783–1789) and Irish lord chancellor, John Fitzgibbon, earl of Clare. The Tory/Anglican-dominated Parliament defeated Grattan's bill 155 to 84, in part because of fears of local upheavals and war with France. Fitzwilliam was forced to resign after only a few months in Ireland. As a consolation, Pitt offered to endow the Maynooth Catholic seminary for two hundred students. Most of the Irish seminaries operating in France since the sixteenth century had been closed because of the revolution. Maynooth soon became a bulwark for Irish Catholic conservatives. Meanwhile, Tone left Ireland for America (1795) and later Paris (1796), seeking French intervention in Ireland. Tone was followed to America and France by the Dublin United Irishman leader Tandy, who openly advocated revolution in Ireland.

Unfortunately for the cause of Irish unity, events in France caused a revival of sectarian emotions. Armed bands of Protestant Peep O'Day Boys (founded 1784) began raiding Catholic settlements in county Armagh, forcing the Catholic Defender militia to become active across northern parts of Leinster and Connacht. The Defenders advocated lower rents for farm tenants and higher wages for agricultural laborers, as well as abolition of Church of Ireland tithes. Peep O'Day Boys and Defenders engaged in frequent skirmishes at public events such as fairs. A more serious "Battle of the Diamond" occurred in county Armagh in September 1795 when Peep O'Day Boys drove off Catholics. Protestants began establishing Orange societies, recalling the Williamite victory over the Jacobites a century earlier, which heightened the sectarian tensions in the effort to protect the Protestant ascendancy.

After the Peep O'Day–Defender violence and the narrow aversion of a French fleet with Tone aboard landing at Bantry Bay in late 1796, the Irish Parliament, led by Lord Lieutenant John Pratt, second earl of Camden, voted to suspend habeas corpus. The following March, British military commander Gerard Lake ordered the surrender of arms in Ulster. Rioting occurred in Belfast. The United Irishmen began to split along religious lines between Catholics and Presbyterians. In Dublin, the government arrested fourteen United Irishmen conspirators in early 1798 and declared a state of rebellion. The United Irishmen were routed at New Ross, Wexford, in early June. Led by a Catholic priest, John Murphy, 15,000 Wexford Catholic peasants beat back the local militia and killed several hundred Protestants before being defeated by Lake's British troops at Vinegar Hill, near Enniscorthy, in June 1798. Leaders of the revolt were captured and hanged. Another June rising erupted in Ulster led by Henry McCracken, a cotton textile manufacturer, and Henry Monro, a linen draper, but their force of 7,000 was beaten in county Down, and both leaders were executed. A small French complement of

almost 1,000 under Jean Humbert accompanied by Tandy landed at Kil-
lala Bay, county Mayo, in August, but they were beaten by superior
British forces under the new lord lieutenant, Charles, marquis of Cornwallis. Tandy and a small contingent of United Irishmen sailing from
Dunkirk briefly occupied the island of Rutland off Donegal before retiring to France. The Royal Navy stopped another potential invasion fleet
of nine ships carrying 3,000 troops led by French General Jean Hardy off
county Donegal, and captured Theobald Wolfe Tone. Denied his preference to be shot by a firing squad, Tone committed suicide in a Dublin
jail a couple of weeks later to avoid being hanged, drawn, and quartered.
Tandy escaped to France, where he was decorated by Napoleon. Tone's
campaign for a united Irish front against Britain turned into an internal
sectarian struggle between Protestants and Catholics, an unfortunate
omen for Ireland's future.

Both Lord Chancellor Clare and Pitt, supported by Cornwallis, envisioned a return to stability in Ireland by replacing an independent Irish
Parliament with Irish representation in the British Parliament, similar to
that accorded Scotland in 1707. In return for a legislative union of Ireland
and Britain, Pitt would push for Catholic emancipation, which would
allow Catholic membership in Parliament. The tactics employed appealed
to Catholics since emancipation appeared impossible in a Protestant-
controlled Irish Parliament. On the other hand, Catholics would not be
a political threat if they were a minority within the British Parliament.
The principal designer of the Act of Union legislation was the Irish chief
secretary, Robert Stewart, viscount Castlereagh, who had previously
supported Grattan as a member of Parliament from county Down. Un-
concerned about the largely apolitical peasant population, Castlereagh
sought to win support from the Irish elites by offering the traditional
bribe of patronage. The staunchly Protestant earl of Clare shrewdly persuaded Castlereagh to drop the provision in the legislation to allow Catholics to vote. Moreover, with Burke's death in 1797, the Catholics lost a
formidable spokesman. Upon passage by the British Parliament of the
Act of Union (1800), the Irish Parliament voted 158 to 115 to accept their
extinction, ending the 1782 constitution. When George III refused to revive Catholic emancipation and Pitt resigned in 1801, Ireland began a
new era with new problems.

Prior to revolutionary troubles after 1795, by almost any measurement
Ireland had progressed dramatically over the previous hundred years.
Although many problems remained, economic improvements combined
with increased cooperation between Protestants and Catholics held the

potential for Ireland to overcome its past disabilities. Yet the Enlightenment inducement toward individualism and idealistic revolutions in America and France had a more profound impact on Ireland than mere material-constitutional progress.

5

From Union to Home Rule, 1801–1870

The primary method of solving European political problems in the eighteenth century had been revolution, and although revolution remained a viable alternative in the nineteenth century, the popularity of liberal-constitutional methods grew apace. The dramatic alteration of the Irish constitution by the Act of Union (1800) replaced a Protestant ascendancy with a British ascendancy—in politics, the economy, and even culture. However, the Union did not resolve accumulated Irish grievances from previous centuries any more than did legislative independence after 1782. Britain intended the Union to contain Irish conflicts, and it did. Yet debate over the Union itself became the axis around which other issues revolved through much of the century. The United Kingdom of Great Britain and Ireland gave rise over the century to "Britain's Irish question" as well as "Ireland's British question." Various attempts to solve these questions through reform failed, leaving revolution once again as an inadequate but decisive approach for the twentieth century.

Reconciling themselves to Union, Henry Grattan and other reformers came to believe that a shift from the goal of a Catholic-majority Ireland to a Catholic-minority United Kingdom could bring unity as well as equal rights for all Irish. Yet Daniel O'Connell's vision rejected the Union as the proper framework for governance because as an Irish nationalist, he viewed Catholics as the majority, which should rule Ireland. Thus, even when Catholic emancipation was eventually achieved, it did not determine the matter of who makes decisions for the Irish: Britain or Ireland. Although O'Connell believed Irish nationalism could exist within a British context, other nationalists after him pushed the movement toward separation from Britain. Because nationalist leaders from O'Connell to John Redmond appealed to Irish Catholic commoners, they often found themselves forced to accommodate the Roman Catholic church in their negotiations with the British government.

THE CATHOLIC EMANCIPATION CAMPAIGN

The Act of Union generously provided Ireland with one hundred seats in the British House of Commons (two representatives each for the thirty-two counties, thirty-five borough seats, and one for Dublin University) and twenty-eight peers and four bishops in the House of Lords. Although the Church of Ireland merged into the Church of England, Britain retained the Irish executive offices of lord lieutenant, chief secretary, lord chancellor, chancellor of the exchequer, and other minor posts. Ireland would contribute about 12 percent (two-seventeenths) of United Kingdom expenses but would continue to pay its own debts separately until debt approximated the proportion of financial commitment to the Union (i.e., two-seventeenths), at which point Irish debt would be rolled into United Kingdom debt. That possibility dimmed as Irish debt quadrupled between 1801 and 1817. Free trade between Britain and Ireland was established, except that 10 percent import duties protected Irish manufactures from British competition. Even while the United Kingdom focused on the defeat of Napoleon Bonaparte, domestic concerns began to emerge in both Britain and Ireland before the wars ended in 1814–1815.

A spirit of romantic nationalism accompanied the Napoleonic wars across Europe, including Ireland. Nationalists argued that state boundaries should contain all people with a common language and culture. Yet an Ireland divided in both language and culture made the application of nationalism problematic. If the Irish nation was defined so as to include only Catholic Irish, the goal of unity pursued by eighteenth-century reformers could not be realized. The romantic poet Thomas Moore in *Melodies* (1808) waxed nostalgic for a mythical ancient Ireland by comparing an idyllic past—featuring the absence of religious division—with the unhappy present. Moore blamed recent British policy, not Irish revolts, for Ireland's return to direct British rule in the Union. Sydney Owenson, Lady Morgan, resurrected the Gaelic cultural heritage, an Arcadian "fair Hibernia," in works such as *The Wild Irish Girl* (1806). Ironically, her writing gained more notice in England than in Ireland.

Romantic nationalism also showed a more dangerous face in the birth of various secret societies beginning in 1806 in Connacht. Unlike earlier extraparliamentary organizations with their middle-class orientation, secret societies appealed to the most aggrieved rural Irish: tenant farmers, cottiers, and laborers. The groups adopted colorful names, such as Lady Clares, Whitefeet, and Molly Maguires. Yet the so-called Ribbon societies, launched first in Ulster (1811) to protect Catholics against the Protestant Orange Order, soon eclipsed the others in size and significance. In many respects a successor to the Defenders, Ribbon society membership tended to be more urban than other secret groups. The appearance of secret societies and their association with agrarian crime led to another round of British coercion, offered in the guise of national security because of the war.

Although aristocratic Irish Catholics continued to labor for emancipation, they did so selfishly, without claiming to represent ordinary Catholics. Catholic commoners had lacked leadership for over a century before Daniel O'Connell (1775–1847) appeared on the scene. His liberal ideals would complement British Whig efforts to reform Parliament. O'Connell was the son of Catholic gentry from county Kerry. During the eighteenth century, the O'Connells had profited from both farming and smuggling. Other family members had served European Catholic governments. Tall, blue-eyed Daniel learned not only Catholic piety but also the Gaelic language in his youth. He briefly attended schools in France, but most of his education took place in London, including training in the law at Lincoln's Inn. During his years of study, the influence of democrat Thomas Paine and anarchist William Godwin led O'Connell to embrace political radicalism as the means of solving Ireland's problems.

In the upheavals of the late 1790s, O'Connell was loosely affiliated with the United Irishmen, though he did not approve of violence. Indeed, he did not hesitate to condemn agrarian crime fostered by secret societies. Hence, he had no sympathy for the abortive 1803 revolt in Dublin led by Robert Emmet. Emmet's brother had been a leader of the United Irishmen, and when Robert was expelled from Trinity College in 1799, he fled to France. Upon his return to Ireland in 1802, Emmet began plans to seize strategic buildings in Dublin but lacked proper preparation and had very few firearms for his would-be rebels. Emmet's hopes for a nationwide popular insurrection did not materialize, forcing him to flee. He was caught, tried, and executed; his impassioned speech on the scaffold would inspire future Irish rebels. Emmet's failed rebellion marked the end of the influence of the United Irishmen and paved the way for O'Connell to emerge as the new Irish leader.

As a Catholic lawyer, O'Connell missed normal opportunities for advancement. Nonetheless, he established a profitable practice, maintained a modest estate at Darrynane, and soon entered the political ranks as a member of the Catholic Committee in 1805. By 1812, O'Connell was the recognized leader of the Catholic Committee. When Henry Grattan introduced a compromise Catholic emancipation bill in 1813, which gave the monarch a veto over the choice of Catholic bishops, O'Connell opposed it. Thus, while most Catholic elites favored the bill and Parliament was disposed to pass it, O'Connell's opposition, backed by the Catholic masses, was sufficient to cause its failure. Even at this early stage, O'Connell linked religion with national unity; Catholic emancipation was only a step toward ending the Union.

In the years following the end of war in Europe, social justice for the industrial working classes became the chief popular cause in Britain. An entrenched Tory government found itself defending the status quo against both parliamentary Whigs and extraparliamentary radicals. In Ireland, the postwar era began on a tragic note, with a potato famine and typhus epidemic in 1816. Meanwhile, Grattan's last effort to enact Catholic emancipation with an 1819 bill similar to the 1813 measure lost by two votes in the House of Commons. William Plunket, MP for Dublin University, sponsored two emancipation bills in 1821 that passed the Commons but failed in the House of Lords. Irish Catholics remained divided over Plunket's bills, O'Connell heading those opposed versus proponents led by Trinity-educated dramatist Richard Lalor Sheil. When George Canning formed a moderate Tory government in 1822, O'Connell decided the time was right to form a new Catholic organization. O'Connell and Sheil reunited in 1823 and joined Waterford merchant Thomas Wyse, educated at Trinity and at Lincoln's Inn with Sheil, to form the Catholic Association. Unlike the gentry-dominated Catholic Committee, O'Connell changed the association membership requirements in 1824 to recruit participants from the Irish lower classes. Membership dues for the Catholic Association were only one penny per month, within the means of many tenant farmers and laborers. Eventually Catholic clergy—as Wyse put it, seeking not to "be buried altogether beneath the stream" of support—gave their blessing to the new organization. Thus, the Catholic Association became the first popular organization of its kind in Ireland. In addition to Catholic emancipation, its agenda included repeal of the Union, security of tenure for tenant farmers, abolition of tithes, nonrestrictive manhood suffrage, and a secret ballot.

At the Catholic Association's founding, O'Connell made it clear to supporters that he would use constitutional measures and oppose revolutionary violence. The British government outlawed the Catholic Association, and despite O'Connell's support, an 1825 Catholic emancipation bill (without previous veto provision) offered by Plunket and radical MP Francis Burdett was defeated in the House of Lords. O'Connell and Wyse founded a new Catholic Association in 1825. The first political action in Ireland by the association came in the general election of 1826, when the group endorsed the pro-emancipation candidacy of Henry Villiers Stuart, a well-to-do landlord, against Waterford County's established political family headed by Lord George Beresford. With Wyse as his campaign manager, Stuart defeated Beresford in a major upset, thereby demonstrating the association's clout. Quickly the association launched similar campaigns backing pro-emancipation candidates for seats in Armagh, Cork, Galway, Louth, Monaghan, and Westmeath. In the aftermath of the election, O'Connell created the Order of Liberators to protect rebellious freehold voters from reprisals by landlords. The title "Liberator" ultimately attached itself permanently to O'Connell. Of course, all of the candidates backed by the Catholic Association were Protestants. The next step was to offer a Catholic candidate to challenge the exclusion of Catholics from political offices.

When the Tory government of the duke of Wellington (a former chief secretary, 1807–1809) in 1828 appointed William Vesey Fitzgerald, MP for Clare, to a cabinet post, a by-election was required. Daniel O'Connell was persuaded by the Catholic Association to challenge Fitzgerald although as a Catholic he could not sit in Parliament. Ironically, Fitzgerald had opposed the Union and supported Catholic emancipation. Framing the contest as one between a Catholic and a Protestant, the freehold electors returned O'Connell by a two-to-one margin, creating a dilemma for Wellington, who hoped to avoid any popular upheaval. Facing the hard choice of coercion or concession, Wellington agreed to a Catholic emancipation bill in 1829. While it opened Irish offices, including Parliament, to Catholics, except lord lieutenant and lord chancellor, it replaced the 40 shilling freehold franchise with a more restrictive £10 property qualification, thereby disfranchising much of O'Connell's constituency by reducing the number of eligible voters from 100,000 to 16,000. Only about half of Ireland's one hundred MPs would be Catholic for several decades. Moreover, Catholic emancipation crippled Irish Protestant national feeling as Protestants felt compelled to identify more than ever with the Union and against O'Connell's Catholic nationalism. Protestant groups such as the Hibernian Society worked diligently to convert Catholics to Protestantism during the 1820s. Nonetheless, O'Connell was elected MP for Clare again in 1830 and became head of the Irish Catholic delegation in the Commons, which included Wyse, MP for Tipperary.

CAMPAIGN FOR REPEAL AND YOUNG IRELAND

Although emancipation had little effect on the lives of most Irish Catholics, it gave the Union a second chance to prove its validity to the Irish. While O'Connell continued to rely on his trademark harsh oratory, he became an important leader of parliamentary reform in the House of Commons. O'Connell joined Whig reformers after 1830 to enact the watershed Reform Bill of 1832, which redistributed seats based on population and doubled the number of eligible voters by lowering and making property qualifications uniform. The middle class controlled the House of Commons as never before. In the case of Ireland, the Reform Act increased eligible voters from 16,000 to 93,000, still lower than before emancipation. Also, the number of Irish seats in the House of Commons rose by 5 to 105. Yet a comparison with Britain was not favorable to Ireland. Only 1 in 22 held the franchise in Irish towns, and only 1 in 115 could vote in the counties, allowing fewer voters than in British constituencies.

Other British reform measures followed: a factory bill to regulate child labor, the abolition of slavery in the empire, and reform of municipal government ending local corruption. After the 1835 elections, the Whigs, with a thin majority, entered into the Lichfield House Compact with O'Connell's party. In exchange for O'Connell's setting aside the anti-union issue, the Whigs promised other reforms for Ireland. Indeed, O'Connell told Irish constituents that he would embrace the Union if Ireland was allowed to become a genuine equal partner with Britain. Equal status would mean solving Irish problems within an Irish, not a British, context. A few reform measures did benefit Ireland directly.

Irish educational efforts after 1815 reflected sectarian divisions. A theoretically nondenominational Kildare Place Society (founded 1811) received public grants for schools. However, the society was controlled by Protestants and thus not supported by most Catholics. Therefore, the papacy funded a Catholic organization, Christian Brothers (founded 1808), headed by Edmund Rice, to maintain Catholic schools. Since almost two-thirds of the male population remained illiterate, Chief Secretary Lord Edward Stanley proposed in 1831 establishing an elementary school system for Ireland with two-thirds of its funding from public revenues. The schools would allow Protestant and Catholic communities to offer limited religious instruction in the curriculum. Catholic clerics Paul Cullen and John MacHale opposed the state schools, charging they were agencies of Protestant and pro-Union propaganda. Cultural nationalists, but not O'Connell, also opposed the state schools for discouraging growth of the Gaelic language. Yet one measure of literacy, newspaper circulation, doubled from the late 1820s to the mid-1840s. The 1851 census reported that more than half the population over age five was literate.

As for O'Connell, when he could muster only thirty-eight votes in the Commons to repeal the Union in 1834, he launched a campaign to eliminate the compulsory church tithe. A veritable tithe war of violent opposition had been raging since 1830. An 1832 act had required landlords rather than tenants to pay the tithe, thereby reducing the number of tithepayers by more than a third. Yet the measure allowed landlords to raise rents on tenants in order to finance the tithe, so that many Catholics and the secret societies remained aggrieved. Because widespread Catholic nonpayment caused the arrears of tithe payments to swell to over £1 million, the Whigs backed a church bill that abolished ten of twenty-two Anglican bishoprics to reduce the costs of maintaining the established church. O'Connell eventually withdrew his support for the bill when a provision to allow excess ecclesiastical revenues to be spent on nonreligious (i.e., social) needs was deleted. Final settlement of the tithe issue awaited a reorganized Whig government after 1835. An 1838 bill transformed 75 percent of the value of the tithe into a property tax.

Although a municipal corporations act (1840) admitted Catholics to the franchise limited by a £10 qualification, the largest issue in the late 1830s was the poor law. An Irish commission report on the poor in 1835 recommended prevention of poverty through enhanced economic development. Modeled to a large degree on the British poor law reform of 1834, Parliament enacted a poor law for Ireland in 1838. One concern of Parliament was that 2.5 million eligible Irish poor might overwhelm the public assistance program. The Irish law divided the country into 130 districts, each with a workhouse to be financed by a poor rate borne equally by landlords and tenants and managed by an elected local board.

Most of the board members outside Ulster were liberal, middle-class Catholics. Implementation was slow; only four workhouses were operating in 1841, but by 1845 Ireland had 123 workhouses with 42,000 residents. Surprising many skeptics, collection of the poor tax from a million ratepayers was rather effective. Despite increased public poverty assistance, private charity continued to be more significant to most Irish poor. Forty percent of the Irish lived in one-room housing. The average life expectancy of thirty-eight years was similar to most other European countries. Despite Irish poverty, except for nonhomicidal violence against persons, the per capita crime rate for Ireland was lower than in Britain.

Meanwhile, though the Irish executive after 1829 remained rather incompetent, a change occurred when Thomas Drummond became undersecretary in 1835. He evenhandedly suppressed the violence of the Catholic Ribbon societies and the Protestant Orange Order. Drummond also stopped the practice of packing juries with Protestants and began recruiting Catholics for the police forces. It was unfortunate for Catholics when Drummond died in 1840. The general election of 1841 reduced O'Connell's anti-union contingent in the Commons from forty to twelve. A new Tory government proved ambivalent toward Ireland, symbolized by a conservative lord lieutenant and a liberal chief secretary. Still, priests and most Catholic bishops backed O'Connell, who resumed the campaign to repeal the Union in 1838. But the torch of Irish nationalist leadership was gradually passing in the 1840s to a new breed. When O'Connell created a new organization, the National (later Repeal) Association, in 1840 only a handful of members joined at first.

The "Young Ireland" movement was led by men grounded less in practical affairs like O'Connell and more in romantic escapism nurtured by writers such as Thomas Carlyle. They joined their political nationalism—envisioning all Irish bound together in self-sufficiency—with pride in Gaelic culture. Young Ireland therefore distinguished Irish rural agrarianism from British urban commercialism; it also pursued a nonsectarian nationalism that envisioned a limited role for the Catholic church. Thus, the leadership included Protestants such as Thomas Osborne Davis and John Mitchel, both educated at Trinity College, and county Clare's William Smith O'Brien, descended from the earls of Thomond and educated at Cambridge University. Catholic leaders included the self-educated Charles Gavan Duffy of Monaghan and county Mayo's John Blake Dillon, a lawyer educated at Trinity College. Although the respected *Dublin University Magazine* (founded 1833) had encouraged an Irish-language literary revival, it defended the Protestant ascendancy and opposed repeal of the Union. Thus, it was quickly eclipsed by a more political journal, *Nation* (founded 1842), edited by Davis and Duffy. Although *Nation*'s byword, "Trust ourselves alone," was similar to the future Sinn Féin republican party, it is not clear that the party name derived directly from the *Nation* usage. The *Nation* not only renewed interest in early Celtic Irish mores, but also romanticized patriot leaders who had resisted foreign invaders such as the Scandinavians, Normans, and Scots. Soliciting original contributors, the *Nation* featured poetry, short stories, history, biography, and nationalist songs. Because the journal editors included both Protestants and Catholics, it offered an ecumenical variety of opinion. Politically the *Nation*'s editorials supported O'Connell's Repeal Association.

O'Connell, however, did not share Young Ireland's obsession with the past and concerned himself only with contemporary matters. Whereas O'Connell believed he could bargain with the Tory government (1841–1845) led by a former Irish chief secretary (1812–1818), Sir Robert Peel, Young Ireland favored confrontation. After serving a term in 1842 as the first Catholic lord mayor of Dublin, O'Connell returned to the repeal campaign. When Peel refused to deal with O'Connell, a mass meeting was scheduled at Clontarf in 1843. Despite efforts of Sheil, O'Brien, and Wyse to block a government coercion bill in Parliament, the measure passed banning the Clontarf meeting. O'Connell reluctantly agreed to obey the order but was still arrested, tried, and convicted by an Irish court. He appealed to the House of Lords, where a narrow majority overturned the court conviction. Despite his pyrrhic victory, the episode demonstrated that O'Connell could no longer command meaningful influence with the British government. Thus, Peel's maneuvering for a settlement in Ireland considered Tory party interests more than Irish concerns. Peel persuaded Parliament to increase its grants to Catholic institutions such as the Maynooth Seminary. He named a parliamentary commission to study agrarian grievances in 1843, but nothing was accomplished before the famine.

SOCIETY AND THE ECONOMY THROUGH THE FAMINE

The population of Ireland in 1800 was about 5 million and predominantly rural. The largest city, Dublin, had a population of 200,000, but the next largest, Cork, had only 80,000. Limerick's population was 60,000, and a growing Belfast totaled only 20,000. Early marriages and high marital fertility caused continued growth to 7 million in 1821 and 8.5 million by 1845. Although the war years, 1801–1814, produced high agricultural prices and increased exports, the Irish poor reaped few benefits. After 1814, prices fell, but exports of products such as flour, pork, and butter continued to grow. The result was that Ireland did not provide, as did Britain, an industrial expansion to employ the growing populace. Nor did government economic policy decisions help the unsophisticated Irish economy. By 1826, British and Irish customs were merged into a single system, ending the 10 percent protective import duties on manufactures, and the two currencies were unified in 1826.

Agricultural output, aided by rapid conversion from wooden to iron ploughs, increased markedly between 1801 and 1845. The potato, totaling about 20 percent of total agricultural production, had become the dietary staple of most Irish by 1800. One acre of land could produce 320 bushels of potatoes, more than enough to feed a large family for a year. By the nineteenth century, one-third of Ireland's population subsisted almost entirely on the potato. About half the potato crop was used to feed livestock. Oats and wheat followed potatoes as the most valuable agricultural commodities, although the bulk of these crops were exported. By 1845, almost one-fourth of agricultural output was exported. Long a benchmark for exports, cattle products remained significant along with dairy products such as butter and milk. Pigs maintained third rank in livestock commodities. The quality of Irish livestock improved greatly in the first half of the nineteenth century, keeping demand strong.

Although agricultural production in Ireland was only half that of Britain, it was just below that of France. Crop yields were almost as high in Ireland as in Britain. The serious deficit for agriculture was the ratio of land to labor and the poor quality of Irish soil (only 30 percent of the highest-quality soil compared to almost 50 percent in Britain). The scarcity of land for small farmers obviously contributed to reliance on the potato. Less than one-half of 1 percent of the population owned the majority of land before the Great Famine of the 1840s. Fifty thousand wealthy owners held about 20 percent of the land in the 1841 census; 100,000 gentry owned 25 percent, and 250,000 family farms accounted for another 25 percent. Three hundred thousand peasant farmers owned an average of five acres but possessed only 7.5 percent of total acreage. Another million poor laborers held an average of one acre. Poverty, like illiteracy, was greatest in Connacht. The situation became worse after the famine, when 2,000 of the wealthiest property owners controlled two-thirds of the land. Since there were virtually no taxes on land or income (until 1853), the landed classes were shielded from major tax responsibility, placing the greater tax burden on small-propertied urban artisans and merchants.

Exports as a percentage of national income more than doubled between 1801 and 1845. Since foreign trade markets stimulated primarily agricultural commodity exports, it hindered the movement of capital and labor to industry. The chief imports were also food items, including sugar, tea, and coffee, while cotton imports increased during the 1830s. Ireland maintained a favorable balance of exports over imports prior to the famine.

Before the nineteenth century, manufacturing for local markets was done almost entirely in the home through the putting-out system, with handtools, so that many workers who might otherwise be classified as an industrial group actually combined their occupations with agriculture. Gradually in the first half of the nineteenth century, as markets expanded regionally, nationally, and internationally, manufacturing moved out of homes into factories, but outworkers in individual homes remained important in Irish industry longer than in Britain. For example, the 1841 census listed 123,000 weavers, of whom a majority were outworkers.

Ulster's contribution to Irish manufacturing remained disproportionately large. Textiles were still the leader in Irish industry, with textile mills employing 15,000 in 1841 compared with 250,000 in England. Cotton was a new industry that pioneered mechanization and challenged the older woolen and linen trades beginning in the late eighteenth century. Cotton output doubled in the Cork area and grew eightfold in east Ulster from 1790 to 1820. Still, cotton production was only 3 percent of Britain's output by 1820. Belfast had been the primary Irish port for textile exports since the 1780s, so it benefited most from textile growth. A noticeable decline in the wool as well as cotton textile industries occurred from the 1820s to the 1840s. By contrast, Ireland's linen production grew, albeit modestly. Clearly the most important industrial export by the 1830s, linen manufacture was also centered in Ulster, with pockets in other places like Cork and Kerry. Employment grew from 3,400 to 17,000 between 1835 and 1845. Unlike fluctuations in textile industries, flour milling and brewing industries grew steadily before 1845 using the factory system modernization. Guinness brewery sales increased tenfold between 1800 and 1845, with over half of sales in the form of exports.

Even with the modest duty protection before 1826, Irish cotton and woolen manufactures could not keep pace with their British counterparts, so that Ireland experienced an industrial decline prior to 1845. Many scholars attribute the primary cause of manufacturing's decline to the end of the 10 percent duty protection in 1826. Whereas low Irish wages should have attracted more industrial investment, Ireland had a shortage of skilled workers available for factories compared with a surplus of workers in Britain. Significantly, where industry declined between 1821 and 1841, especially in regions such as Connacht, there was a corresponding lowering of the standard of living.

As industry began to depend on coal-fueled steam engines, Ireland was at a disadvantage since it had to import most of its coal at double the cost of its meager domestic production. Still, Ireland's several rivers provided ample water power, which served as a viable substitute for its factories. Water also provided the cheapest form of transportation, and some canal construction aided inland transport. The Grand Canal, connecting Dublin with Barrow in 1791, was extended to the river Shannon by 1804, allowing 250,000 tons of material to be shipped annually. The ninety-two-mile Royal Canal from Dublin to Longford, completed in 1817, also contributed to increased internal trade. Despite considerable public funding, however, the Irish canal system did not approach the success of British canals. Steamship routes began regular service across the Irish Sea by the 1820s to ports in Scotland, Wales, and England. The first transatlantic steamer sailed from Cork to New York City in 1838. Land transport advanced more than any other area, with improved roads reducing travel time connecting major port cities with the interior. The government mail service improved as a direct result of better roads. Reduced passenger and freight rates resulted from competition, with the Purcell and Bianconi transit coach firms reaping the greatest profits. Purcell also later operated a major railroad company. Railroad expansion grew slowly, the first lines connected Limerick-Waterford (1826) and Dublin-Kingstown (1834). By the time of the famine, only three profitable lines existed: Dublin-Kingstown, Dublin-Drogheda (opened 1843), and Belfast-Portadown (completed 1842).

A major problem for all Irish nonagricultural development was the difficulty of attracting investment capital. The maturation of the banking system in the first half of the nineteenth century offered the potential for improvement. The government-chartered Bank of Ireland effectively became a central bank regulating private operations by the early nineteenth century. By issuing paper notes, the Bank of Ireland led the nation gradually to lessen its reliance on the old specie (i.e., coins) system. Private banks also increased in number in the early nineteenth century. Belfast banking grew more than other localities because of its expanding commercial economy. Half of Ireland's private banks failed in the financial crisis of 1820; none was left in Munster or outside of Dublin, in Leinster. A financial reorganization promoted new banks in the mid-1820s, so that only one new bank failed before the famine of the 1840s. Irish banks tended to be more conservative than average in their loans, but much of the needed investment capital in Irish banks came from England. Loans began to increase to the food processing, flour milling, and brewing industries. Gradually the Bank of Ireland began establishing branches; eighteen branches had opened by 1845, when Ireland boasted 173 banks and branches.

Prior to the 1840s, the worst Irish famine had occurred in 1739–1740, when perhaps 300,000 died. Although there were food shortages in 1801, 1816–1818 (65,000 deaths), 1822, and 1831, conditions improved to the point that the 1841 census reported only 117 deaths from starvation. The potato blight, a fungal disease, was imported to Europe from Peru. It appeared first in Germany and in Britain perhaps as early as 1842. In fact, the 1845 blight migrated from southern England to Ireland when the crop was first infected and, made worse by heavy rains, partially lost, averaging one-third in 1845. The 1846 crop began without problems, but the blight spread in July all across Ireland. Often the harvest was unaffected until it was dug up. Farmers soon learned to separate good potatoes from the bad and store them in dry places. Between 1846 and 1848, the potato harvest averaged only 1½ tons per acre compared to the typical 7 tons.

With each bad harvest came a reduction in seed available for the next planting season and thus less acreage than normal under cultivation. Thus, problems in the 1847 season hardly concerned the blight at all but resulted from significantly reduced plantings—about 11 percent of the 1845 acreage. Although more seed was available for the 1848 season, the blight returned to reduce the potato yield to about half of the 1847 harvest. Worse, the grain harvest was very poor in 1845, so there was little to compensate for the loss of the potato crop. In 1848, the grain crop was even lower. Wheat production between 1847 and 1852 declined by 52 percent. Only the oat crop kept its production levels steady. Moreover, exports of grains from Ireland to foreign markets continued even after the famine began, often under armed guard.

The British government of Sir Robert Peel responded about as well as a government might under the circumstances. Constables in 1845 were instructed to monitor crop losses. One measure, much too inadequate, arranged for the importation of American corn into Ireland, selling at a penny per pound. In early 1846, the government shipped 20,000 tons of unmilled corn and oatmeal from India, and other private stocks followed. By mid-1846, Peel's Irish officials had established 650 local committees to distribute food. Although the number of relief workers rose from 114,000 in late 1846 to 734,000 by March 1847, too often government relief officials were both incompetent and untrusted by the Irish poor. Peel also set up public works projects in 1846 designed to provide employment to the Irish poor as well as improve infrastructure. Most work involved roads, but other projects on harbors and land reclamation gave employment to about 140,000 Irish.

The Whigs, with Lord John Russell as prime minister, replaced Peel's Tory government in July 1846. Henry Labouchere became chief secretary for Ireland with a place in the cabinet. The elevation of the chief secretary showed how important the famine had become in British policy. O'Connell told his colleagues in the Commons, "If you do not save [Ireland], she cannot save herself." Urgency of action still being needed, Russell decided within six months to cancel Peel's ongoing public works projects and concentrate on direct relief. Although additional food imports were scheduled, they did not arrive before much starvation occurred. Concerned about landlord fraud in the distribution of relief, Parliament prohibited anyone holding at least one-quarter acre of land from receiving handouts, a policy that excluded a huge segment of those in need. The census of 1851 estimated that 1 million died during the famine, many more from disease caused by malnutrition than outright starvation. The poorest region, Connacht, had the highest proportion of deaths, about 40 percent with Mayo enduring the greatest mortality for counties at 58 percent. Munster counted 30 percent losses, Ulster 21 percent, and Leinster was lowest with 8.5 percent, while Dublin was the least affected county.

The most decisive response to the famine was emigration. Emigration between 1801 and 1845 had been brisk, even unprecedented, totaling 1.5 million, most of it to America and Britain. The largest categories of pre-famine emigrants were males and children. Probably more than two-thirds were laborers, at the bottom of the Irish social scale. Thus, the famine merely stimulated an established pattern. Furthermore, high evictions and heavy poor taxes acted in conjunction with the famine to stimulate emigration. One hundred thousand left in 1846, double the 1844 numbers. Two hundred thousand departed in 1847, and annual emigration between 1849 and 1852 averaged 200,000. Another 1 million emigrated between 1852 and 1861. Most counties lost more than 15 percent of their population from the combination of famine and emigration between 1841 and 1851. Two-thirds of postfamine emigrants went to the United States, where they combined with earlier arrivals to constitute a significant minority in cities such as Boston, New York City, and Philadelphia on the East Coast. Only a small percentage of postfamine emigrants were skilled workers. Thus, both before and after the famine, the vast majority of Irish emigrants came from the lower social classes and were typically unskilled, Catholic, and Gaelic speaking.

Predictably the famine led to an increase in agrarian violence by secret societies that targeted landlords. Russell was forced to request another coercion bill from Parliament. He also brought forward a tenants' rights' bill to limit landlord depredations in 1848, but it died in a House of Commons committee. Parliament preferred to make indebted landlord estates subject to foreclosure and resale to create opportunity for those most affected by the famine. Although favored also by Irish radicals, the redistribution of land did not attract new investors. In the decade following 1849, almost 9,000 new purchasers acquired the available land, but the result was simply to replace one set of repressive landlords with a new group.

In the aftermath of the terrible famine, Queen Victoria visited Ireland in 1849 and was received cordially. Whig Prime Minister Russell persuaded Parliament to lower the property requirements for the franchise in the counties from £10 to £5. Yet Parliament rejected Russell's proposal to abolish the mostly ceremonial office of lord lieutenant.

POSTFAMINE NATIONALISM: YOUNG IRELAND TO FENIANS

The tension between Daniel O'Connell and Young Ireland led to a split in late 1846. When O'Connell insisted that all members of the Repeal Association take an oath against the use of violence, most Young Ireland leaders, including Charles Gavan Duffy, Thomas Francis Meagher, and William Smith O'Brien, withdrew from the association. In January 1847, they formed the Irish Confederation, made up mostly of middle-class nationalists. The confederation organized chapters in many Irish towns. Meanwhile, despite O'Connell's age, he began a tour of the Continent, seeking backing for his failed Irish repeal campaign. He died in May 1847 while in Genoa, Italy. Throngs crowded the streets of Dublin for his funeral, paying homage to the Liberator one last time.

Meanwhile, divisions developed in the confederation between the Ulster Unitarian attorney, John Mitchel, and Duffy. Mitchel had come under the influence of the radical nationalist James Finton Lalor, an occasional contributor to the *Nation*. Lalor believed that Ireland's most pressing need was land reform rather than repeal of the Union. Mitchel took up Lalor's idea of refusing to pay the poor tax as a protest against denial of tenant rights. Duffy and O'Brien were alarmed at the strategy of Mitchel, who was forced to resign from the board of the *Nation* in December 1847. A majority of the confederation backed Duffy and O'Brien, causing Mitchel and his followers to withdraw from it.

Mitchel, joined by Devin Reilly, founded in February 1848 a new nationalist newspaper, *United Irishman*, which favored an Irish republic. With the outbreak of the 1848 revolution in France, Irish nationalists tried to overcome their differences. Mitchel rejoined the Irish Confederation, but when O'Brien outlined a rebellion in narrow political terms rather than concentrating on Mitchel's concern for tenant rights, Mitchel resigned from the confederation again. Fearing violence, British authorities arrested O'Brien, Mitchel, and other nationalists in May. Juries initially refused to convict the Irish leaders, but a coercion bill allowed the manipulation of the juries, which led to a conviction of Mitchel, whose sentence was transportation to Australia. In July, after the suspension of habeas corpus, Duffy and O'Brien called for rebellion despite lacking either a strategy or preparations. The only serious rising occurred at Ballingarry, county Tipperary, where a local police force routed O'Brien's pathetic contingent and arrested him. O'Brien, Meagher, and several others were sentenced to be hanged for treason, but the sentences were commuted to transportation to Australia in 1849.

Mitchel escaped to the United States in 1853, published a journal, and later became a southern leader opposed to the abolition of slavery. He wrote for Confederate newspapers during the American Civil War and was elected, in absentia, MP for county Tipperary in the 1870s. Meagher also made his way to America, where he became an officer in the Union army during the Civil War and later served as governor of the Montana Territory. O'Brien was pardoned in 1854 and eventually made his way back to Ireland.

Certainly Mitchel helped make tenants' rights the burning political issue in the 1850s and 1860s. Local tenants' rights clubs had formed all over Ireland by 1850. Released from jail in 1849, thanks to efforts of his Protestant attorney, Isaac Butt, Charles Gavan Duffy revived the *Nation* but turned away from repeal of the Union to land reform. Duffy combined with two other journalists, John Gray, Protestant editor of the large-circulation *Freeman's Journal* (founded 1763), and Frederick Lucas, editor of the Catholic weekly *Tablet* (founded 1840), to organize the nonsectarian Irish Tenant League in 1850. The league's method was to seek redress through Parliament with a platform including security of tenure and credit for improvements made by tenants, as well as abolition of arrears of rent from the famine era. Because the league appealed to all religious groups, Archbishop Cullen and other Catholic clerics refused to endorse it.

Targeting Parliament, the league solicited and gained support from forty-eight MPs in the election of 1852. However, the vitality of the reform movement withered when the sectarian Catholic Irish Brigade was established around a different Irish issue, the ecclesiastical titles bill, which proposed to penalize Irish Catholic clergy who accepted papal appointment to British ecclesiastical titles. The Irish Brigade, led by MP George H. Moore, threatened to withhold crucial voting support from Lord John Russell's Whig government, the very government Duffy counted on to produce a tenants' rights bill. When John Gray offered assistance to the Irish Brigade, it forced Duffy to forge an alliance between the league and the brigade. Yet the dilution of issues in the alliance caused the tenants' rights movement to dissipate; Duffy resigned as editor of the *Nation* and left Ireland in 1855 for a new political career in Australia, where he became prime minister of the state of Victoria. By the election of 1859, conservative landlord interests returned fifty-seven MPs and reduced the independent Irish MPs to twelve. The remnant of Duffy's party, led by ex–Young Irelander John Blake Dillon, soon joined the British Liberal party, formed largely from the ranks of the old Whigs.

The retirement of the last key leader of Young Ireland left a void in the nationalist leadership, which was soon filled by the Protestant James Stephens of Kilkenny, himself a former member of Young Ireland. After the abortive 1848 rising, Stephens fled to France with Limerick's John O'Mahony, who had studied Gaelic literature briefly at Trinity College. In France, they came under the influence of liberal and socialist ideology. Both agreed in 1855 to begin recruiting participants for an Irish rebellion—Stephens in Ireland and Britain and O'Mahony in the United States—in partnership with another Irish expatriate, Michael Doheny. In Dublin, Stephens founded in 1858 a secret society, the Irish Republican Brotherhood (IRB), which merged with the Phoenix Society of Cork. In America, O'Mahony in 1859 transformed the Emmet Monument Association (raising money to build a monument to revolutionary Robert Emmet) into the secret Fenian Brotherhood (from Gaelic *fianna*, ancient mythical Irish warriors). The origins of the Fenians and IRB derived from numerous secret society networks operating since 1811. Together the two societies had perhaps 50,000 members.

The IRB was the first Irish organization that became dependent for financial support on Irish Americans, a pattern that would continue through the creation of the Irish Free State in 1922. The Fenian-IRB movement distinguished itself from previous nationalist movements by its refusal to participate in the constitutional-electoral process. The new republican campaign appealed initially to unskilled urban laborers and spread to rural areas by the 1860s. The social implications of republicanism not only highlighted the familiar Catholic religious elements but also community engagements ranging from recreational activities to group propaganda lectures and common meals replete with music and dancing.

Although elder statesmen of Young Ireland, such as O'Brien in Ireland and Meagher in the United States, condemned republican ideology and tactics, the real threat to Fenian-IRB influence was the Catholic church. In the years following the famine, the Catholic hold on the common classes became even firmer thanks to the work of Paul Cullen. While some Catholic clerics such as John MacHale had sympathized with the nationalist cause, Cullen detested not only the British and Protestants but also Irish nationalism. He was able to impose his control more easily because of Catholic losses during the famine through death and emigration. The church's role in shaping conservative social patterns after the famine included encouraging later marriages and even celibacy, as well as discouraging premarital sexual relations, to help prevent another cycle of overpopulation. Also notable in the postfamine ultramontane (papal-centered) church was a new devotional piety among the laity, which incorporated religious symbols such as the rosary, novenas, vespers, jubilees, pilgrimages, shrines, and medals. A major church-building phenomenon increased the number of new church structures by 1,400 between 1865 and 1905.

Cullen's own heritage from yeoman stock caused him to identify with the privation of the lower classes. He retained strong papal favor, which allowed him to move even higher in the Irish hierarchy, from archbishop of Armagh (1849), to archbishop of Dublin (1852), to Ireland's first cardinal (1866). Papal connections permitted Cullen to control most bishopric appointments, but he also promoted Catholic schools and improved the discipline of priests. In the process of extending Catholic influence, Cullen inadvertently caused an even greater popular identification of nationalism with Catholicism. Because the papacy viewed British reform measures as beneficial to the Catholic church, Cullen condemned the Fenian-IRB republican campaign. The fact that the new breed of republicanism was secular also worried a Catholic hierarchy that feared losing its influence with the masses.

The response of the republicans to clerical Catholic opposition was to adopt an anticlerical stance. As editor of the chief republican newspaper, *Irish People*, Charles Joseph Kickham (1826–1882) of county Tipperary gently urged the Catholic populace to ignore the clergy when they moved into political matters. Also a well-known romantic novelist, Kickham tried to convince the Irish that church interference in nonecclesiastical policy issues would likely harm rather than help the nationalist cause. Some priests sympathetic to the republican campaign defied Cullen, but most clerics took their cue from Cullen.

Following the American Civil War, which gave many Irish republicans military experience, the republican movement planned a frontal assault on British power. One Civil War veteran, John Devoy, initiated a recruitment campaign in Ireland among Irish soldiers in the British army and gained a following of several thousand. American Fenians reorganized in 1865, giving greater democratic voice to policy decisions by creating their own congress. Led by William Roberts, the Fenians decided to invade British Canada, expecting French Catholic residents to back their effort. Control of Canada would make it a bargaining chip to gain independence for Ireland. Stephens was arrested in Ireland but escaped and decided to sail for America to seek direct aid for an Irish rebellion. Despite stimulating recruitment, Irish-American Fenians resented Stephens's attempt to subvert their plans and removed him from leadership. The attempted invasion of Canada by the Fenians in the spring of 1866 did not produce either an alliance with French Canadians or a takeover of the British government there.

The British government began a new round of coercion to block the IRB campaign in 1865 by suspending the publication of *Irish People* and arresting its editor, Kickham. Though Stephens escaped arrest after his return from America, he was unsure whether to pursue armed rebellion. Finally, some Irish republicans launched a futile rising in February 1867. In every location—Dublin, Cork, Tipperary, Limerick, Clare—the republican bands were defeated easily by the British army and its loyal Irish constabulary. Although British repression caused sympathy for the republicans, even among Catholic clergy, the British lobbied for and obtained a papal condemnation of the republican violence. Public opinion also worked against the Fenians in actions such as the bombing of a London jail in December 1867 intended to free Fenian prisoners; twelve people died, and over a hundred were injured. Despite the popularity of the republican cause among ordinary Irish, the Fenian-IRB era effectively ended in 1867.

GLADSTONE AND REFORM

The attempt of revolutionary republicanism to liberate Ireland spurred British liberals to scrutinize the Irish question more seriously. By 1868 the British Liberal party leader, William E. Gladstone, encouraged those seeking ordered change in Ireland. He was assisted in recruiting Irish Catholics to his cause by the old radical John Bright. Gladstone was determined not merely to resolve but to do justice to social, economic, and religious grievances in Ireland aimed at undercutting the republican appeal for Irish independence and binding the Irish to the Union. Liberals such as Gladstone were opposed to traditional imperialism and thus considered various imperial reform ideas that would give British colonies a greater degree of self-government. Gladstone came to view Ireland as a part of such reform. The home rule concept evolved gradually, but Gladstone wanted to show the Irish that Britain sought to address their grievances about land, religion, and education with positive policy.

Leading the parliamentary opposition in 1868, Gladstone advanced several resolutions dealing with the disestablishment of the Church of England in Ireland. The Conservatives proposed state endowment of both Catholic and Presbyterian churches to make them equal with the Church of Ireland, but the proposal required increased taxes. When Gladstone's measures gained majorities in their first reading, Conservative party Prime Minister Benjamin Disraeli pushed through a new parliamentary reform bill that lowered the property qualifications in Irish boroughs significantly. Yet Gladstone's maneuver ultimately forced Disraeli to dissolve Parliament and call for new elections in late 1868. With broad Catholic approval, the Liberal party won 66 of the 105 Irish seats in the House of Commons, helping Gladstone to become prime minister. He named C. S. P. Fortescue chief secretary (1868–1871) to assist in formulating Irish policy. The previous resolutions became the basis for legislation known as the Irish Church Act, passed in 1869. Effective in 1871, the Church of Ireland would become an independent entity, and half its property would be transferred to an appointed commission. Thus, much of the former state church's property was offered for sale to tenants of the church supported by government loans. About six thousand tenants bought land under the act. The Presbyterian church was paid a one-time settlement of £1 million to compensate for the end of its annual subsidy from the Church of Ireland, the regium donum (i.e., crown grant).

Disestablishment was viewed gravely by the Church of Ireland's defenders since it promoted the very principle of separation of church and state that had been championed by Union opponents, Young Ireland, and the republicans. Church defenders pointed out that the Church of Ireland had been an integral part of the constitutional arrangements in the Act of Union, based on the principle of a Protestant monarchy, so that its removal would endanger the entire Union structure. The Irish Church Act also caused Presbyterians in Ulster, not normally defenders of the state church, to condemn the measure as ending the Protestant ascendancy in Ireland. Gladstone, on the other hand, considered the measure a necessary gesture to show Catholics that the Union could respond to their concerns. Thus, Gladstone saw disestablishment as merely an adjustment, not a fundamental change, in the social relationships in Ireland.

The second plank in Gladstone's Irish agenda was the tenants' rights cause, which had grown to major proportions since the famine of the 1840s. Tenant demands concentrated on the "three F's": fair rent, fixity of tenure, and free sale. Irish farmers organized a second Irish Tenant League at Tipperary in 1869 with Isaac Butt as president. John Gray, editor of *Freeman's Journal*, held meetings to promote the cause. Some Fenians, viewed with suspicion by farmers, tried to disrupt the tenants' rights campaign, but Butt succeeded in calming the two sides.

Gladstone's approach in the Land Act of 1870 was to sanction property custom where it existed such as in Ulster and thus not upset existing arrangements. The so-called Ulster custom, operating since 1849, allowed local councils of tenants to protest unfair landlord evictions or excess rent increases. Gladstone knew that members of his own cabinet were skeptical of government regulation of private property, which might obliterate most landlord authority. The act provided that tenants receive from the landlord compensation for any improvements made on the leasehold. Security of tenure for the length of the lease was also guaranteed except for nonpayment of rent. Perhaps most important, the act provided government loans up to two-thirds of the purchase price for tenants who wanted to buy their interest.

The Land Act did discourage arbitrary evictions of tenants, but it left a loophole of eviction for nonpayment of rent that landlords used in response to the measure. Since the legislation did not prevent landlords from raising the rents, they could hike the payments to unreasonable levels, forcing tenants to give up the parcels due to their inability to pay exorbitant rents. Also, property owners could not be forced to sell, and most would not. Thus, the land bill did not satisfy Irish tenants in the long run and left landlords secure in their control of property. Rumors filled the air about a revival of Fenianism, which alarmed the government. Moreover, Catholic clergy viewed the Land Act as an indication that the British government was scared and would be willing to make other major concessions.

The Catholic church had not responded positively to the creation in the 1840s of several queen's colleges in different cities supposedly open to Catholic students. Thus, Gladstone sought to appease the clergy more effectively with his 1873 university bill. The idea was to end the queen's colleges (tax supported) and replace them with a new Catholic division of the University of Dublin. However, the measure contained no endowment for the new college comparable to the support given the Catholic Maynooth Seminary. Thus, Cardinal Cullen urged opposition to the bill, and most Irish Liberal party MPs voted against the bill, helping to cause its defeat. Yet the very defeat of a measure intended to aid Irish Catholics caused the collapse of Gladstone's government in 1874 and brought back an unsympathetic Conservative regime headed by Disraeli. By the time Gladstone and the Liberals returned to power, the issue of Irish home rule had emerged to become the next great cause célèbre.

6

The Home Rule Era, 1870–1918

By the 1870s, Ireland seemed greatly settled from the seismic upheavals of the Great Famine and the Fenian republican threat. The economy was stabilized and actually helped in the case of agriculture by the continuing emigration, which served as a safety valve, and corrective measures stimulated by the potato crisis of the 1840s. Industry, at least in Ulster, continued to expand, offering the opportunity for Ireland to become a normal participant in the European economic system. The appearance of another strong reform leader in William E. Gladstone, who took Ireland's grievances seriously, also boded well for solving problems through the constitutional framework of the Union. For example, the lingering land reform problem was tackled again and finally largely resolved by the end of the century.

Yet too much had changed as a result of the rise of Irish nationalism since the O'Connell era, and Irish Catholic attitudes toward the Union were not much more optimistic than they were after emancipation. Catholic nationalists believed the nation-state should be controlled by the religious-cultural majority, whereas British policymakers strove to make Ireland part of a diverse, multicultural political entity. The two objectives were not mutually exclusive, but they were not compatible. By the 1870s, the definition of Irish nationalism revolved around the unifying theme of home rule. The advent of the home rule campaign in the 1870s forced Gladstone to abandon the never-ending cycle of conciliation and coercion. He made a politically risky decision to incorporate home rule into the Liberal reform agenda. Home rule was never so much about Ireland's governance as it was bound up with other issues—social and economic—involving the relationship of Ireland to Britain and the empire. Indeed, six of the seven parliamentary home rule proposals between 1870 and 1920 were introduced by British political leaders. That campaign, however, not only met firm opposition from the Conservative party and its Protestant allies in Ulster but also split Gladstone's Liberal party. Moreover, the leading Irish parliamentary home rule strategist, Charles Stewart Parnell, proved controversial and in the end detrimental to achieving the goal.

In the aftermath of the Gladstone-Parnell era, a revival of Irish republicanism frightened Ulster Protestants, and both groups organized to pursue constitutional and then violent means to sustain their interests. The passage of the third home rule bill in 1914 did not lead to settlement since it was suspended because of World War I and Ulster Protestant objections. Thus, leading Ireland to the verge of legislative independence without completion allowed radical Irish republican elements to seize the initiative. A rebellion in 1916 showed that constitutional methods could not create both an independent and a unified Ireland.

Following World War I, the daunting task of the government of Prime Minister David Lloyd George was to satisfy both republican claims of independence and Protestant Ulster's desire to remain in the United Kingdom. The 1921 treaty provided for a partition, but many Irish republicans were unsatisfied with self-government for the South and determined to annex the North to create a single Ireland. Thus, the stage was set for a pattern of tension and crisis over Northern Ireland that continues to this day. To be successful, home rule needed support from all Irish elements and a willingness among the varied Irish communities to accept differences. As events transpired, neither of these goals was achieved. Ireland illustrates the generalization that ethnic and cultural minorities within complex states develop an aggressive response to perceived economic exploitation. It seems that each time Britain loosened its political hold on Ireland to mollify nationalist agitation, it was in response to economic hardships. Yet solving one dilemma produced the expectation among the Irish of yet more solutions.

GLADSTONE, PARNELL, AND HOME RULE

Protestant lawyer and long-term MP Isaac Butt founded the Home Government Association in 1870 to advocate legislative independence for Ireland as a substitute for the repeal campaign in the O'Connell era. The son of a Protestant clergyman and graduate of Trinity College, Butt had shown political tolerance in his appeal for the release of Fenian prisoners. Recalling the late-eighteenth-century experience of legislative independence, Butt argued that a separate Irish Parliament, rather than the imperial Parliament, should legislate on internal Irish matters. He did not insist on eliminating the lord lieutenant, the crown's representative, or terminating Ireland's representation in the British Parliament. In effect, Butt proposed the creation of a federated system of governance for the United Kingdom. Initially, Butt's proposals were considered by all Irish political divisions—Conservatives and Liberals, Protestants and Catholics, unionists and republicans. Still, Liberals and Protestants dominated the executive committee of the Home Government Association. Most important, Butt proved less effective as a political leader than as an organizer of the campaign for Irish home rule.

After failing to win several by-elections in 1873, pressure mounted to reshape the Home Government Association into an extraparliamentary popular institution like O'Connell's Repeal Association. Hence, in November 1873, Butt reorganized the Home Government Association into a broader movement known as the Home Rule League. The home rulers won fifty-nine seats in the general election of 1874, though lacking good balance: all but a dozen were from Leinster and Munster, and forty-six were Catholic. Nonetheless, the Liberals lost their majority in the election to the Conservatives, who were decidedly opposed to home rule. Further, the league's agenda did not elaborate its plan beyond legislative independence. It lacked a vision of what structure would exist in a new constitution and what it might achieve if established. Butt's hopeful waiting approach during the 1874–1880 Conservative government did not satisfy many in the home rule party. Only thirty-one MPs attended the party's annual meeting in 1876. One member, Joseph Biggar, began a one-man strategy of obstructing Disraeli's government, which appealed to other home rulers. Furthermore, in 1876, the Irish Republican Brotherhood voted narrowly to urge good republicans not to sit in Parliament. Thus, home rule's potential for creating unity appeared illusory. Political division on tactics and strategy remained fractious—Conservatives, Liberals, unionists, republicans, Catholics, and home rulers all stubbornly distinct and only occasionally crossing each other's boundaries. Although Butt introduced a home rule bill every year, when it finally got to the floor for a vote in 1877, the bill was defeated decisively, 417 to 67. The next year, Butt resigned as leader of the home rule party. He was succeeded as parliamentary chairman by William Shaw, MP Cork.

By 1877, Butt's leadership of the home rule campaign was eclipsed by the emergence of Charles Stewart Parnell, another Protestant first elected to Parliament in an 1875 by-election as MP for county Meath. Parnell had favored Biggar's approach and thus showed little confidence in Butt while respecting the need for organization. Gladstone's Secret Ballot Act of 1872 inadvertently created the conditions that allowed Parnell to become a powerful spokesman for home rule. He recognized the potential of using the secret ballot, which protected the integrity of individual votes by preventing undue external pressure, to mold an effective party. Another obstacle to unity on home rule, the Catholic Union (founded 1872), became less imposing after the death of Cardinal Cullen in 1878. Parnell was selected president of the Home Rule League of Great Britain in 1877 and named chairman of the Irish parliamentary party in 1880, when he defeated Shaw twenty-three to eighteen.

The turning point in Parnell's rise to power, other than the passing of Butt, was the 1879 "New Departure" agreement with John Devoy, leader of Clan na Gael, founded in 1867 as successor to the Fenian Brotherhood in America, and previously opposed to pursuing constitutional strategies. The new departure connected the home rule movement with tenants' rights agitation. Parnell and Devoy agreed to push for a parliament without regard to republican wishes, to demand self-government through an Irish Parliament and executive, and to form a home rule parliamentary party. To these home rule positions, the "New Departure" added the goal of achieving compulsory land purchase legislation for tenants. The concern for the welfare of Irish tenant farmers therefore came to possess a political meaning equal to its economic implications. Thus, it was not mere coincidence that Parnell was elected president of the newly founded and Fenian-dominated Irish National Land League in 1879. The league was the brainchild of Michael Davitt, who lost an arm in a textile mill accident at age eleven, served seven years (1870–1877) in prison for Fenian activities, and first met Devoy in 1878.

The "land war" of 1879–1882 became the largest popular enterprise in Irish history and thus the catalyst Parnell used to gather momentum for his home rule quest. The relative prosperity of tenant farmers since the

1850s did not produce euphoria, for many did not believe it could continue. Three consecutive years of bad harvests (1877–1879) produced excessive evictions. Yet more blame was placed on the landlords than during the Great Famine of the late 1840s. Evictions rose from 2,177 in 1877 to 10,457 in 1880. The conflict began in county Mayo, one of the poorest regions of Ireland, with a call for reduced rents and the threat of nonpayment if relief were not forthcoming. The Land League organized demonstrations against and denied business to landlords who evicted tenants. It also provided aid to removed families. The most famous case of resistance to landlords was a successful tenant campaign to ruin financially Captain Charles Boycott of county Mayo—hence the application of economic pressure to achieve social goals thereafter being known as "boycotting." Yet violence also ensued, with 1880 being the highwater mark for agrarian crime by secret societies collectively labeled "Captain Moonlight" by Parnell.

Davitt, the recognized leader of the agitation, was joined by Fenian-IRB sympathizer John O'Connor Power, MP county Mayo, and tenants' rights advocate James Daly, editor of the *Connaught Telegraph*. Yet it was Parnell who bound up repressed republicans and Davitt's agrarian following into a political as well as protest movement. The goal of the National Land League was peasant proprietorship, and its motto, "The land for the people," echoed throughout rural Ireland. The land agitation also had the backing of many Catholic priests, though not bishops, and the sympathy of British Liberals. The Conservative government's response was to arrest Davitt and other Land Leaguers, charging them with sedition, but they were acquitted in a trial.

In early 1880, Parnell traveled to North America to solicit aid for the Land League. Although his tour was advertised as a fund-raising venture for the Land League, in fact it was primarily to beat the drum for home rule. At his appearance in Montreal, future MP Timothy Healy (1855–1931) dubbed Parnell "the uncrowned king of Ireland." Parnell was even invited to address the U.S. House of Representatives. Meanwhile, a general election in Britain resulted in a Liberal majority. Gladstone, who had been received cordially during a 1877 visit to Ireland, became prime minister, and W. E. Forster was named Irish chief secretary. As chairman of sixty Irish home rule members, Parnell was determined to keep his party independent. Gladstone pledged no new coercion legislation in response to the land war. Instead, he agreed to support Power's Compensation for Disturbance Bill, which would allow evicted tenants to claim financial compensation for their improvements to the property.

The measure passed the Commons but was defeated in the Lords. In frustration and in an effort to demonstrate political credibility with constituents, Parnell and thirteen other Land League members were arrested and indicted for conspiracy to foster nonpayment of rent. Unable to empanel juries that it could control, the government dropped the charges. Another coercion bill passed in early 1881, allowing the suspension of habeas corpus to round up suspected agitators.

Meanwhile, the government's Bessborough Commission submitted a report that favored a new land law. Gladstone's Liberal government enacted the Land Law Act of 1881, which created a three-member commission to review rent charges to determine if they were fair, fix rentals for fifteen years, and ensure compensation for improvements made by tenants. The act also provided government loans of up to three-fourths of the purchase price to enable tenants to buy their holdings. The act did not, however, cover about one-third of Irish tenant farmers whose rent payments were in arrears. The Land Act did not pacify Irish leaders. Indeed, further agitation led Chief Secretary Forster in October to label the Land League a "criminal association" and order the arrest, among others, of Parnell, Davitt, and John Dillon, MP for Tipperary and son of John Blake Dillon. In response to the arrests, agrarian violence increased another 60 percent.

Seeking to end Parnell's martyrdom, Gladstone's diplomacy produced the Kilmainham Treaty of April 1882 providing for the release of Parnell and other jailed MPs. The Irish leadership promised to call an end to the land war in exchange for an amendment to the Land Act that would effectively cancel arrears of rent for 100,000 tenants. Forster resigned in protest over the settlement, and Conservatives charged Gladstone with entering into a corrupt bargain to gain Irish votes. The temporary peace was disrupted immediately by the assassination of the newly arrived chief secretary and the under secretary in Dublin's Phoenix Park. The murders were orchestrated by a previously unknown secret society, the Invincibles, an IRB splinter group heavily financed by Irish Americans. Other murders followed, until in 1883, seventeen Invincibles were arrested, convicted, and executed. Parnell, who feared the Phoenix Park attack was aimed at him, began to chart a more moderate course, seeking to deal with the next chief secretary, George Otto Trevelyan. Dillon and Davitt also condemned the Invincible violence and favored negotiation.

The Land League was dissolved and replaced by the National League, which got off to a slow start with only 371 locals in 1882. Yet by the end of 1885, the league had 1,261 local chapters and showed its viability as

the most representative Irish nationalist organization. The Liberals enacted more conciliatory legislation. A Labourers Act in 1883 provided
government assistance for peasant housing, and the Ashbourne Land
Purchase Act of 1885 allotted a substantial amount in loans to tenants
wanting to buy their holdings. Davitt urged the government to set a
"fair" purchase price equal to no more than fifteen years' rent. Meanwhile, agrarian crime was reduced from about 4,500 incidents in 1881 to
fewer than 900 in 1884.

Irish representation gained a major boost from the Third Reform Bill
of 1884, which abolished all property qualifications and thus gave the
vote to all adult males. The number of Irish voters increased from 126,000
(about 4.4 percent of the population) to 738,000 (16 percent of the population), with Irish tenant farmers and laborers thereafter the majority of
the electorate. The Conservative party leadership realized that Ireland
should not be left entirely to the Liberals. Some Conservatives such as
Lord Randolph Churchill wanted an accommodation with Ireland and
were willing to make some concessions, though retaining Ireland in the
United Kingdom. Parnell actually preferred dealing with the Conservatives, partly because they controlled the House of Lords. Not only did
most Conservatives not support home rule as an alternative, but also
many unionist Liberals, led by Joseph Chamberlain, opposed home rule,
making it difficult for Gladstone to succeed.

In the 1885 general election necessitated by the Reform Act, Parnell
urged Irish voters in Britain to back the Conservatives. Yet the Liberals
won 335 seats, the Conservatives 249, and the Irish home rulers 86 (85
from Ireland and 1 from England). Gladstone thus needed the Irish votes
to sustain a government and privately decided to favor home rule. He
encouraged Parnell to maintain good relations with the Conservatives to
ensure success on home rule. The premature public revelation of Gladstone's backing of home rule ended the Parnellite-Conservative alliance
and endangered home rule itself. To avoid the appearance of an alliance
with Parnell, Gladstone drew up the first Irish home rule bill in 1886. It
would have created a unicameral Irish assembly of 309 members divided
into two "orders," with separate voting. One order would have 28 appointed Irish peers and 75 members elected to ten-year terms by £25
franchises. The other division would be composed of 206 members
elected under the 1884 Reform Act franchise (i.e., no property qualifications). Parliaments were limited to five years, and the Irish executive
would be responsible to a majority in the Parliament. Catholics would
be eligible for the office of lord lieutenant, and no religion would be

endowed. The powers excluded from the home rule Parliament included crown privileges such as copyright law, postal service, coinage and currency regulation; defense; and foreign policy, which would include customs and the laws of trade as well as diplomatic matters. Finally, the imperial Parliament at Westminster would retain control over the Royal Irish Constabulary (RIC).

Although Parnell was in many ways delighted with the turn of events, he was not consulted in the drafting of the home rule bill and thus had some objections. Specifically, he did not like the separate voting by the two orders. He opposed the clause allowing the imperial Parliament to control customs duties and was not satisfied with the Irish contribution (one-fifteenth) to imperial expenses. Finally, he felt the RIC should be under Irish control. Yet Gladstone's most imposing opposition came from the unionists whose anti-Catholic motto, "Home rule meant Rome rule," reflected fears of the Ulster Protestants. In the end, the home rule bill was defeated by a vote of 343 to 313, with 93 Liberals voting in the negative. The home rule defeat led to the collapse of Gladstone's government and new elections in 1886. The outcome was a Unionist majority with 317 Conservatives and 77 Liberal Unionists. Gladstone's Liberals won only 191 seats, and Parnell sustained the 85 Irish home rule seats.

The Irish nationalists responded by launching the so-called plan of campaign in 1887. Parnell introduced a tenant relief bill that would stop evictions if half the rent was paid. It was defeated in the Commons, and land agitation in Ireland resumed, though without Parnell's blessing. The plan of campaign was outlined by John Dillon in the newspaper *United Ireland* (founded 1881), edited by MP William O'Brien. The Conservative government along with the papacy condemned the plan, yet the arrest of Dillon and O'Brien again failed to secure a conviction. A new chief secretary, Arthur James Balfour, had the confidence of his uncle, Prime Minister Lord Salisbury. Balfour acted decisively in repressing the plan of campaign and restoring law and order. O'Brien and Dillon were indicted in 1890 but fled to America. However, 650 others were arrested, reflecting Balfour's vigor.

Then something unexpected happened with the 1887 *London Times* publication of a series entitled "Parnellism and Crime." The essence of the articles revolved around letters purportedly written by Parnell that condoned the violence, including the Phoenix Park murders, of the preceding years. Parnell denied the charges on the floor of the House of Commons but refused at first to sue for libel. However, when the

Conservative-controlled Parliament would not investigate the *Times*, Parnell did bring suit in late 1888. In the end, under court examination, a Dublin hack journalist, Richard Pigott, confessed to forging the letters sent to the *Times*. Parnell won his case and became a hero again. The Conservative government even became more malleable in passing the 1891 Land Purchase Act, which subsidized loans for tenants to purchase their holdings. The act also created the Congested Districts Board designed to stimulate the agricultural and commercial economy for 500,000 Irish poor in parts of eight counties. In the days leading up to the next election, home rule looked to be in an unbeatable position, but another unforeseen event turned the tables once more.

In December 1889, Captain W. H. O'Shea, independent MP, filed for divorce from his wife, Katharine, and named Parnell as a corespondent in the divorce petition. Mrs. O'Shea had been engaged in an extramarital affair with Parnell for almost a decade. She had also been the key intermediary in political discussions with Gladstone during the 1880s. Captain O'Shea won his divorce in 1890, and Parnell married Katharine O'Shea. Gladstone responded by urging Parnell to resign as Irish party chairman, and Tim Healy made a blistering attack on his former mentor. Parnell refused to step aside and lashed out at Gladstone. The dilemma led to a split in the Irish party, with former House of Commons clerk John Redmond rallying twenty-six members loyal to Parnell and journalist Justin McCarthy heading 44 anti-Parnellites. Even with Parnell's death in October 1891, the remaining split cast a giant shadow over future home rule strategy.

The final episode in home rule during the Gladstone era came after the 1892 general election gave Liberals a slight majority. Gladstone's home rule Liberals won 274 seats along with 81 from the Irish party. The Conservatives were reduced to 269 but could count on 46 Unionist Liberals to oppose home rule. Now almost eighty-three years old, Gladstone formed his fourth government, disappointed that he did not have a greater margin favoring home rule. Nonetheless, working with the chief secretary, John Morley, a second home rule bill was drafted in 1893. In most respects, it was similar to the 1886 bill, the main difference being that Irish MPs would remain in the Westminster Parliament but vote only on Irish or imperial matters. John Redmond gave an impassioned speech supporting home rule, yet the margin in the Commons supporting the bill fell from forty-three on the second reading to thirty-four on passage. All concerned knew that the measure was doomed in the House of Lords, where it went down, 419 to 41. Gladstone had staked his political fortune on Irish home rule, and it cost him control of the government twice. The Gladstone-Parnell era came to a close in 1893.

THE GAELIC CULTURAL REVIVAL

Even before the failure of the first home rule bill in 1886, a new twist in the evolution of Irish nationalism emerged. Inspired by the romantic Gaelic renaissance in the first half of the nineteenth century, a related movement emerged in the 1880s that was more independent of political influences of the 1830s and 1840s. Irish cultural nationalism reflected a pattern also apparent in two other Celtic fringe areas, Scotland and Wales. Yet because of the home rule campaign underway at the time, the Irish trend held greater potential. The leaders of the Gaelic revival fell into two categories: those who wanted to express their views in English and those who preferred to revive the Gaelic tongue. William Butler Yeats was the leader of the former, and Douglas Hyde became the recognized authority for the latter. Separate organizations to revive the Gaelic language were established in 1876 and 1880.

An important impetus for the Gaelic revival, other than the political campaign for home rule, was the spread of social Darwinism being promoted by several Anglo-Saxon writers of the day. The notion of "survival of the fittest" determining purportedly superior and inferior races was often used in the imperial language of the late nineteenth century to justify control by the Anglo-Saxon English over colonial peoples. The Celtic groups in the British Isles were thus thrown into the same category as African tribes. The racial themes were seized on by Anglo-Irish Protestants anxious about maintaining their privileged position in Ireland over the native Gaelic people. Protestants sought a new identity because they felt ostracized by Gaelic Catholic nationalism. The failure of the first and second home rule bills, combined with political divisions in the Irish parliamentary party, caused many younger generation Irish to turn away from political and toward cultural nationalism as a more viable outlet.

Writers such as Young Ireland poet Samuel Ferguson and historian Standish O'Grady favored using the theme of Gaelic culture as a replacement for, rather than a complement to, political nationalism. They failed to get an endorsement from either Protestant or Catholic communities. Increasingly Catholic clergy backed the trend toward Gaelic nationalism, while most Protestants defensively clung to their Anglo-Saxon cultural ties. Michael Cusack founded the Gaelic Athletic Association (GAA) at

Thurles in 1884 with the Catholic archbishop of Cashel, Thomas William Croke, as patron. Cusack made the GAA an exclusively Gaelic membership openly hostile to Anglo-Saxons. A Gaelic-speaking native of county Clare, Cusack had started a hurling club in Dublin in 1883, which he hoped would raise the Irish national consciousness. The GAA began in the rural part of Ireland promoting native Irish sports such as football and hurling while rejecting popular English sports such as rugby and soccer. GAA members proudly distinguished themselves by carrying a *caman* (hurling stick). Although Cusack's irascibility caused friction, which led to his forced retirement as GAA head in 1886, he had launched a powerful cultural trend.

The tendency took on a somewhat different emphasis with the founding of the Gaelic League in 1893 by a Protestant, Douglas Hyde, and a Catholic, Eoin MacNeill. The league's scholars proved more dedicated to revitalizing the Gaelic language than the earlier Young Ireland movement, dominated as it was by politically oriented journalists. Hyde's *Literary History of Ireland* (1899) became a classic, reclaiming Ireland's cultural past. Hyde also helped establish the Irish Texts Society (1898), edited its first volume (1901), and served as president of the society until his death. Hyde and MacNeill saw language as part of a broader cultural identity that would set Ireland apart from Britain. Indeed, the league's writers openly assailed the social Darwinist myths of Anglo-Saxon superiority. The Gaelic League drew most of its following from the middle class, and its writers congregated in Dublin, which hosted the first Irish Literary Festival in 1897.

In response to the anti-British tone of the Gaelic League, some Irish intellectuals continued to use English as their language of expression, in part to gain a wider audience. These writers included especially the poet-playwright William Butler Yeats, county Mayo novelist George A. Moore, comic playwright Lady Augusta Gregory of county Galway, and Dublin playwright John Myllington Synge. Part of the rich Anglo-Irish tradition, Yeats's father was a painter and member of the Royal Hibernian Academy. Disturbed by Young Ireland's journalists' treating literature as an adjunct to politics and thus creating a false image of the Irish, Yeats championed literature as the essence of Irish culture. He organized Irish literary groups in both Dublin and London, and he was joined by Hyde and other cultural leaders in founding the National Literary Society (1892) to promote Irish writers.

As a racehorse owner and MP, Moore's father was able to support his son's venture to Paris in 1873 to study painting. Instead, Moore turned to writing realistic novels such as *A Modern Lover* (1893) and *Esther Waters* (1894). Upon Moore's return to Ireland in 1899, he joined Yeats in launching the Irish Literary (later National) Theater, soon permanently housed in Dublin's Abbey Theater (1904). Also instrumental in establishing the Irish Theater, Lady Gregory was artistic director of the Abbey Theater in its early years. She wrote many of the comedies performed there, including *Hyacinth Halvey, The Rising of the Moon*, and *Spreading the News*. The Irish playwrights revived the short, one-act play as a distinctive feature of the Irish stage.

Another product of Anglo-Irish bloodlines, Synge was born on the outskirts of Dublin and educated at Trinity College. He met Yeats in Paris, where Synge was encouraged to write about his native Ireland. He then returned to spend some time on the bleak Aran Islands to contemplate his subject matter. Works such as *Riders of the Sea* and *Deidre of the Sorrows* reflected Synge's Aran perspective. The work of Yeats and Synge was not always received favorably by Gaelic audiences. For example, Synge's play *The Playboy of the Western World* (1907) was accused of demeaning Irish poor and women and met resistance in productions in Ireland and America. Even Yeats was disturbed by Synge's lowering of Irish tastes. Yeats's own *Countess Cathleen* (1892), which opened the Abbey Theater era in 1899, was deemed to be anti-Catholic or at least antireligious to some. Hence, there were differences about the applications of the cultural revival of the late nineteenth and early twentieth centuries, especially culture's role in politics. Moreover, scholars such as Yeats failed to understand that Ireland was composed of not one but several cultures.

In another arena, Irish writers such as Oscar Wilde and George Bernard Shaw framed their literary expression more through English than Irish lenses. Despite his prominent Irish parents, a surgeon father and a nationalist poet mother, Wilde wanted to escape Ireland after taking a degree at Trinity College. Yeats accused Wilde of abandoning his youthful Irish experiences. In London, Wilde used satire to ridicule the deterministic social mind-sets of Victorian England. In his best play, *The Importance of Being Earnest* (1895), Wilde criticizes conventional social class attitudes as naively simplistic. Still, Wilde was unwilling to challenge Irish social stereotypes openly, even though he believed that the differences between a typical Irishman and Englishman were not nearly so great as both sides assumed. Shaw's *John Bull's Other Island* (1904), written at the request of Yeats, is about the plight of landless Irish laborers struggling against English landlords. In the play, Shaw demonstrates the fixity of opinion by the Irish of the English and vice versa, each depending on the other's predictable stance to maintain the necessary divide, when in fact they were missing an opportunity to gain an understanding of each other. He has his cynical Irish and romantic English characters take on the very characteristics of their opposites in order to satirize national stereotypes. In the end, despite their knack for witty commentaries, Wilde and Shaw preferred to portray an English aloofness rather than an Irish seriousness. After all, they were writing for an English, not an Irish, audience.

There were other diverse and even discordant notes of cultural pursuit prior to World War I. Sir Horace C. Plunkett and George William Russell offered a socioeconomic cultural approach to Irish problems. The son of Anglo-Irish aristocracy, Plunkett was educated in England at Eton and Oxford University. Upon graduation from Oxford, he spent ten years farming in the United States, returning to Ireland in 1889. Immediately, he took note of Ireland's backward economy and began to devise a self-help program, believing that the nation's difficulties stemmed much more from economic than political woes. Plunkett founded the Irish Agricultural Organization Society in 1894 with the goal of assisting tenants to become successful independent farmers by providing them with the best information about agriculture. Also elected to Parliament from county Dublin in 1892, Plunkett hoped to gain some cooperation from the Parliament. He was instrumental in getting legislation passed in 1899 creating the Department of Agriculture for Ireland and being named its head.

Meanwhile, sociologist and poet George William Russell, who wrote under the pen name "AE," became interested in Plunkett's campaign. Russell grew up in Dublin and, like so many others in his generation, was enthralled by the issue of nationalism. Russell believed that the goal of economic self-sufficiency through reliance on cooperatives was the best way for the Irish to make themselves independent from Britain. His published works, *Cooperation and Nationality* and *The National Being: Some Thoughts on an Irish Policy*, outlined the means of establishing cooperatives in both the urban and rural economies. In 1905, Russell became editor of *Irish Homestead*, the journal of the Irish Agricultural Organization Society, and began working closely with Plunkett. As a Unionist MP, Plunkett alienated the parliamentary home rule party, which feared self-help ideas would detract from the objective of self-government. Thus, Plunkett resigned as head of the Department of Agriculture in 1907. The political agendas of home rule and republicanism eclipsed the campaign for self-help. Still, Irish political philosophy did not ignore the economic element.

David Patrick Moran (1871–1936) used his weekly journal, the *Leader* (founded 1900), to challenge virtually all versions of nationalism current since the early nineteenth century. Partly because he was so controversial, Moran gathered a considerable readership. He was opposed to any Irish accommodation with Britain so he assailed not only current nationalist leadership but also the revered Daniel O'Connell and Young Ireland from an earlier era because of their willingness to cut deals with the British government. Moran mostly favored Irish industrial development, which made him similar in certain respects to the initiatives of Plunkett and Russell. Yet he also admired the Gaelic-language revival and was a staunch Catholic. Indeed, Moran's monthly *Catholic Bulletin* (founded 1911) contained virulent anti-Protestant diatribes. His book, *The Philosophy of Irish Ireland* (1905), became a best-seller in the attempt to reshape the nationalist tradition. Moran believed that Ireland had been a conquered nation for so long it had forgotten that Gaelic culture was superior to and older than Anglo-Saxon culture. It was foolish, Moran asserted, that Yeats and his followers sought merely to make Irish writings a branch of English literature. He saw the issue as a battle between Irish and Anglo-Saxon civilizations rather than one of cultural fusion. Moran's anti-British sentiment contributed to the growth of a republican spirit.

Thus, although the Gaelic cultural revival of the post-Parnell era profoundly influenced the debates about Ireland's future, it did nothing to bring unity to the cause. Indeed, the Gaelic culturalists, like their nationalist brethren, tended to foster a mythical picture of a beleaguered Irish peasantry enduring their pains with a stoical Christian indifference. As with almost every other area of Ireland's modern history, culture was as problematic as religion, social class divisions, or economic opportunity. The idea of blending various Irish cultures into one entity failed because the native Irish would not recognize the cultural leadership of the Anglo-Irish, the differences between cultures were greater than their common elements, and politics rather than culture had become the preeminent concern of most Irish of all stripes.

HOME RULERS VERSUS REPUBLICANS

The rise of Gaelic national culture, combined with the failure of home rule in 1886 and 1893, allowed the latent republican sentiment to be resurrected in the late 1890s. By 1898, Arthur Griffith (1872–1922), editor of the *United Irishman*, began unveiling the core of a quasi-republican philosophy soon known by the Gaelic label *Sinn Féin* (ourselves) given to the movement by Maire Butler. Griffith sought to build on Daniel O'Connell's social and political theme of Ireland for the Irish. He also hoped to politicize the Gaelic cultural phenomenon by establishing in 1900 Cumann na nGaedheal, an organization to promote economic development and Gaelic culture. Griffith did not believe that Ireland was strong enough to force Britain to allow Ireland to become an independent republic. Thus, he initially thought in terms of the Hungarian status within the Austrian Empire, achieved during the revolution of 1848–1849 by Louis Kossuth. Hungary had acquired its own constitution and the right of internal self-rule while remaining part of the Austrian Empire. The format Griffith presented therefore was halfway between a genuine republic and the home rule formula.

Griffith did not advocate violent revolution but rather passive resistance to persuade Britain to create a Hungarian model for Ireland. The key element in his strategy was to make the Irish economy self-sufficient and to institute essentially protectionist means to keep British imports to a minimum. Between 1905 and 1908, through various amalgamations with Cumann na nGaedheal, the Sinn Féin political party emerged. Like so many other Irish leaders, Griffith was an elitist rather than a liberal democrat. He did not, for example, have any sympathy for the rights of industrial laborers, since in order to attract needed investment to build an industrial base, cheap labor was a prerequisite.

Industry, especially in Ulster, continued to expand, led by the shipbuilding industry and companies like Harland and Wolff (founded 1858) and Workman and Clark (founded 1879). Workman and Clark led in the development of turbine engines. By the turn of the century, Harland and Wolff was headed by the innovative shipbuilder William James Pirrie. Pirrie designed for the White Star line the two largest ships ever constructed, the *Titanic* and the *Olympic*. Railroad expansion and consolidation facilitated industrial growth. The Great Northern Railway was created in 1876 through a merger of four lines: Dublin-Drogheda, Dublin-Belfast, Irish North Western, and Ulster.

With urban industrial expansion came typical problems of difficult working and poor living conditions, which inspired labor organization efforts. Founded in 1894, the federated Irish Trade Union Congress was modeled after its British counterpart. The leading figure of the Irish labor movement was a former Liverpool dock worker, James Larkin, who had

studied the anarchistic syndicalist ideas current on the European continent. Larkin founded the Irish Transport and General Workers Union
(ITGWU) in 1908 with the help of a deserter from the British army, James
Connolly. As a Marxist, Connolly started the first Irish socialist newspaper, *Workers' Republic,* in 1896. After several years in America learning
labor agitation techniques, Connolly returned to Ireland in 1910. Eventually about 10,000 workers joined the ITGWU.

Through effective strikes, the ITGWU won concessions from some
Dublin employers. But Larkin met his match in United Tramway Company owner and MP William M. Murphy. Also owner of Ireland's largest
circulation daily newspaper, the *Irish Independent* (founded 1905), Murphy supported the home rule movement. He locked out the union after
a 1913 strike and forced strikers to surrender without any gains. The
Irish union movement got virtually no political support and only modest
backing from the British Trade Union Congress. In frustration, Larkin
sailed for the United States to raise funds for the union and promote an
anti-British trade policy among Irish-American workers. Connolly, much
more of a nationalist, took control of the ITGWU. The failure of Larkin's
aggressive methods caused most Irish laborers, following Connolly's
lead, to reject socialist ideology in favor of Irish nationalism. Thus, the
republicans could count on yet another ally to their cause.

Griffith's republicanism was not the only element of the renewed
trend. Older organizations such as the Irish Republican Brotherhood,
largely moribund since the 1870s, found new leadership in Thomas J.
Clarke. A follower of Fenian John Devoy, Clarke endured a lengthy imprisonment from 1883 to 1898 for his part in Fenian bombing incidents.
Clarke's efforts to revitalize the IRB after his release from prison contributed to a modest increase to about 1,500 members by 1900. The IRB
also sought to infiltrate and control the Gaelic League, heretofore a nonpolitical group. The revived IRB was preparing for its entrance onto the
national scene in the 1916 rebellion.

Before republicanism became dominant, there were successful attempts to establish the home rule cause within the Irish parliamentary
party. The initial hurdle was to resolve the split that occurred on Parnell's death in 1891. William O'Brien founded the United Irish League
in 1898, based in county Mayo, using the same formula so successful in
Parnell's strategy, blending land reform with self-government. The platform of the league concentrated on breaking up large farms to allow
more land distribution to tenant farmers. Much of the problem by the
late 1890s concerned relatively prosperous Catholic tenant farmers clash-

ing with Catholic landless laborers, replacing the old dichotomy of Protestant landlord versus Catholic tenant. O'Brien's league grew steadily from 8,000 members in 1899 to 86,000 by the end of 1900. The league's agenda also advocated political home rule, an endowed Catholic university, support for Gaelic instruction in schools, and better housing for the urban poor.

The reunification of the Irish parliamentary party occurred in 1900 after the retirement of factional leaders Justin McCarthy and John Dillon. The party membership elected the old Parnellite stalwart, John Redmond, as chairman of the party. A few months later, Redmond was also named president of the United Irish League, thus replicating the posts held by Parnell with the parliamentary party and the Land League. At the time of Irish parliamentary reunification, the Conservatives were in power. Conservatives, following their old formula as well, sought to pacify the Irish MPs with various reform measures to keep them from joining the Liberals. Still searching for a new Irish policy following the death of Gladstone, the Liberals made no overtures to the Irish party.

In the general election of 1900, the Conservatives won a significant majority, while the Irish home rulers returned eighty-two members. Although supportive of the sixteen Irish regiments in the British army in South Africa, the Irish party criticized Conservative policy during the Boer War (1899–1902). By 1902, under their new leader, Sir Henry Campbell-Bannerman, the Liberal party demonstrated more sympathy toward Irish concerns but was not yet prepared as a body to back home rule again. The Liberals proposed instead a kind of devolved government in which elected county councils would have more authority. They also favored ending corruption within the Irish executive at Dublin. Fearing another alliance between Liberals and the Irish party, Conservative Chief Secretary George Wyndham pushed through Parliament a Land Purchase Act in 1903 with the backing of the United Irish League. The act allowed the sale of entire estates if three-fourths of the tenants agreed to buy their holdings with government-financed loans. The better-off tenant farmers were the major beneficiaries, and agrarian violence dropped off noticeably after 1903.

The land settlement buoyed Irish hopes for a political solution. However, the United Irish League's campaign for creation of a Catholic branch of the University of Dublin failed to secure support from most of the Irish MPs. O'Brien reacted by resigning from the party in late 1903. A new Conservative initiative in 1904 sought to placate the Irish party. The Irish Reform Association headed by an Irish landlord, W. T. W.

Quin, fourth earl of Dunraven, crafted a devolution scheme featuring locally elected Irish councils between Parliament and the Irish executive to distribute public funds. Redmond offered only lukewarm support, and Dillon opposed the idea. It was finally rejected by Chief Secretary Wyndham. The Conservative government lost its majorities in 1905, and a Liberal government led by Campbell-Bannerman assumed office in preparation for the general election of 1906.

The results of the election gave the Liberals one of their largest majorities ever, with 399 members. The Conservatives and Liberal Unionists held 156, the new Labour party elected 29 members, and Irish home rule candidates won 83 seats. Unfortunately for the Irish leadership, the margin of the Liberal victory meant they were not dependent on the Irish votes for their program and thus could not be forced to resurrect home rule. Dillon presented the Irish agenda to the Liberal chief secretary, which included further progress in land sales to tenants, a housing act, the end of coercion, support for Gaelic instruction in the schools, and a publicly funded Catholic university. The Irish gains were meager. A housing measure gave urban tenants the same rights held by rural tenants against landlords and funding to build 300,000 new public housing units. Another bill in 1907 provided public assistance to evicted tenants. The failure of the Irish party to gain major concessions from the Liberals before the election of 1910 made it easier for republican organizations to snipe at the parliamentary leadership.

The Liberals followed the Conservative lead in 1907 by introducing another council bill to establish local agencies independent of Parliament and the executive to deal with local needs. Redmond and a majority of the Irish party rejected the proposal. The parliamentary leadership was encouraged in 1908 by the return to their fold of former leaders William O'Brien and Tim Healy. Soon after the replacement of Campbell-Bannerman as prime minister by Herbert Henry Asquith in 1908, the Liberals enacted a university bill establishing the basis of Ireland's modern university system. Trinity College in Dublin and Queen's University in Belfast were unaffected, but the National University was created by merging colleges in Galway and Cork with a new Catholic university in Dublin. The National University was effectively Catholic with state funding and satisfied a long-held objective of Catholic nationalists.

The general election of 1910 resulted in losses for the Liberals, which gave the Irish party more leverage. Liberals won 275 seats, and the 40 Labour members held a margin of 315 to 294 over Unionist forces (Conservatives and Irish Unionists). Thus, the 83 Irish home rule members were again needed by the Liberals to keep their edge. Before the election, O'Brien had established his All-for-Ireland League, which stood for home rule, continued tenant purchases from landlords, lower taxes, and cooperation with Protestants. The league won 8 seats in the new Parliament. Unionists responded to the election by advancing the idea of American federalism as an alternative to home rule.

Because of the battle over the Parliament bill to alter the constitutional status of the House of Lords, another election was called in December. Liberals lost four more seats and depended more than ever on the eighty-four home rulers. Prime Minister Asquith offered nominal support for home rule, but the devil obviously would be in the details of the plan. One new factor for the Liberals by 1910 was that government spending in Ireland exceeded revenues collected there. The eventual passage of the Parliament Act in 1911 meant that the House of Lords could only delay legislation passed by the Commons. Specifically, the Lords could force reconsideration of a Commons-passed measure twice, but if the Commons passed it a third time, it became law without the Lords' approval. The constitutional change was important to Ireland since the Lords had blocked the second home rule bill in 1893.

Rapidly emerging from the background in the preliminaries leading to a third home rule bill was the rise of the Ulster Unionist political organization. Sir Edward Carson, a Trinity-educated lawyer and MP for Ulster, became chairman in 1911 of the Ulster Unionist Council (founded 1905). He was assisted by other Presbyterian Orangemen, including Sir James Craig, MP for county Down since 1906. Ulster Unionists took the initiative before the home rule bill was crafted by demanding a partition of Ulster from the rest of Ireland. The Ulster opposition proved powerful and effective, especially because it gave the Conservative party a legitimate vehicle to obstruct home rule while appealing to public sentiment.

A Liberal cabinet committee was assigned the task of drafting a home rule bill in early 1911, but the committee was divided between home rule and federalism as the appropriate framework. Another dilemma was how to finance home rule since public Irish expenses were £2 million over revenues by 1911. The Liberal party wanted Ireland to assume responsibility for solving the budget deficit. Ulster opposition to what was called an "all-around" (all of Ireland) home rule bill intensified as the drafting process moved forward. Unionist clubs in Britain multiplied from 14 in 1911 to 371 by 1914, and over 5,800 propaganda meetings were held. Carson spoke to an anti–home rule crowd of 50,000 at Craigavon, Ulster, in late 1911. The new Conservative party leader named in

November 1911, Andrew Bonar Law, had Ulster roots and expressed open sympathy for the Ulster Unionists.

The final draft of the home rule bill was presented to the cabinet in April 1912. The 1912 bill was similar in structure to the 1893 proposal. A bicameral legislature would be composed of 164 members in the House of Commons (128 county, 34 borough, and 2 university seats). The upper house senate would include 40 appointed members with eight-year terms. The executive was made responsible to a majority of the Parliament. A British presence would be continued through the office of lord lieutenant and lesser posts but would act mainly as a liaison between the Irish and British governments. Ireland's representation in the U.K. Parliament would be reduced to 42 seats. Finances would be managed by a joint Irish-British board, but Ireland would not control its own finances until the deficit was extinguished. The implication of the financial clauses was that either fewer public services or higher taxes must be accepted to balance the budget.

Carson's Unionist criticism focused on specific parts of the legislation deemed discriminatory to Ulster. Dillon and Redmond expressed reservations about the financial ingredients but supported the bill overall. After the bill's second reading, Ulster Unionist amendments were offered in committee that would exclude Ulster or parts of it from the bill. Those amendments did not gain a majority, and the bill passed its third reading in January 1913 with a 110-vote margin. The House of Lords, as expected, turned the bill down, 326 to 69. The Liberals moved ahead with a second passage in the Commons in July by the same margin as the January vote. The Lords rejected it a second time, so that if the Commons passed the bill a third time, it would become law.

In October 1913, Conservative leader Bonar Law told Prime Minister Asquith that the Conservatives would support home rule if Ulster was excluded, but Redmond opposed such a provision. Back in Ireland, the Ulster Volunteer Force organized by the Unionists recruited 77,000 paramilitary members in 1913. Alarmed at the development, some Irish nationalists, led by D. P. Moran, Patrick Pearse, and Eoin MacNeill, organized the National Volunteers at Dublin in November 1913. Both Unionist and nationalist militias were rapidly collecting arms and prepared to use violence. In early 1914, the Liberal cabinet approved the native Welsh David Lloyd George's amendment to allow counties to opt out of the home rule arrangement for six years with a simple majority vote. The Commons passed the Lloyd George amendment to the home rule bill, but the House of Lords changed it to exclude the nine Ulster counties without a required vote.

Prime Minister Asquith convened a home rule conference at Buckingham Palace with Lloyd George, Conservative leader Bonar Law, Irish home rulers Redmond and Dillon, and Ulster Unionists Carson and Craig present. They could not reach agreement on the issues. Sporadic violence began cropping up in Ireland as a result of Volunteer activity. In August 1914, the United Kingdom declared war on Germany and entered World War I, whereupon Redmond suggested using Protestant and Catholic Volunteers as a defense force. Asquith's government now sought quick passage of home rule to remove the issue in order to concentrate on the war. The original home rule bill was passed but suspended for the duration of the war, and Lloyd George's amending bill for Ulster was delayed until the war ended. When Asquith proposed creation of a coalition war cabinet in May 1915, Redmond refused to join, while Carson and Conservative leader Bonar Law agreed to participate, thereby increasing Unionist influence in the government.

Both Protestant and Catholic Volunteers continued to operate as militias after the war began. Fears about conscription ended in early 1916 when Redmond secured Ireland's exception from Britain's military draft legislation. Even so, by late 1915, 80,000 Irish males were serving in the British military, about evenly divided between unionists and nationalists. Some Irish republicans sought Germany's aid in overthrowing British rule. An Ulster Protestant who had turned radical nationalist, former British consul Sir Roger Casement, tried to organize an Irish army from prisoners of war in Germany. Despite German promises, no help for the Irish rebels was forthcoming. When Casement landed in Kerry from a German submarine in 1916, he came to warn the rebels that German backing had dissipated. He was captured by British authorities, and the Volunteers in Dublin canceled plans for an Easter rising.

Yet, some IRB republicans persevered naming Patrick Henry Pearse "president of the Irish Republic." A member of the Gaelic League, Pearse had operated a Gaelic-speaking school and promoted the Irish cultural revival before joining the IRB in 1915. Although a nonviolent intellectual, Pearse came to accept rebellion as a legitimate act while seeking as the author of the proclamation of the republic to restrain elements of "inhumanity" in the violence. In the end, a small contingent of die-hards seized the General Post Office in Dublin and fought British troops for four days before surrendering. There was little national sympathy for the rebels; Redmond, who was in England at the time, as well as Carson condemned the revolt in Parliament. Not surprisingly, the leading newspapers—*Irish Independent* (pro–home rule), *Freeman's Journal* (pro–home rule), *Cork Examiner* (pro–home rule), *Irish Times* (unionist), and the *Daily Express* (unionist)—condemned the rising to one degree or another ("insane and criminal," according to the *Independent*; "a communistic disturbance" in the *Examiner*). Fifteen leaders of the rebellion, including those who had signed a document declaring Irish independence, were executed as traitors, along with Volunteer commanders. Among the victims were Casement, Connolly, Clarke, and Pearse. Seventy-five others initially sentenced to death including Eamon de Valera, were imprisoned. Redmond warned about and John Dillon correctly predicted that the British lust for punishment and the drawn-out schedule of executions would inflame the nation. Hence, the so-called Easter Rebellion of 1916 not only would live in the memory of Irish republicans for decades afterward but also eventually in the wider nation.

The Irish rebellion gave ambitious David Lloyd George an excuse for reviving home rule and creating trouble for his rival, Asquith. While Asquith created a royal commission to investigate the rebellion, Lloyd George began personal negotiations separately with Carson and Redmond. He told Carson the exclusion of Ulster would be permanent and Redmond that it would be only temporary, so that both agreed to immediate home rule for twenty-six counties, excluding six Ulster counties whose future would be determined by an imperial conference after the war. Lloyd George's solution was backed by the Conservative leadership though still opposed by southern Unionists, who wanted any action delayed until after the war. Their opinion was voiced by a cabinet member, the marquis of Landsdowne. When Redmond was told by Lloyd George and Unionists that the exclusion of Ulster must become permanent, the Irish party withdrew its support, and the plan was scuttled. The failure of the 1916 negotiations permanently undercut Redmond's constitutional nationalists and effectively doomed home rule. Most Irish home rule MPs deserted Asquith's government. In reaction to the British repression of the rebellion, Sinn Féin candidates began to win by-elections in 1917.

A Liberal split between Asquith and Lloyd George came to a head in December 1916, leading to Asquith's resignation and Lloyd George's formation of a national government. Irish concerns seemed suddenly buried even further beneath the war and British politics. Nonetheless, Lloyd George announced the convening of an Irish convention for July 1917 at

Trinity College to consider Ireland's future. Meanwhile, following his release from prison in June, Eamon de Valera was elected president of Sinn Féin and head of the Irish Volunteers in October 1917. Sinn Féin refused to participate in the Irish Convention as did Irish party leaders Healy and O'Brien. But fifty-two Irish nationalists attended, along with forty-three Ulster and southern Unionists. There were fifty-three Catholics and forty-two Protestants among the delegates. Sir Horace Plunkett, elected chairman of the convention, pledged that all viewpoints would be aired. Differences in the convention between republicans and home rulers dominated the discussions and prevented any unanimity. Although twenty-one draft resolutions were approved by a divided vote of forty-four to twenty-nine, the numbers did not yield strong enough support. Redmond died in March 1918 and was replaced by John Dillon, but the convention ended its deliberations the next month without reaching a common position. Although the war served as a distraction during the convention, it was not a substantive factor in the failure to reach an Irish settlement.

Lloyd George proposed in early 1918 to extend the military draft to Ireland in exchange for granting home rule. He hoped to get Conservatives in his national government to back him. But the Irish parliamentary party walked out of the Commons and allowed Sinn Féin to gain the upper hand. Irish nationalists opposed to conscription organized a one-day general strike across the country in April, and it was most effective. The British government ordered the arrest of Sinn Féin leaders including de Valera and Griffith in May, charging them with participating in a German plot, though there was virtually no evidence to support the accusation. By July 1918, Lloyd George announced that he was no longer pursuing home rule for Ireland. In the general election of December 1918, Sinn Féin won 47 percent of the popular vote and 73 seats of the 105 Irish total. The home rule party returned only 6 members, and Unionists won 23 seats, all from Ulster. The era of home rule had passed.

The home rule era, which held such potential for permanently resolving Irish differences, ended with Ireland divided in both the literal and figurative sense. Britain's Irish question had not been solved but merely reshaped for the twentieth century. By the time a majority in Parliament came around to agreeing with Gladstone's concept of home rule in 1914, Catholic Ireland had been converted to republicanism. Also, home rule served as the last best hope for Protestant participation in a unified Irish solution. Home rule was intended to establish a devolved British role in

Ireland, yet the establishment of a Protestant-controlled Northern Ireland actually increased the likelihood of future British involvement in Ulster affairs. Thus, home rule as a potential unifying force proved too simplistic for such a complex society.

7

The Irish Free State, 1918–1938

The 1916 Easter Rebellion proclamation of a republic created a national mythology for Ireland, just as the storming of the Bastille did for France in 1789. With the second declaration of an Irish Republic by Sinn Féin following the end of World War I, the British government was more determined than ever to resolve the "Irish question." Although Great Britain supported the Paris Peace Conference's principle of national self-determination, it had difficulty applying the same principle to Ireland. The British were experts at international diplomacy, but the Irish showed their own propaganda skills by exploiting postwar anti-imperial sentiments. Partition of Ireland seemed inevitable because of Ulster Protestant opposition to a united Ireland. Thus, the task of David Lloyd George and his government was to persuade southern Ireland to accept dominion status without the inclusion of most of Ulster. The "war for independence" between 1919 and 1921 drained both sides, so that Britain and most Irish republicans were ready for a treaty in 1921, even though it created two Irelands instead of one. The Irish Free State was merely an interlude on the road to a republic, and the British seemed to understand that better than Sinn Féin, which fretted over symbolic language. After 1922, the Irish Free State set aside the matter of Ulster to build a self-governing state.

Eamon de Valera initially resisted the Free State status and clung to the dream of a republic. For some time after 1922, the Irish political landscape was shaped by the pro- and antitreaty parties. The protreaty party, Cumann na nGaedheal (Community or League of Irishmen), held power until 1932 when de Valera's reconstituted Sinn Féin party, Fianna Fáil (Soldiers of Destiny), gained a majority. Biding his time until Britain was again distracted by war clouds in Europe, the declaration of Éire rather easily was accepted by the Chamberlain government in 1937–1938. Thus, internal Irish politics more than British overlordship became the focus of attention during the 1920s and 1930s. The quest for Irish self-sufficiency and a distinctive national identity was evident in the politics, economics, and culture during the era.

ORIGINS OF THE FREE STATE, 1918–1922

Although Sinn Féin won seventy-three Commons seats—including the first woman MP—in the United Kingdom general election of December 1918, members decided not to sit at Westminster but to convene in Dublin as the Irish republic's Dáil Éireann (Irish Parliament). The proclamation of a republic in 1918 was much more significant than the Easter Rebellion claims of 1916 because republicans were united and had the backing of a large portion of the southern Irish electorate. The British government of David Lloyd George unwittingly facilitated the claim of a republic in March 1919 by releasing the Sinn Féin prisoners of 1916. Eamon de Valera, who escaped from jail, was named president of the republic.

Although the Dáil was declared illegal in September, it began to function without interference in most parts of southern Ireland. Sinn Féin dominated district and county councils, collected taxes, and operated its courts completely outside British governmental structures. Most Irish accepted the republic and gave it tacit approval. Nonetheless, Sinn Féin's peaceful coexistence plan was undermined by the Irish Republican Brotherhood, which reestablished the defunct National Volunteers in January 1919, renamed the Irish Republican Army (IRA). The IRA commander, former postal clerk Michael Collins of county Cork, participated in the Easter Rebellion and was imprisoned for several months. The IRA launched a war for independence from British rule and obtained ample financing from Irish American groups. Collins proved to be an expert at gathering intelligence to keep the British off-guard. The IRA numbers have been difficult to ascertain, with claims running as high as over

100,000. In practice, the tactical squads never had more than a few thousand in active service. Yet Collins's IRA targeted isolated but vulnerable British operations such as police stations or convoys to keep the initiative.

The British army maintained about 50,000 troops in southern Ireland, complemented by 10,000 Royal Irish Constabulary. However, they had to cover all parts of the country, which spread them thin, and the British were not accustomed to fighting guerrilla-type conflicts. By 1920, Britain created an auxiliary force of 7,000 nicknamed the "Black and Tans," mostly ex-soldiers, which matched the terrorist tactics of the IRA, thus creating a public relations disaster for the British. By the end of the conflict in 1921, about 750 Irish had been killed and 230 British soldiers and police died. Hundreds more on both sides were wounded.

On the political front, David Lloyd George persuaded Parliament to pass the Government of Ireland Act in December 1920. The British had decided to ignore objections of southern Protestants and northern Catholics about partition but to give both Ulster unionists and southern nationalists what they wanted: a piece of Ireland. The act thus provided for a divided Ireland with separate parliaments—twenty-six counties in the south and six in Ulster (Antrim, Armagh, Derry, Down, Fermanagh, Tyrone) totaling 5,476 square miles or 17 percent of the island. Ulster's Carson agreed to reduce Northern Ireland from nine to six counties largely because it would enhance Protestant majorities. Protestant minorities (18 percent) in the excluded Ulster counties of Donegal, Monaghan, and Cavan felt as betrayed as Catholics (33 percent) in the six counties of Northern Ireland. Both Irish governments would have a reduced representation in the United Kingdom Parliament at Westminster (thirty-three seats for the south and thirteen for Northern Ireland). A Council of Ireland with delegates from both Irish governments would seek a formula for reunification. Sinn Féin immediately rejected the 1920 act, while Ulster Unionists agreed to accept the legislation even while refusing to participate in the Council of Ireland. Unionists proclaimed "a Protestant nation for a Protestant people." King George V insisted on personally opening the Northern Ireland Parliament—Unionists won forty of fifty-two seats—at Belfast in June 1921 with an appeal for reconciliation.

In the interim after the 1920 act, despite Sinn Féin's opposition, de Valera began secret negotiations with the British government to break the political impasse and end the fighting. The two sides signed a ceasefire in July 1921 when Britain offered dominion status for the south. Sinn

Féin continued to press for a republic, but Lloyd George was committed to salvaging the imperial connection, necessitated by his dependency on Conservative votes in the coalition government. An October conference was held in London with Collins, Griffith, George Gavan Duffy, Eamon Duggan, and Robert Barton representing Sinn Féin and Lloyd George, Austen Chamberlain, and Winston Churchill leading the British representatives. De Valera decided to remain in Dublin for strategic purposes, since any position the Sinn Féin delegates might take must be presented to the Dáil. Curiously, Sinn Féin seemed more concerned about the oath of allegiance to the crown than the dominion structure that Lloyd George proposed. Sinn Féin offered an alternative to the oath known as "external association," by which Ireland would merely recognize the king as head of the British Commonwealth, but Lloyd George rejected external association.

The ice seemed to be broken when Lloyd George proposed to include Ulster in a unified dominion structure, and Sinn Féin accepted. But Conservative Unionists threatened to withhold their electoral support for Lloyd George, and he backed down. Lloyd George then suggested to Sinn Féin that a British boundary commission could be created to survey the division between northern and southern Ireland and that the commission would reduce the size of Ulster so much that an independent Ulster would become untenable, leading Unionists to ask to join the Free State. In response, Sinn Féin's delegates submitted Lloyd George's terms to the Dáil in December, but the Dáil rejected the plan because of the oath. When the Irish delegation returned to London, Lloyd George gave them an ultimatum: agree to his proposals or face all-out war. Viewing the offer as preferable to continuing the war, Collins and Griffith persuaded the other three delegates to accept, and they signed a treaty on December 6, 1921. The treaty created a dominion, the Irish Free State, with financial, judicial, political, and educational independence. Britain would retain three ports for use of the Royal Navy and remain in control of foreign policy. Oddly, the agreement provided that the Dáil Éireann, which Britain deemed illegal, would be the agency for ratification on the republican side.

Ratification by the Dáil was not certain since de Valera, clinging to the republic, led opposition to the Irish Free State status. Nonetheless, many were tired of fighting, including Collins, and the Dáil approved the treaty by sixty-four to fifty-seven in early 1922. De Valera resigned as president of the Dáil and was succeeded by Arthur Griffith. The transfer of power to a provisional government occurred in March, and the elections to Parliament (the so-called pact election) were held in June. Collins preferred to characterize the elected body as a constitutional convention. Almost three-fourths of those elected to the assembly, 109 to 44, were in favor of the treaty. Although de Valera opposed violence, Rory O'Connor led insurgent IRA forces to defy the Free State and occupy a government building in Dublin, the Four Courts, in April 1922. With about half the old IRA reconstituted as Free State forces, commander-in-chief Collins did not move to attack the insurgents until they kidnapped one of Collins's deputies. The Free State assault on the Four Courts in June 1922 began a new civil war, pitting Irish against Irish. The insurgents, known as Irregulars, recruited new soldiers, who included de Valera. The Irregulars, commanded by Liam Lynch and Earnan O'Malley, gathered arms, manned outposts, and prepared for war. Ten months of fighting ensued, with Free State forces holding the upper hand but unable to deliver a decisive defeat to the Irregulars. Almost two hundred Protestant residences, dubbed "Big Houses," were burned by the IRA during the civil war, causing many Protestants to lose confidence in the government's promises of protection. Because Collins led the Free State forces, he became a target of Irregular efforts and was killed in August 1922. In October 1922, the Dáil voted special powers for the army to establish martial law and use capital punishment for illegal possession of firearms. Over the next several months 12,000 suspects were arrested and detained as security risks. Seventy-seven Irregulars, including leaders such as Erskine Childers and Rory O'Connor, were executed.

The fighting continued until April 1923 when Irregular leader Lynch was killed. De Valera persuaded the new chief of staff, Frank Aiken, to halt the armed resistance. Born in county Armagh, Aiken joined the Volunteers in 1914, became a commander in the IRA in 1921, and was promoted to chief of staff in 1923. There was never any surrender, negotiations, or treaty ending the civil war; it just stopped. However, the civil war left deep and bitter divisions among those who had previously been allies for so long against their common enemy Britain. De Valera went to prison for a year as punishment for his resistance. The conflict caused considerably more destruction than the 1919–1921 war for independence. Estimates of deaths have yet to be authenticated and range from 600 people to 4,000; property damage was widespread and extensive. The Free State government was forced to spend about £17 million to prosecute the war, thereby diverting important funds from other needs.

THE COSGRAVE ERA, 1922–1932

While the fighting raged, the Dáil drafted a constitution that was approved by the Westminster Parliament in December 1922. The constitution included elements of individualism such as a bill of rights and the grass-roots tools of the referendum and initiative, which required 75,000 signatures to become operative. The official launching of the Irish Free State (Saorstát Éireann) came on December 6. Longtime nationalist Tim Healy was named governor-general, the crown representative, by the king. The last British troops left Ireland in December. The Oireachtas (Parliament) was bicameral. The lower-house Dáil of 153 members was elected by proportional representation, intended by Britain to protect Protestant minority interests. Proportional representation provided for a "single transferable vote" in multimember constituencies. Voters could choose several candidates in order of preference. If a first choice was eliminated, the vote could be transferred to the next preference. The Free State had thirty multimember constituencies, one having nine members (Galway) and others from three to eight members. The Dáil also had three university seats each for Trinity College and the National University, the electors being the alumni. The upper-house senate, or Seanad, was composed of sixty members, half appointed by the president (prime minister) of the executive council (cabinet) and half elected by the Dáil. The Seanad's powers, mirroring the British House of Lords, were limited to delaying or amending Dáil bills.

The first president of the executive council, Arthur Griffith, died in August 1922 and was succeeded by Easter Rebellion veteran William Thomas Cosgrave. Dublin-born Cosgrave was a founding member of Sinn Féin in 1905, joined the Volunteers (1913), served a prison term for participation in the Easter Rebellion (1916–1917), and was elected to the Dáil (1918). His Cumann na nGaedheal (CNG) party won 63 of 153 seats in the 1923 Dáil elections in which 59 percent of eligible voters participated. Sinn Féin won 44 contests but refused to take their seats because of opposition to the oath of allegiance. The revived Labour party (founded 1914), which did not participate in the 1918 elections in deference to Sinn Féin, won 14 seats behind the leadership of the pragmatic moderate Tom Johnson. Johnson was a former president of the Irish Trade Union Congress and served as Teachta Dála (member of the Dáil, TD) for county Dublin (1922–1927). The political wing of the Farmers Union, the Farmers' party, secured 15 seats from rural constituencies. The Farmers' party favored free trade and a limited role for government.

Independents accounted for the remaining 17 seats. Richard Mulcahy succeeded his former commander Collins as minister of defense. A former postal worker from Waterford, Mulcahy had served a prison term for participating in the Easter Rebellion. He was TD for Dublin (1922–1937). Kevin O'Higgins was named minister of home affairs. The son of a physician and educated at Maynooth, O'Higgins joined Sinn Féin in 1918 and was TD for Dublin after 1922. O'Higgins had been most outspoken in criticism of the Irregulars as mere opportunists out for their personal aggrandizement rather than seeking the nation's needs.

Despite many nationalists being disappointed at having to accept dominion status, the Irish participated vigorously in the commonwealth conferences during the Free State's existence. Delegates such as O'Higgins and the ministers of external affairs—Desmond Fitzgerald to 1927 and Patrick McGilligan after 1927—were active in collaborating with their colleagues from other dominions such as Canada and South Africa. A poet-playwright, Fitzgerald lived in France as well as England before joining the IRB at Kerry in 1914. He was TD for Dublin (1922–1937) and afterward a senator. The son of an MP, McGilligan hailed from county Derry and received his education at University College, Dublin. He was TD for the National University (1923–1937). Their combined efforts pressuring Britain to allow greater independence led to the passage by the British Parliament of the Statute of Westminster in December 1931 defining dominion status simply as a free association of sovereign nations with allegiance to the British crown. The Free State was the first dominion in the commonwealth to establish a permanent consulate at the League of Nations in Geneva. Against the wishes of the British, the Free State sent its own diplomatic representatives to several commonwealth nations, France, the Vatican, and the United States. Free State citizens traveling abroad were issued Irish, rather than British, passports. Thus, more than any other area of government activity, the Free State's foreign policy laid the foundations for the eventual break with Britain in 1937–1938.

Security remained a high priority for the new government, even after the civil war ended. The Gárda Síochána (Civic Guard) police force numbered about 4,500 by mid-1923 and merged with the Dublin Metropolitan Police in 1925. Army rolls totaled more than 50,000 in mid-1923, but the government wanted it cut in half to reduce costs. There was resistance, mainly among officers, to Mulcahy's reduction-in-force plan. A threatened rebellion was accompanied by an ultimatum by officers—Liam Tobin and C. F. Dalton—demanding that the government halt the military reductions, dismiss the army council, and commit to moving toward a republic. Tobin and Dalton were arrested, but an investigation of army administration was also authorized. The confusing attempts to squelch the mutiny episode ultimately led to the resignations of Mulcahy and three of his senior officers in March 1924. Gárda commissioner Eóin O'Duffy succeeded as army chief of staff. Other army resignations followed an investigation of the mutiny.

Republican hopes for gains from the boundary commission were misplaced, despite pledges by Lloyd George and other British leaders before the treaty was signed. A British Conservative government was in power when the commission was appointed in late 1924, and Conservatives had no intention of sacrificing Ulster. Northern Ireland refused to appoint its representative on the commission, while the Free State named Minister of Education Eoin MacNeill as its member. When the commission's report proposed to incorporate 183,000 acres of Ulster with a population of 31,000 into the Free State and remove 49,000 acres in the Free State with a population of 7,600 to Northern Ireland, MacNeill resigned in protest. Having built up expectations of major territorial gains from the revised boundary, the Cosgrave government could not afford to allow the report to become public. Thus, in December 1925, the three governments agreed to revoke the treaty clause about the boundary commission, and the matter was dropped. Thus, there were no changes in the existing boundary between Northern Ireland and the Irish Free State. Due to the opposition of Northern Ireland, the Council of Ireland never functioned, and it was also abolished in the December agreement. Although Cosgrave had met on several occasions with his counterpart from Northern Ireland, Sir James Craig, to seek solutions to their common problems, there were no more meetings between the two heads of state after the boundary debacle until 1965.

At the very moment that Cosgrave's government was grappling with financial strictures emanating largely from the civil war, the president faced a previous commitment to liquidate debts owed to Britain. The Free State had agreed in 1923 to pay land annuities dating from decades before World War I and to fund pensions for the now-defunct Royal Irish Constabulary. The total obligation amounted to £5 million. In 1926, Cosgrave made good on these commitments even though his political opponents criticized the decision. Further controversy surfaced in a reduction of old-age pensions by 1 shilling per week in 1924, though the original proposal called for twice the actual amount approved.

By 1926, de Valera had a change of heart toward participation in the politics of the Free State after consultation about the oath of allegiance with papal advisers in Rome, especially the rector of the Irish College, Monsignor John Hagan. At Sinn Féin's *ard-fheis* (party convention), de Valera urged the party to challenge their political enemies, Cumann na nGaedheal, by contesting Dáil seats in the next election. A boisterous debate ensued in which a slight majority, 223 to 218, opposed de Valera's strategy. Repudiated by Sinn Féin, de Valera resigned in May 1926 and created a new party, Fianna Fáil, to enter the Free State political arena. Fianna Fáil's platform called for creation of a united Ireland under a republic, revival of Gaelic language and culture, equal opportunity for all, land redistribution, and a self-sufficient economy. De Valera's supporters within Sinn Féin joined Fianna Fáil to become the core of the new entity, which prepared to campaign for the Dáil elections of 1927. De Valera correctly concluded that the Cosgrave government's unpopular record made CNG vulnerable.

The election results in January 1927 reduced CNG to forty-seven seats, Fianna Fáil won forty-four, the Labour party held twenty-two, four lesser parties totaled twenty-five seats, and fourteen elected members were not affiliated with a party. Four women were elected to the Dáil. Fianna Fáil members were denied their seats in the Dáil after refusing to take the oath of allegiance. Cosgrave allied with one minor party and the independent members to form another government. In July, unidentified IRA assailants assassinated the most controversial member of Cosgrave's government, Kevin O'Higgins. He had held the offices of vice president, minister of justice, and minister of external affairs. De Valera condemned the murder of O'Higgins, but the Dáil passed a public safety act that called for suppression of republican organizations and their publications, widened police search-and-seizure powers, and established special courts to impose the death penalty for illegal possession of firearms.

The Dáil also passed a constitutional amendment requiring future candidates for elective office to sign a pledge to take the oath of allegiance if elected or be disqualified. De Valera determined that his party was being marginalized and decided in August to take the oath with Fianna Fáil TDs and enter the Dáil. The political situation changed immediately, with Labour's Tom Johnson calling for a vote of no confidence. A tie vote was broken by the chairman of the Dáil siding with the government. His governing majority having evaporated, Cosgrave dissolved the Dáil and called for new elections in September. In the second vote within a few months, the smaller parties suffered most. CNG improved its position, winning sixty-two seats, but Fianna Fáil also did well, taking fifty-seven contests. The Free State had come close to establishing a two-party system, thereby reducing the impact of proportional representation.

Although most Irish nationalists in the Free State favored economic self-sufficiency in the abstract, in practice it proved unrealistic, especially since the main industrial region of Ulster had been separated from the south. Existing economic conditions had tied Ireland more directly to the British economic system, particularly in the area of agricultural exports from Ireland to Britain. Thus, if the nationalists had applied protectionist tariffs against Britain, it could have caused grievous harm to Ireland's agricultural economy. In the event, a six-month dockworkers' strike in 1923 crippled Irish exports at a crucial moment.

The fact that Ireland's economy was dominated by an agricultural system beset with backwardness should have been offset by the conclusion of persistent landlord-tenant tensions. Most tenant farmers had obtained ownership of their farms prior to 1921, and the remainder purchased their holdings under the 1923 Land Act. Furthermore, the proportion of agricultural laborers had dropped to about one-fifth of the agricultural population according to the 1926 census. Thus, farm divisions no longer revolved around the landlord-tenant or even producer-laborer relations but rather between small farms (mainly in north and west) and large farms (mainly in south and east). Also, farmers lacked political clout in the Dáil. Not until the 1930s did a farmers' party of note, Clann na Talmhan (Children of the Land), show any electoral strength. Perhaps the main problem for agriculture was a reluctance to adopt new technologies and scientific methods. Half of the Free State workforce was engaged in agriculture, which had production twice as great as industry. Minister of Agriculture Paul Hogan urged farmers to reduce their costs and improve quality, and called on the government to reduce taxes on agriculture. The Dáil established the Agricultural Credit Corporation in 1927 to make government loans to farmers, but too many of the recipients still resisted any modernization.

In the financial realm, a Dáil-appointed Coinage Committee's recommendations became the basis of the Coinage Act of 1926. The first Irish coins (silver and copper) minted in 1928 under the act were imprinted with various animal symbols rather than more traditional Irish symbols such as round towers or shamrocks. The coins were designed by Percy Metcalfe. The Parker Willis Banking Commission recommendations in 1926 became the basis of the Currency Act of 1927. The Irish pound, in seven denominations, was pegged to British sterling at the ratio of one to one, establishing a fixed exchange rate with Ireland's chief trading partner. The government would maintain 100 percent sterling reserves to back the new pound issues, a safe, if very conservative, policy. Finally, a Currency Commission rather than a central bank would operate mainly to supervise the new currency. Since the seven-member commission, chaired by Joseph Brennan, was not empowered to regulate interest rates, private banks set their own rates, which remained higher for loans and lower for personal accounts compared to British banks.

The wage scale for Ireland's embryonic industries was far below that of Britain, so many workers, especially disillusioned Protestants, continued to emigrate to Britain for better-paying jobs. Urban slum tenements, mainly in Dublin, were another factor stimulating emigration; about 800,000 Irish poor lived in inadequate, overcrowded housing. Dominion status therefore did not forestall the level of emigration, which held back Ireland's economic development. Emigration averaged 33,000 per annum during the 1920s, then slowed to an annual average of 14,000 during the depression years of the 1930s. A pattern of late marriages, dating from the postfamine era, made it easier for unmarried young people to leave Ireland. The 1926 census showed that 80 percent of males and 62 percent of females between the ages of twenty-five and thirty were unmarried. The total population of the Free State declined by fewer than 3,000 from 1926 to 1936. Only a few bright spots appeared, such as the sugar beet industry, which spread gradually from south Leinster to most of the Free State. The largest employer after agriculture was the brewing-distillery industry, followed by textile manufacturing. Industrial employment grew from about 60,000 in 1926 to almost 100,000 in 1936. Export values, however, could not grow beyond 1924's £51 million. The Dáil in 1924 approved the merger of twenty-seven railroad companies into the Great Southern Railways Company, thereby ensuring an effective, though uncompetitive, transport system.

Electric power development also lagged in Ireland, with many urban areas still without electricity in the 1920s. Despite opposition from within the cabinet and the Dáil, the minister of industry and commerce, Patrick McGilligan, got approval in 1925 to hire a German engineering firm, Siemens, to build a dam and hydroelectric plant at Andracrusha, outside Limerick, along the Shannon River. The power station began operating in 1929. The government-operated Electricity Supply Board, established in 1927, helped spread electric power to most parts of the nation. Yet relatively high electric costs kept the rate of increase for new electric customers to about 10 percent per annum until power was available throughout the nation in the 1950s.

Irish labor unions were still in their infancy in the 1920s. Their membership potential was limited by only 13 percent of the workforce being industrial. After serving three years of a ten-year jail sentence in the United States, former labor leader James Larkin returned to Ireland in 1923 to resume leadership of his old union, the Irish Transport and General Workers Union, whose membership William O'Brien (not the home rule William O'Brien) had increased to 100,000. O'Brien helped found the ITGWU in 1908 and served several terms as president of the Irish Trade Union Congress (1913, 1918, 1925, 1941). Larkin's dyed-in-the-wool socialism (some called it communism) led to his ouster from the ITGWU. He then formed a second major union and party, the Workers' Union of Ireland (WUI), in 1924 and served as TD in the Dáil (1927–1932). The Communist party of Ireland, founded in 1921 by Liam O'Flaherty and others, was ordered by Moscow's Communist International to merge into Larkin's group. Yet communism never attracted a large following in Ireland. Industrial workers constituted virtually the sole constituency of the Labour party, which lost support to Fianna Fáil after 1927. An unemployment rate averaging 6 percent during the 1920s remained a source of concern to the unions.

SOCIETY AND CULTURE IN THE FREE STATE

Because of the historic intertwining of the Roman Catholic church and nationalism, church-state cooperation in the Free State was implicit, despite a clause in the 1922 constitution guaranteeing separation of church and state. The 1926 census revealed that 92.6 percent of the Free State population was Roman Catholic. Reflecting its effective status as a confessional state, the Irish Free State accommodated the Catholic church in social policy. There were 14,000 Catholic clergy in the Free State, most of whom emulated their rural conservative social milieu. Cosgrave's cabinet contained only one non-Catholic, and most of the clergy supported the Cumann na nGaedheal party, though one bishop voiced sympathy for de Valera in 1924. The archbishop of Dublin, Edward Byrne, made his views known to the government, and the church strongly influenced political issues as well as social mores. Despite traditional Irish moral puritanism, the church urged limits on the importation of loose moral tendencies from Europe in movies, dress styles, literature, and sex. The Dáil passed the Censorship of Films Act (1923) and laws in 1923 and 1927 to limit the sale of liquor. The introduction of private divorce bills on the British model was opposed by the Dáil with the church's influence a major factor, much to the dislike of the Free State's 7 percent Protestant population. A high point in the Catholic church's prominence came in 1932 with the convening of a eucharistic conference. Prelates from forty nations attended the week-long gathering in Dublin. The climax of the conference was an open mass in Phoenix Park, where 500,000 participated.

Although equal opportunity existed in theory, few women made their mark in the early years of the Free State. The Catholic church's opposition to abortion, contraception, and female priests were not challenged during the Free State era. A legal ban on married women serving in the government remained in effect until 1973, and a marriage bar affected teachers in state schools from 1934 until 1958. Fianna Fáil's first executive committee included six women. One of those, Hanna Sheehy Skeffington, helped found the Irish Women's Franchise League (1908) to promote women's suffrage, which was implemented in the 1922 constitution. Mary Hayden, an exception to the male dominance in academe, was professor of history at University College, Dublin, and coauthor of the primary history textbook used in schools until the 1960s. Female members of the Dáil never grew to more than a handful, and no woman served as a government minister until 1979.

The church also promoted the Dáil's Censorship of Publications Act (1929), which banned "indecent or obscene" books as determined by a censorship board. The measure met with stiff resistance from Irish writers, led by W. B. Yeats (recipient of the Nobel Prize for literature in 1923), George Bernard Shaw (Nobel laureate for 1926), and in George Russell's *Irish Statesman*. On the eve of the act's passage in 1928, Shaw warned that Ireland was in a "position of special and extreme peril" if the measure became law. Later in 1932, Shaw and Yeats founded the Irish Academy of Letters to combat state censorship. Expatriate James Joyce's *Ulysses* (Paris, 1922), with its 1904 Dublin setting and Irish characters, was controversial but not banned. Indoctrinated in Catholic nationalism, Joyce had never sympathized with the revival of Gaelicism and showcased his skepticism in *Ulysses*. Joyce had remarked on a sense of "paralysis" in Irish culture and politics earlier in *Dubliners* (1914). Also, in *A Portrait of the Artist as a Young Man* (1916), Joyce assailed the false facade offered by Irish religion and social institutions. There was no formal censorship of the theater, but pressure often was felt, such as against Protestant Sean O'Casey's play, *The Plough and the Stars* (1926). The largely self-educated O'Casey had been a member of the Gaelic League, but when he left Ireland for London in 1926, his influence on the Irish stage ended.

Most of the younger Irish writers in the 1920s came from a working-class background, which contrasted with the Anglo-Irish leadership during the Gaelic renaissance a few decades earlier. The mentor of many in the group was novelist-playwright Daniel Corkery, professor of English literature at University College, Cork (1930–1947). Embittered by the war for independence, Corkery became an obsessive nationalist repudiating the Anglo-Irish contribution. Corkery's novel, *The Hidden Ireland: A Study of Gaelic Munster in the Eighteenth Century* (1924), and his play, *Resurrection* (1924), made plain that the Irish identity was determined by Catholicism, nationalism, and the land. Gaelicists such as Corkery felt Ireland was unique in Europe since it had preserved a native primitivism by avoiding the imperial influence of Rome and the decadence of Western civilization. Corkery therefore did not respect Western-oriented Irish writers such as Yeats, Russell, and Joyce.

Corkery-influenced authors included Frank O'Connor, Liam O'Flaherty, and by the late 1930s Sean O'Faolain. Born in Cork and taught by Corkery, O'Connor's short stories and his biography of Michael Collins (1937) doused romantic notions of the republic. O'Connor later served as director of the Abbey Theater in Dublin (1935–1939). A native of the bleak Aran Islands and educated at University College, Dublin, O'Flaherty traveled in the Americas after World War I and began writing, upon taking up residence in London in the early 1920s. His novel *Thy Neighbor's Wife* (1923), reflected a provincial realism devoid of romantic sentimentality. Also an opponent of censorship in *The Puritan*, O'Flaherty was a founding member of the Academy of Letters. A great champion of democracy and native of Cork, O'Faolain's novel *King of the Beggars* (1938) assailed what he called the Gaelic myth and exalted pragmatic political reformers such as Daniel O'Connell. Thus, the new authors tended to be less idealistic and more realistic, reflecting deep disillusionment with the social, political, and economic developments of the post-treaty period.

The Free State offered only modest public funding of the arts, including the National Gallery (opened 1864), the Science and Art Museum and National Library (opened 1890), and the Royal Dublin Society's School of Design (1849), but that was as much due to the dire financial straits of the budget than to a hostility toward the arts. A state radio system, Radio Éireann, began broadcasting at the beginning of 1926 in

Dublin, and Cork in 1927, but its bureaucratic director, T. J. Kiernan, had little artistic sense of radio's potential. Radio Éireann played mostly live concerts. The number of radio receiving licenses grew threefold from 1935 to 1941 after a powerful transmitting station was opened at Athlone.

Budget constraints also led to inadequate support for the national schools, administered by the Department of Education. Sixteen thousand teachers' salaries were cut by 10 percent in 1923. Still, school systems themselves were well organized under Ministers of Education Eoin MacNeill (1923–1925) and John O'Sullivan (1926–1932). MacNeill had assisted Douglas Hyde in founding the Gaelic League in 1893, and edited its journal. Later he was named professor of history at University College, Dublin, and served as chairman of the Irish Manuscripts Commission from 1928 to 1945. Although Irish literacy approached 100 percent, a 1926 Dáil act required compulsory school attendance for children between the ages of six and fourteen. A Gaelic-language initiative followed the constitution's designation of Gaelic as the national language. Only about 10 percent of the Free State population could speak Irish in 1922. MacNeill strongly supported the language effort as did Mulcahy, who served as chairman of the Gaeltacht Commission, which was charged with preserving certain Irish-speaking areas in Munster and Connacht as a means of encouraging the nation to imitate their tradition. The government plan called for compulsory courses in Gaelic to be offered first in the National University and gradually spread down to the secondary and primary schools. By 1934, all students had to pass a Gaelic-language skills test before receiving a diploma, a stipulation that remained until 1973. All employees of the government, the military, and the police were required to be proficient in Gaelic. The native language would be used in government communications, Dáil debates, and legal proceedings.

Not only did the Gaeltacht Commission have to work diligently to make the appeal of Gaelic studies attractive outside Irish-speaking areas, but within the Gaeltacht, the government met hostility to its modern educational methods. Few who learned Gaelic in the schools outside the Gaeltacht domain used native Irish in their daily communication. A 1929 study showed little progress in spreading language usage, and teachers complained that excessive time devoted to language instruction left too little for other courses in the curriculum, some of which were deleted. Yet the government remained adamant that the emphasis would continue. By 1939, the number of Gaelic-speaking Irish was half the 1922 figure. The Gaelic League, which had led an earlier language emphasis, declined from 819 chapters in 1922 to 139 by 1924. Between 1881 and

1926, Irish speakers had shrunk by 41 percent, though a good portion of that was due to emigration. Other Gaelic revivals under the Free State included the Irish folklore society, An Cumann le Bealoideas (1927), and Irish folk music.

Despite being a private agency, the Gaelic Athletic Association rose to its greatest prominence during the Free State era. It continued to ban British sports such as soccer, cricket, and rugby until 1971. The GAA tried to operate in both the north and the south. It had 1,000 clubs in 1924 and increased to 1,700 by 1932, the largest number in Leinster and Munster, but Ulster had 200 as well. Relations between the GAA and the Cosgrave government were not always friendly because the GAA attempted to remain nonpolitical. The GAA claimed tax exemptions that were tacitly allowed until the Dáil's Finance Act (1927) gave the GAA a legal tax exemption that continued over the next fifty years. Despite GAA opposition, the Football (i.e., soccer) Association of Ireland (founded 1921) maintained a large following and held events in cities such as Dublin, Belfast, Cork, and Limerick.

Anglo-Irish society clearly was enervated from the outset of the Free State, if not before. The old aristocracy felt isolated and ostracized, practically like foreigners. Of course, the Protestant population was not evenly distributed: Connacht had only 2.6 percent Protestants, Munster 3.6 percent, and Leinster 10.1 percent. Business and professional Protestants accounted for 40 to 50 percent of some Dublin suburbs. The Royal Dublin Society became a cultural haven for the Anglo-Irish in the capital, sponsoring lectures and concerts. Membership in the society increased from 2,200 in 1919 to 7,000 in 1926. The old cultural center of Trinity College experienced financial troubles and decaying campus buildings during the 1920s and 1930s. These and other factors led one-third of the Free State Protestant population to leave by the late 1920s. One disgruntled Anglo-Irish resident in 1929 described the Free State as run by a medieval priesthood. The Seanad included several Anglo-Irish members, but they never attempted to establish a political organization. Anglo-Irish literary contributions were centered in the *Irish Statesman*, resurrected in 1923 with George Russell as editor. The *Statesman* remained an aesthetic beacon, cultivating Ireland's place in a larger European cultural context and thus often at odds with the Gaelic nationalists. Russell, though not alarmed by a Gaelic-language revival, touted great Irish literature written in English. The two languages, like Protestant and Catholic religions, need not be mutually exclusive in Ireland's mixed cultures.

FIANNA FÁIL RULES, 1932–1937

Preparing the way for the rise of Fianna Fáil was the establishment of the polemical *Irish Press* in 1931, edited by the innovative Frank Gallagher. Deliberately friendly to revolutionary nationalist movements outside as well as inside Ireland, the *Press* reached its circulation goal of 100,000 within its first couple of years of publication, surpassing its rival, the conservative *Irish Times* (founded 1859). Gallagher also strove to make the *Press* more inclusive of other parts of Ireland beyond Dublin and of multiple constituencies such as women. Before the election of 1932, the *Press* faced prosecution under the Special Powers Act and was fined for criticizing government treatment of political prisoners. More seriously, Gallagher soon faced financial problems brought on by reduced advertising during the depression. He resigned as editor in 1935, succeeded by M. J. MacManus.

In addition to the controversial policies of Cumann na nGaedheal, the advent of the Great Depression after 1929 undermined CNG's popularity. Irish Free State unemployment rose to 30,000 by 1932, with many of the new industries failing. Cosgrave faced a delayed red scare in 1931 as a result of some dissident IRA members, led by Peadar O'Donnell, Seán MacBride, and Frank Ryan, founding Saor Éire (Free Ireland), Ireland's independent Marxist organization. James Larkin's Irish Workers League (1927), backed by Moscow's Communist International, never gained a popular following. Born in county Donegal, O'Donnell joined the ITGWU in 1918 and the IRA in 1920. He was elected a Sinn Féin TD in 1923 and edited the IRA newspaper, *An Phoblacht*. O'Donnell also published seven novels in the 1920 and 1930s, the most notable, *Islanders* (1928), reflected an almost fanatical nativism. MacBride was born in Paris and joined the IRA in 1918. After serving a prison term, he held the post of chief of staff in the IRA until 1936. Ryan was from county Limerick, educated at University College, Dublin, majoring in Gaelic studies. He later fought with Spanish republicans in their civil war (1936–1938).

At the inaugural convention, 120 delegates met to draft a constitution for Saor Éire. Reflecting international communist aims, Saor Éire was committed to overthrowing the government of the Free State, though the purported purpose would be to set up a workers' utopia rather than a republic; the enemy was capitalism. Other communist front organizations such as Comhairle na Poblachta (Council of the Republic), founded in 1929 by, among others, MacBride and Ryan, promoted the destruction of the Free State. Thus, Cosgrave felt compelled in 1931 to ask the Dáil to ban organizations such as Saor Éire, Comhairle na Poblachta, and the Labour Defense League (founded 1929). Included in the list of proscribed organizations was the IRA, which caused Fianna Fáil to vote against the measure and criticize the Cosgrave measure. The Catholic church, which had condemned Saor Éire, gave only nominal support to the law, with its military court allowing capital punishment to enforce the political ban. The extreme nature of the legislation furthered the growth of Cosgrave's unpopularity.

Aware of electoral dangers, Cosgrave called an election in February 1932 about six months before a constitutionally mandated election would have been required. De Valera and his Fianna Fáil party were well prepared for the election, even though it was held earlier than expected. Cleverly, de Valera's campaign promised to abolish the oath of allegiance and terminate the land annuity payments to Britain. Though he lacked a resonant voice, de Valera began using the radio effectively to communicate with the nation. Cumann na nGaedheal ran on its record but also showed desperation in charging the opposition with endorsing Marxist ideology and violence. Voter turnout reached a new high of 75 percent, helped in part by a more friendly press for Fianna Fáil. Thus, Fianna Fáil triumphed in the election, winning seventy-two seats in the Dáil to fifty-seven for CNG. Lesser parties won twenty-four seats and held the balance of power, but de Valera gained the backing of seven TDs in order to form a government. A new party with a new leader unveiled plans for ending the dominion connection with Britain.

De Valera's palpable threat of creating a republic and fostering economic nationalism caused the British prime minister, Ramsey MacDonald, to form the Irish Situation Committee in 1932 to track de Valera's actions and prepare responses. The committee met regularly until 1938. One item on Fianna Fáil's agenda was to terminate the land annuities, repayment of loans made from 1891 to 1909 allowing tenant farmers to purchase land. The debt payments totaled £3 million per annum. In addition, the Free State was obligated to pay £250,000 per annum for sixty years to compensate for property damage caused during fighting from 1921 to 1925. Since the property damage payments had not been approved by the Dáil, de Valera simply ordered them stopped, along with a suspension of annuity payments. Pursuing an agrarian mythology, de Valera envisioned a revitalization of small farms that would keep Irish youth from emigrating. When no agreement could be reached between the Free State and Britain, the British treasury ordered a 20 percent import duty on Irish agricultural products. The income from the tariff would be used to pay Irish debts. The Free State responded by imposing tariffs on British imports, beginning a trade war that would prove quite harmful to a Free State economy already reeling from the effects of the depression.

Caught in the trade struggle, Free State agricultural exports to Britain declined by two-thirds from 1929 to 1935, but de Valera was unapologetic for the trade losses. De Valera's attempt to find alternative markets for Irish exports and stimulate new domestic industry proved largely unsuccessful, as non-British exports increased only 1 percent between 1929 and 1935. British trade was also hurt by the conflict but not nearly so much as damage to the Free State economy. A partial settlement of the trade war occurred in 1935 with the coal and cattle agreement. Britain raised its quota for Irish cattle imports by one-third, while the Free State agreed to purchase all its coal imports from Britain (averaging 1 million tons per annum). Economic woes caused by the depression and the trade war continued, with the rural poor enduring the brunt of hardships. Unemployment in 1933 rose from 30,000 in March to 80,000 by October, and reached a peak of 145,000 by the end of 1935. Industrial output grew by 40 percent from 1931 to 1936 at the expense of agriculture, but industry represented less than 15 percent of the economy. Because the Guinness Company built a brewery near London in 1936, its exports from Ireland were cut in half. It seemed that de Valera had chosen an inopportune time to pressure Britain for Irish nationalist principles.

Fianna Fáil's leading economic thinker as minister for industry and commerce (1932–1939, 1941–1945) was Sean Lemass. Lemass had learned economics as a prisoner following the 1922 Four Courts episode. A believer in state economic planning, he coordinated an expansion of the welfare state in Ireland, made easier by the impact of the depression. Unemployment benefits were extended to tens of thousands out of work, and public housing additions averaged 12,000 units per annum between 1932 and 1942. The Industrial Credit Company (1933) provided business loans to companies threatened by the economic problems. Lemass also increased the number of vocational schools and helped create the state airline, Aer Lingus, in 1936.

De Valera sought to replace the oath of allegiance to the British crown with his post-World War I theory of external or unrestricted association with Commonwealth nations. The Dáil passed legislation to abolish the oath in May 1932, but the Seanad delayed its implementation for a year. A general election was called in January 1933 as de Valera hoped to strengthen his party's majority. Fianna Fáil won seventy-seven seats in the Dáil compared to CNG's forty-eight, Labour's eight, Centre's eleven, and nine independents. With continued backing from Labour, Fianna Fáil had secured a strong majority. Quickly after the election, de Valera began to ostracize the governor-general, James MacNeill. The British government agreed to remove MacNeill, who was replaced by a Fianna Fáil member, Donald Buckley. Two constitutional amendments stripped the powers of the governor-general. De Valera also sought to terminate the right of appeal from Irish courts to the British privy council. Another constitutional amendment decreed an end to the right of appeal, and the privy council actually sanctioned the move.

Not only did Free State politics experience left-wing communist movements in the early thirties, but fascism also appeared on the scene. It began with a veterans' organization, the Army Comrades Association (ACA), founded in 1932. The ACA was politicized in July 1933 when former Gárda commissioner (1922–1932) Eóin O'Duffy became head of the ACA and changed its name to the National Guard. O'Duffy had been trained as an engineer but joined the IRA in 1917 and became chief of staff in 1922. O'Duffy created the blueshirts paramilitary organization, imitating other continental fascist movements. The ideology of the National Guard was anticommunist and pro-Christian. Alarmed at the potential for violence, Minister of Defense Frank Aiken authorized a raid in August 1933 to round up blueshirts, and the National Guard was banned. De Valera's government also had trouble with radical IRA elements. A series of IRA-sponsored murders continued in 1933. A split in the ranks occurred in 1934 between Ryan and O'Donnell on one side (created the Republican Congress) and Seán MacBride on the other. Continued violence finally prompted the Free State to declare the IRA an illegal organization in June 1936.

Meanwhile, a political reorganization took place in September 1933 with the creation of a new party, Fine Gael, combining the existing parties of CNG, the Centre party, and the National Guard. O'Duffy became president of Fine Gael, which had three vice presidents: CNG's Cosgrave, Frank MacDermot, and James M. Dillon. MacDermot was educated at Oxford University and became a practicing lawyer in Britain, serving in the British army during World War I. He returned to Ireland from France in 1929 and was elected an independent TD in 1932 when he founded the National Centre party to seek improved relations with Northern Ireland and Great Britain. The Centre party won eleven seats in the January 1933 election. Born in Dublin and educated at University College, Galway, Dillon managed his family's mercantile business before entering politics as a TD from Donegal in 1932. De Valera persuaded the Dáil to pass legislation banning the wearing of uniforms by the blueshirts in February 1934. The Seanad rejected the measure, so that its final passage was delayed by eighteen months. The action of the Seanad was a prime factor causing de Valera to push through a constitutional amendment to abolish the upper legislative house in 1936. The first electoral impact of Fine Gael came in the 1934 county council elections. Fianna Fáil gained majorities in fifteen councils while Fine Gael prevailed in eight councils. Of the combined membership in the twenty-three councils, Fianna Fáil totaled 728, Fine Gael 596, Labour 185, and others 371.

In 1935, O'Duffy resigned as head of Fine Gael following an internal dispute. He founded the National Corporate party, but soon left Ireland in 1936 to fight with Franco's Spanish fascists in the civil war. Labeled the "Irish Don Quixote" by an Irish journalist, O'Duffy commanded an Irish brigade of 700. Cosgrave was elected to take O'Duffy's place as leader of Fine Gael. Though Fine Gael and the Catholic church favored anticommunist Franco, de Valera assumed a neutral position toward the Spanish Civil War.

De Valera continued his quest to sever ties to Britain in additional Dáil legislation. The Irish Nationality and Citizenship Act of 1935 ended British citizenship in the Free State but allowed a dual citizenship with the Free State and other countries. The Aliens Act of 1935 decreed that British citizens in Ireland must assume alien (i.e., noncitizen) status. At the same time, de Valera issued an executive order exempting British subjects already living in Ireland from coming under the law.

When the British government learned that de Valera was drafting a new constitution for the Free State in 1936, the cabinet began to outline the British position on anticipated issues. Britain would agree to abolish the office of governor-general and end the trade war in exchange for recognition of the king's constitutional position in Free State affairs and an agreement that there would be no union of north and south without mutual consent. The royal abdication crisis of 1936 gave de Valera an unexpected opportunity to push his constitutional agenda. In order to marry a commoner, King Edward VIII abdicated in favor of his brother, who became George VI. The commonwealth dominions were required to pass their own act of abdication before recognizing the new monarch. The Dáil offered amendments to the abdication bill, which would remove the crown from the Free State constitution and acknowledge the crown as head of the commonwealth free association of nations. Fine Gael's attack on the proposals was led by John A. Costello, educated at University College, Dublin. As a student of the law, Costello had served as attorney general for the Free State (1926–1932) and as TD for Dublin (1933–1937). Costello noted the inherent contradiction in the bill to remove the king from the constitution but not from the state. The bill passed 79 to 54 in the Dáil.

The introduction of a new constitution (Bunreacht na hÉireann) in 1937 followed the abdication crisis. The constitution omitted reference to the king or the commonwealth but did not describe the state as a republic. The name was changed from Irish Free State to Éire, that is, Ireland, designated as including Ulster but applying at the time only to the Free State territory. Éire's structure of government included a largely ceremonial president elected for a seven-year term. The Taoiseach, or prime minister, would be more powerful than the president of the executive council under the Free State constitution. A deputy prime minister, the Tánaiste, was also created. The Dáil retained its Free State format, but the Seanad of sixty members was altered somewhat following the 1936 suspension. The Taoiseach would appoint eleven members, three each would be elected by the alumni of Trinity College and the National University, and the Dáil, in consultation with the county councils, elected the remainder. The religious article granted freedom of religion while recognizing the Catholic church as holding a "special position." Parochial schools as well as secular schools were to receive state aid. Archbishop of Armagh Joseph MacRory pushed hard for a state church, but the papacy remained neutral.

In June 1937, the Free State Dáil approved the proposed constitution sixty-two to forty-eight and scheduled a popular referendum. The referendum results ratified the new constitution by a vote of 685,000 to 527,000, and the constitution took effect on September 29, 1937. Britain's Irish Situation Committee, chaired by Conservative Prime Minister Neville Chamberlain, met but made no statement about the Éire constitution. The British choices seemed to be either to accept the constitution or expel Éire from the Commonwealth. De Valera quickly moved to call a general election in 1937. The results gave Fianna Fáil sixty-nine seats, Fine Gael forty-eight, Labour thirteen, and eight independents were elected. De Valera took some pleasure in the defeat at the polls of Fine Gael's Richard Mulcahy and Desmond Fitzgerald.

In January 1938, de Valera came to London seeking a settlement of issues with Chamberlain. De Valera took a hard line, insisting on the end of the partition of Ireland as well as a settlement of the trade war.

Chamberlain was equally firm that no unification of Ireland would occur without the consent of Ulster Unionists. De Valera assumed that Britain would make the decision without consulting Ulster, but he underestimated the power of the Unionist influence still present in the Conservative party. The so-called Anglo-Irish Agreement signed in April called for Britain to withdraw from its three treaty ports, for Éire to pay 10 percent (£10 million) of the outstanding annuity debt, and a trade agreement largely establishing free trade between Éire and Britain.

Although some internal differences about Fianna Fáil electoral strategy surfaced during the next general election in 1938, de Valera's party gained strength, winning seventy-seven seats. Fine Gael remained viable with forty-five, but Labour's hopes for gaining leverage with Fianna Fáil fell short when they won only nine seats. Independents won the remaining seven seats in the Dáil. With de Valera's endorsement, Gaelic-language enthusiast Douglas Hyde was elected Éire's first president. Britain relinquished control of the treaty ports in July amid great celebrations across Éire.

NORTHERN IRELAND, 1920–1939

The Government of Ireland Act (1920) was accepted by the Unionist majority in Ulster as the basis of a type of home rule. Ulster Unionists realized that Northern Ireland would be neither a nation nor a state and that Northern Ireland's creation was an act of British expediency. Yet it was the best arrangement the Unionists could obtain. A governor was the crown's representative, but most power would be wielded by a bicameral parliament. A forty-eight-member Commons would be elected by proportional representation, as prescribed for the Free State later. The Senate of twenty-four members would be appointed by the Commons. Symbolically, the government convened at Stormont Castle, an imposing structure on a hill overlooking Belfast. The "reserved powers" held by Britain were similar to those in the Free State constitution, including especially foreign and fiscal policy. Northern Ireland retained twelve MPs in the United Kingdom Parliament at Westminster, though they would be elected by the direct vote system used in Britain. The Ulster Unionist party dominated the government from the outset, led by Prime Minister Sir James Craig (created Viscount Craigavon in 1927), who served until his death in 1940.

Northern Ireland exhibited an obsessive concern from security against nationalist threats. In addition to the constituting of the Royal Ulster

Constabulary, the regular police were supplemented by three auxiliaries. The A-specials were full-time adjuncts until their disbandment in late 1925. The B-specials, part-time constables in their local communities, became infamous in using vigilante-style methods until their disbandment in 1970. The C-specials were a standby force for emergencies; their recruitment ended in early 1926. Although Catholics were eligible for participation in the special constabulary, few were enrolled, and the B-specials soon became wholly Protestant.

Determined to secure Unionist control of government against the Catholic nationalists, Craig's government terminated proportional representation in the elected local councils in 1922. When the Westminster Parliament objected, Craig threatened to resign, and the matter was dropped. The ability of the Unionists to alter the constitution obviously set a bad precedent and gave a green light to further encroachments on minority rights. In the event, nationalist majorities in local councils were reduced by a dozen to only eleven out of seventy-three. Furthermore, Unionists began gerrymandering local district lines so as to maximize Protestant authority. The next logical step came in 1929 with the abolition of proportional representation for elections to the House of Commons. The rationale for this change was slightly different. The Unionist majority party was being challenged by two other unionist parties, the Labour party and the Independent Unionist party, which could have eroded the majority party's strength under the proportional system. The veritable one-party rule produced a stagnant, defensive political elite. One reason the majority Unionists became so anti-Catholic in the early history of Northern Ireland was that a precondition to joining the Unionist party was membership in the Orange Order. Working-class Protestants deferred to an elitist social leadership of Unionism in order to maintain unity in the face of Catholic nationalism. Thus, a sectarian definition of political parties limited the scope of positions they might take on other issues.

Northern Ireland did not receive fair treatment from the United Kingdom regarding its finances. The great bulk of taxes from Ulster—income and sales—went into the U.K. treasury, some of which would become Northern Ireland's contribution toward costs of defense and debt service. The Northern Ireland Parliament assumed the greater responsibility of financing welfare state services—education, health, social security—as well as police and transportation costs, but without authority over income, customs, and excise taxes. The postwar economic recession and the depression of the 1930s placed an undue burden on local financing.

Social spending increased from one-third of the total in 1923–1924 to one-half by 1938–1939. A 1934 means test was established for receiving unemployment benefits to ease the pressure somewhat. Taxes produced lower revenues during economic downturns, while social obligations naturally increased during such periods. Northern Ireland's government lacked the flexibility to deal with its fiscal dilemma because it was tied to U.K. policies. Even if Northern Ireland had been able to reduce benefits, politicians such as Craig would have found it difficult to justify.

8

Éire and the Republic, 1939–1973

No sooner had Fianna Fáil and de Valera triumphed over their longtime nemesis Great Britain than Éire faced a major decision about World War II. The same anti-British and pro-German sentiment in Ireland that appeared during World War I revived again in the second war. Yet de Valera had to be practical about the possibility of Germany's using Ireland to attack Britain, so that national security rather than ideology drove the government's policy. Ireland's neutrality was controversial also because of the participation of soldiers from Northern Ireland in the war. Éire was not able financially or in military preparedness to join the conflict so that those considerations also influenced de Valera's decisions. Neutrality reflected Éire's internal conflict to reconcile its heritage with the tide of world events. The powerful influence of the broadcast media combined with war to bring the outside world closer than ever before to the Irish.

After the war, Éire moved fairly quickly to terminate the remaining links to Great Britain. Fianna Fáil's triumph in the 1944 elections convinced the party it would become a permanent majority. Yet Fianna Fáil always seemed conflicted between a mystical concept of republicanism and a populist agenda. From the declared intention to create a pure republic in 1948 until the final severing of ties with Britain in 1949, the

British cooperated except to declare again their intent to protect Northern Ireland from unification with Éire except by majority mandate. Because a postwar malaise continued until the 1960s, economic expansion remained the great challenge for the Republic of Ireland. A significant economic revival occurred in the 1960s, only to wane by the 1970s in the face of inflation.

ÉIRE IN WORLD WAR II, 1939–1945

After Britain declared war on Germany in September 1939, de Valera persuaded the Dáil to declare Éire's neutrality in a unanimous vote. Even after the United States entered the war in December 1941, de Valera adopted a "friendly neutrality." Public opinion also seemed to favor the policy, although circumstances of the war ultimately determined Éire's fate. Another consideration for Fianna Fáil was the deplorable condition of Éire's military, reduced in previous years to lessen costs. Although the chief of staff, General Dan McKenna, maintained a disciplined force, the army had only two brigades at full strength totaling 7,600; another 11,000 reserves could be mobilized fairly quickly, though most were ill-prepared to fight. There were also shortages of weapons, ammunition, and antiaircraft batteries. The navy was virtually nonexistent, except for a few patrol boats, and the air corps had just a few fighter aircraft and no bombers. Many members of the Irish military deserted to serve in the British army during the war, largely because of better pay. Perhaps 30,000 residents of Éire fought with the allies during the war.

A cabinet reorganization to deal with the war situation put Frank Aiken in charge of government censorship, which had three branches: mail, telegraph, and press. Joseph Connolly (to 1941) and Thomas Coyne (after 1941) directed the day-to-day activities of the Censorship Board. Easter Rebellion and war for independence veteran Oscar Traynor became minister of defense, and Sean Lemass moved from industry and commerce to manage supplies until 1941, when he returned to his former post. The staunchly anti-British Joseph Walshe served as minister of external affairs.

Even before the war began in September 1939, Éire had to contend with a renewed threat from the outlawed IRA, which hoped for German assistance to create a unified Irish republic. At the end of 1938, de Valera had instructed the Ministry of Justice to prepare legislation outlining treasonable offenses. Ironically, the civil service secretary at the Ministry of Justice, Stephen Roche, argued that Ireland should uphold the English tradition of respecting individual liberties and avoid special military tribunals in peacetime. As a fresh IRA bombing campaign got underway in Britain, de Valera tried to avoid appearing to restore the 1931 Cosgrave Public Safety Act. The resulting Offences Against the State Act of June 1939 allowed the government to suppress planned IRA marches on the eve of the European war.

De Valera established the Committee on Internal Security, mainly to monitor the IRA. Much of the excellent work of Dan Bryan as assistant head (1939–1941) and then head (after 1941) of G2 military intelligence involved tracking IRA and German contacts. Also, Minister of Justice Gerry Boland, TD for Roscommon (1923–1961), himself a former IRA man, favored a vigorous policy toward threats of violence. Several IRA raids on munitions depots occurred, the most significant in Dublin's Phoenix Park in December 1939. By January 1940, the cabinet approved an internment policy, with a camp at Curragh, which operated under the Emergency Powers Act (1939). A Gárda member was killed in January, and two IRA terrorists were hanged in Britain for a bombing that killed five in Coventry. As IRA leaders were jailed in Éire, they resorted to hunger strikes, which tested the government's resolve. After releasing one hunger-striking prisoner, Patrick McGrath, only to have him murder two policemen shortly after, de Valera, with Boland's blessing, took a firm stand against releasing any more of what the IRA claimed were political prisoners. Three prisoners died of hunger while imprisoned; six IRA members were executed for murdering government officers during the war, and another 1,100 were imprisoned or detained.

The concern about IRA contacts with the Nazis focused initially on a February 1939 visit to Ireland by Oscar Pfaf, a German spy who contacted IRA leaders and the right-wing Eóin O'Duffy during his stay. Thereafter, at least fifteen Nazi agents operated in Ireland during the war, and several IRA leaders visited Berlin. The IRA chief of staff, Sean Russell, died during a German submarine trip from Ireland in 1940. Ex-IRA leader Frank Ryan, captured in the Spanish Civil War, was released to German custody in July 1940 and continued as liaison with the IRA until his death in 1944. A proto-fascist party, the People's National party (PNP), was established in 1940, with several prominent Irish leaders, including O'Duffy, as members. Party leaders met regularly in a Dublin restaurant, but G2 kept track of their movements, so the PNP never presented any serious security threat.

Domestic troubles also surfaced in labor relations. The most serious incident was a 1940 strike by 2,000 Dublin municipal workers that threatened to paralyze the capital. The anti-union minister of industry and commerce, Seán MacEntee, was born in Belfast and educated as an electrical engineer. He served as TD for Dublin (1927–1969) and held the post of minister of finance (1932–1939). MacEntee negotiated with the Irish Trade Union Congress to end the strike before additional problems arose. The Trade Union Act (1941) set rules for future labor disputes, aiming to avoid costly strikes, by designating the largest union in any industry as the negotiating agent for the lesser unions. The government ordered wages frozen in mid-1941. Because wages were higher in Britain, which had plentiful jobs in war industries, almost 200,000 Irish workers emigrated to England during the war, the greatest number in 1942. Young, unmarried women also began to make up a greater percentage of emigrants during the war. Éire's industrial production fell by one-fourth during the war, and unemployment reached 15 percent in 1939–1940. Between 1938 and 1947, national income increased by only 14 percent compared to an 84 percent increase in Northern Ireland.

Meanwhile, petrol rationing in Éire began in September 1939, and ration books for bread, tea, and sugar were issued in March 1942. Rationing did not end until 1948. Food rationing in Northern Ireland began in January 1940. The Agriculture Department required farmers to increase the acreage planted in wheat so that output doubled from 1939 to 1944. Although government spending increased 30 percent during the war, as a proportion of the gross national product it fell 20 percent. Thus, the war could hardly be described as costly for Éire, especially in comparison to the economic hardships of Europe's warring states.

Once Lemass returned as minister of industry and commerce in 1941, economic planning received greater attention. As director of supplies (1939–1941), Lemass helped alleviate Éire's tiny merchant marine (41,000 tons) by establishing the state-operated Irish Shipping Company to acquire additional ships. When the Committee on Economic Planning was created in December 1942, Lemass favored appointing economic experts, but de Valera insisted that planning be controlled by politicians. Lemass pressed for major spending on infrastructure, increased agricultural production, and greater attention to exports, all of which he believed would improve the standard of living. Because Lemass's ideas deviated from traditional Fianna Fáil policies, only his Department of Industry and Commerce backed the proposals. De Valera rejected and thus killed Lemass's agenda.

Fianna Fáil had shown dissatisfaction with the 1927 Currency Act soon after assuming power in 1932. A new Banking and Currency Commission (1934), with Joseph Brennan as chairman, reported in 1938 calling for establishment of a central bank to replace the Currency Commission. The Central Bank Act (1942) created the Central Bank of Ireland, which began operations in February 1943 with Brennan as its governor (1943–1953). Yet there was little change in the purpose of the Central Bank from the previous Currency Commission; its primary duty was to protect the currency. Thus, the Central Bank did not regulate private banking policies, and the Bank of Ireland continued to handle government accounts.

Another socioeconomic approach that gained popular currency in the war years was vocationalism, sometimes called corporatism. As an alternative to the ideological clash of capitalism and socialism, vocationalism would organize democratic guilds according to specialized skills and promote cooperation among social classes. It seemed to gain a boost in the 1937 constitution's Senead, wherein forty-three of sixty senators were intended to represent vocational interests. However, because the Dáil could and did choose an electoral alternative that allowed political parties to dominate the selection process, vocationalism did not gain prominence. Among Fianna Fáil leaders, only MacEntee favored skewing the selection of senators toward vocations. Vocationalism's advocates included the Catholic church hierarchy, Fine Gael party, and the *Standard*, a Catholic newspaper. A 1939 Commission on Vocational Organization with twenty-five members was chaired by the bishop of Galway. The commission's detailed 1943 report suggested a hierarchy of elected vocational councils as an alternative to an impersonal, appointed government bureaucracy, but the report was ignored. Fianna Fáil seemed determined not to deviate from its founding premise of pursuing a very conservative social and economic policy.

German bombs began to fall sporadically in Ireland by 1940. In August, bombs destroyed a creamery in Wexford, killing three girls, and three women died in another German bombing at Carlow in January 1941. There was also bomb damage in Dublin during 1941, killing thirty-four. Because Northern Ireland was part of the British war effort, Belfast received much heavier attacks—one in April 1941 killing 700 and another in May costing 150 lives. Éire sent fire brigades to the north to assist in dousing flames from the German bombs. A number of Allied and German planes crash landed in and around Ireland during the war. Éire typically detained the downed pilots, but most Allied pilots were released in short order, whereas thirty-three Luftwaffe pilots surviving sixteen crashes were interned until the end of the war.

The possibility of a German invasion of Ireland was taken seriously by the government of Éire. British intelligence warned of a possible invasion in early 1940, and quietly Allied and Irish military intelligence worked together to anticipate threats. Britain's military was prepared to repel any German invasion threat to Ireland and even considered a plan to invade Ireland to establish bases. Because of security concerns, Great Britain made an offer to negotiate Irish unification in exchange for Éire's entering the war against Germany and Italy, but de Valera rejected the proposal. When James Dillon, deputy leader of Fine Gael, favored Éire's entering the war on the side of the Allies, he was drummed out of his party. Dillon's position not unexpectedly received support from the U.S. envoy to Éire, David Gray, whose nation, like Britain, wanted to use Irish ports. During an early 1941 visit to the United States, Éire spokesman Frank Aiken refused the entreaties of President Franklin Roosevelt to assist the British. Moreover, External Affairs Minister Walshe believed in 1940 that Germany would defeat Britain, so entering the conflict would be risky. Walshe's caution gained backing from leaders of the Catholic church, including the former archbishop of Armagh (1928–1929), Cardinal Joseph MacRory, and the newly elevated archbishop of Dublin (1940), John Charles McQuaid, a conservative who promoted Catholic welfare projects but did not speak out on the moral issues of the war, including anti-Semitism.

Obviously culture took a backseat to the emergency of the war, but the tone of postwar themes emerged nonetheless. A young author, Patrick Kavanagh, wrote one of the most important Irish poems in the twentieth century, *The Great Hunger* (1942). Drawing on his childhood experiences in county Monaghan, Kavanagh pinpointed the pathos of rural peasant life in stark realism. The peasants were tough, but economic realities were causing more and more to consider emigration. Kavanagh also cited the power of the Catholic church in curtailing social change in Ireland. Seán O'Faolain founded a new journal of social science, the *Bell*, in 1940 and edited it until 1946. O'Faolain used hard facts rather than sentiment to argue his points against government censorship and a monolithic Gaelic culture. The Censorship Board remained vigilant, banning Kate O'Brien's *The Land of Spies* (1941) and Eric Cross's *The Tailor and Ansty* (1942) because of earthy language and sexual references. Criticism of Gaelic-language emphasis in the schools increased during the war years. A 1941 study by the Irish National Teachers' Organization emphasized ongoing damage to the overall curriculum caused by the inordinate time spent teaching Gaelic. University College, Dublin, grad-

uate and civil servant Brian O'Nolan, writing under the pseudonym My-
les na gCopaleen, published *An Béal Bocht* (The Poor Mouth) in 1941. It
was a brilliant satire on the "Gaelic morons" whose singlemindedness
in the pursuit of the native language blinded them to larger cultural
issues. O'Nolan also used his pseudonym in a popular *Irish Times* col-
umn, "Cruiskeen Lawn," which continued for twenty years. For later
novels, he adopted yet another pseudonym, Flann O'Brien. Still, scholarly use of Gaelic grew with new journals such as *Comhar* (1942), featuring poetry and short stories, and *Inniu* (1943), a weekly news journal.

The general election of June 1943 proved a crucial test of wartime
leadership for Fianna Fáil, which lost ten seats to a total of sixty-seven.
Fine Gael, which had been divided on various issues including neutrality, fared no better, being reduced to thirty-one seats. Labour increased
its representation from nine to thirteen and doubled its popular vote
from 1938. A new farmers' party, Clann na Talmhan (Children of the
Land), was founded in 1938 by Michael Donnellan of Galway and Joseph
Blowick of Mayo. The Clann won fourteen seats, mostly in Connacht.
Eight independents made up the balance. Minister of Industry and Commerce MacEntee accepted some blame for unpopular measures, such as
the Trade Union Act, and the overall sluggish economy, and submitted
his resignation. He was given a lesser cabinet post by de Valera. Fine
Gael leadership changed as well, with Cosgrave stepping down as leader
in favor of Richard Mulcahy. Further changes included the withdrawal
of Éire's largest union, the Irish Transport and General Workers Union,
from the Labour party to form the National Labour party headed by
William O'Brien in January 1944.

Because of Fianna Fáil's reduced majority, after being defeated on a
transportation bill in May 1944, de Valera surprised everyone by calling
another general election. The suddenness of the vote combined with in-
stability among the other parties gave Fianna Fáil seventy-six seats and
49 percent of the popular vote, although voter turnout was the lowest
since 1923. Fine Gael's weak leadership was evident in Mulcahy's preelection offer to align Fine Gael with Labour and Clann na Talmhan
absent negotiations with either. Fine Gael was reduced to thirty seats.
Labour carried only eight contests, and the National Labour party won
four, while Clann na Talmhan garnered eleven seats, and nine independents won.

A major development in the labor unions occurred in April 1945 when
the ITGWU bolted from the Irish Trade Union Congress to form a new
body, the Congress of Irish Unions. Labor unrest reflected the rise in

unemployment at the end of the war to 70,000. Germany surrendered to the Allies in April, and the following month de Valera paid a courtesy call on the German ambassador to express condolences at the death of Adolf Hitler. Winston Churchill used the occasion to assail Éire's wartime stance of neutrality. A test of Fianna Fáil's wartime popularity was occasioned by the presidential election of June 1945. The Tánaiste, Seán T. O'Kelly, was persuaded to stand for Fianna Fáil; Seán Lemass filled Kelly's old post behind de Valera. Fine Gael's candidate was controversial—an ex-blueshirt and former army chief of staff (1928–1929), Seán MacEoin, TD for Sligo and later Longford (1929–1965). The republican candidate, Patrick McCarten, made a better showing than anyone expected. O'Kelly won with 538,000 votes, MacEoin had 335,000, and McCarten was a strong third with 213,000 votes. O'Kelly ran uncontested for reelection in 1952 and retired as president in 1959 after two terms.

POLITICAL AND ECONOMIC STAGNATION, 1945–1959

Despite the absence of economic growth, Lemass's efforts to impose an industrial efficiency policy failed to obtain cabinet support. Although industrial employment grew by 10 percent between 1946 and 1948, unemployment remained very high, at 9.3 percent in 1947. Fianna Fáil confronted one political crisis after another following the war. Perhaps the most difficult was the teachers' strike of 1946. The Irish National Teachers' Union, representing almost 11,000 teachers, had been perhaps the staunchest supporter of Fianna Fáil before the war. When a government-approved wage increase for civil servants in 1944 did not include the teachers, they were furious. Despite sympathetic public backing from Archbishop MacQuaid and Catholic bishops, negotiations with the education minister, Tom Derrig (1932–1939, 1940–1948), himself a former teacher, broke down in March. The INTU authorized 1,200 teachers in 140 Dublin county schools to strike. It was a public relations nightmare for the government. The *Irish Independent* and *Irish Times*, neither a union supporter, criticized Fianna Fáil's position. The government finally offered an acceptable wage settlement, and the strike ended in late October, but political damage had been done to Fianna Fáil.

Another potentially troubling political development for Fianna Fáil was the formation of a new party in 1946, Clann na Poblachta (Children of the Republic), headed by ex-IRA hardliner Seán MacBride. The new party served as a catch-all for dissident elements ranging from communist to fascist. Clann na Poblachta's wide-ranging platform sought a restoration of confidence in democratic government and a lessening of patronage and bureaucracy. The party called for a minimum wage, improved housing and public transportation, better distribution of electric power, state regulation of the means of production of staple commodities, limits to emigration, agricultural cooperatives, and even a national theater and film company. Clann's electoral manifesto advocated free education from the primary schools through technical and university levels and raising compulsory schooling through age sixteen. Clann na Poblachta benefited from organized labor's division between two parties and won several by-elections in 1947, heightening expectations for the 1948 general election.

Fianna Fáil also faced legislative controversy in the revival of its 1945 public health bill in 1947, modeled after British Labour government welfare schemes. The measure aimed to improve public health in two specific areas: obstetrics and infectious disease. The drafting of the legislation owed much to the newly created cabinet post of minister of health and social welfare filled in January 1947 by James Ryan. Ryan took his medical degree at University College, Dublin, helped found Fianna Fáil in 1926, and was TD for Wexford. The bill proposed that public health centers and schools monitor infections through mandatory inspections. Mothers and children would have no choice about the medical doctors treating them, which displeased the medical profession as well as many potential patients. Fine Gael's James Dillon even raised the possibility of constitutional questions about the bill. The most troublesome opposition came from Catholic bishops, who sent a protest to de Valera citing concerns about potential violations of patient and family rights. Although the Health Act (1947) passed, it was unclear which portions would be implemented.

The general election of February 1948 promised to be interesting. An electoral bill in 1947 increased the number of Dáil seats from 138 to 147, even though the population did not justify it. The number of three-member constituencies increased from fifteen to twenty-two, tending to favor larger parties like Fianna Fáil. Despite a flurry of activity with ninety-three candidates, Clann na Poblachta won only ten seats. Although Fianna Fáil was reduced to sixty-eight members in the Dáil, it retained the largest number of seats because Fine Gael languished with only thirty-one seats, and labor's two parties could manage only a total of nineteen victories. The divided results allowed Fine Gael to forge a coalition government. Former attorney general John Costello, rather than the controversial Mulcahy, replaced de Valera as Taoiseach but Costello depended on a precarious coalition that included the two labor parties, Clann na Talmhan and Clann na Poblachta, for a majority. The main glue that held the coalition together was their dislike of de Valera.

Clann na Poblachta's MacBride held the high-profile post of minister for external affairs and immediately thrust Éire into the international spotlight at the onset of the Cold War. The Soviet Union had blocked Éire's petition to join the United Nations in August 1946, no doubt because of Irish neutrality and IRA links with the Nazis during World War II. Éire would not become a member of the U.N. until 1955. Soviet hostility combined with a staunchly anticommunist papacy led Éire to identify with the West in the ensuing Cold War.

De Valera had already prepared the way for a permanent severing of ties to the British Commonwealth by stating in June 1947 that Éire was "associated" with but not a member of the commonwealth. In September 1948, on a MacBride motion supported by Costello, the Dáil passed a measure that terminated the muddled 1936 External Relations Act, and in December the Republic of Ireland was created. Although British Prime Minster Clement Attlee was not consulted, a formal separation from the British Commonwealth occurred with British approval in April 1949. In a significant victory for MacBride and Costello, the Republic retained its Commonwealth status of joint citizenship and trade privileges in what the Anglo-Irish agreement called a "special relationship." Immediately after, the Republic joined the Council of Europe as a full-fledged member.

When the North Atlantic Treaty Organization (NATO) was created behind U.S. leadership in 1948 to provide security for Western Europe against a potential Soviet attack, the Republic was invited to join. MacBride calculated that the invitation could become a bargaining point for an end to partition. De Valera in opposition had begun to press the issue of ending partition in public statements and during a visit to the United States. Fine Gael's Dillon led a group that wanted to join NATO without conditions. MacBride hoped the United States would serve as an intermediary with Great Britain to negotiate the issue of partition. However, having plunged into the Cold War with the Soviets, the United States did not want to alienate its ally Britain, so the United States took a hands-off approach to partition. MacBride also applied for the U.S. Marshall Plan aid for European postwar reconstruction despite not having fought in World War II. The Republic received $18 million from the fund and also borrowed $128 million from the United States.

The trend toward economic centralization continued with nationalization of the transportation industry. The 1944 Transport Act allowed the state to operate the Great Southern Railways Company and bus transportation, which employed 20,000. An independent six-member board, Córas Iompair Éireann (CIE), regulated rates. A Land Reclamation Act drafted by Dillon's department aimed to restore 4 million acres of land, mainly in Connacht, for arable use. Dillon also promoted state-sponsored improvements in cattle breeding. At the direction of Mac-Bride, the Dáil also created the Irish News Agency in 1949 to coordinate dissemination of state information. There was concern that the world press portrayed Ireland in a negative light. Journalist-historian Conor Cruise O'Brien became director of the INA, but it was terminated by Fianna Fáil in 1951. These and other expenditures led to an increase in the budget of 1949–1950 to £73 million, an excessive amount according to Fianna Fáil. Further centralization of the welfare system proposed in a 1949 white paper report recommended the consolidation of national health and unemployment insurance with the widows and orphans fund. The estimated cost would be £10 million the first year and £12 million the second. The white paper recommendations were not acted on until the 1952 Social Welfare Act by a Fianna Fáil government.

The coalition government began to founder in 1950 when National Labour rejoined the Labour party, strengthening the position of the minister of industry and commerce, William Norton, the Labour party leader since 1932. Precipitating the collapse of the coalition was the so-called mother and child crisis stemming from Ryan's Health Act of 1947. After 1948, Taoiseach Costello and other ministers, such as MacBride, became quite cozy with Archbishop McQuaid, who soon felt like a member of the cabinet. The Catholic hierarchy resented Clann na Poblachta's minister for health, Noel Browne, because he was a graduate of Trinity College. Browne's department worked vigorously to stamp out diseases such as tuberculosis. But controversy erupted with Browne's 1951 proposed implementation of the 1947 mother and child provisions allowing free medical care for pregnant mothers and children up to age sixteen. Although mothers' acceptance of state health care would be voluntary, the Catholic hierarchy revived earlier objections about invasion of the family domain, which the church felt was its jurisdiction. Led by Archbishop McQuaid, the Catholic hierarchy appealed to Taoiseach Costello. The bishops deemed unsatisfactory a Department of Health response to the clerical concerns. The Irish Medical Association also objected to the movement toward socialized medicine. Browne used national radio to explain the plan in 1951, but the entire cabinet rejected Browne's agenda, and he was forced to resign. The power of the Catholic church in social policy remained unrivaled.

The 1951 election results returned Fianna Fáil to power with sixty-nine seats to forty for Fine Gael. Labour won sixteen, Clann na Talmhan carried only six seats, and fourteen independents were elected. The big loser in 1951, Clann na Poblachta, was reduced to two seats—one held by MacBride. At age sixty-nine, de Valera was elected Taoiseach by a vote of seventy-four to sixty-nine. Lemass became Tánaiste as well as minister for industry and commerce, Aiken took over External Affairs again, and MacEntee headed the Finance Department.

Economic and financial concerns were paramount for this Fianna Fáil government with its narrow majority. Lemass tried to invigorate the Industrial Development Authority, established in 1949 to study ways to enhance foreign trade and domestic industry, by promoting industry in the rural areas of Connacht and Munster. Shannon's duty-free airport (created 1947) would become the hub of this stimulus. Lemass also sponsored scientific studies for improved crop and livestock yields and established a Tourist Board (1955) to promote tourism as a new economic development. Yet real wages continued to fall during the 1950s, and emigration did not let up. Indeed, economic stagnation raised emigration to its greatest levels since the 1880s. Total emigration between 1951 and 1961 was 409,000 compared to 187,000 from 1936 to 1946. Britain remained the primary destination for Irish emigrants. Most male emigrants were agricultural laborers, and most female emigrants were domestic servants. The Republic's population fell from 2.96 million in 1951 to 2.82 million in the 1961 census.

Finance Minister MacEntee opted for a politically calculated deflationary policy in his fiscal 1952 budget by raising the income tax as well as sales taxes on petrol, bread, sugar, tea, and beer. MacEntee blamed the previous government for the necessity of dramatic budget adjustments. Buttressed by the founder and longtime secretary of the Department of Finance (1927–1953), James J. MacElligott, MacEntee justified the tax increases to reduce the fiscal 1951 deficit, which was almost double the 1950 deficit. In fact, the imbalance in foreign trade already was correcting itself, and Finance Department forecasts on trade figures for 1951 and 1952 were inaccurate. The actual trade deficit for 1951 was 15 percent lower than Finance's predictions in an October white paper and were anticipated by the April improvements ignored in the report. Increases in cattle exports for 1952 in particular were off base in the white paper projections. Many of MacEntee's contemporaries as well as later scholars believed that his budget worsened the economic depression. Certainly the budget assumptions discouraged industrial and export expansion and spelled electoral trouble for Fianna Fáil.

With James Ryan returning to the Ministry of Health, the mother-child issue was revived. A 1952 white paper underscored mother-child health needs, but it was again attacked by the Catholic hierarchy as well as the Irish Medical Association. Informed that the bishops would accept a means test to eliminate subsidized care for wealthier citizens, Ryan introduced a revised bill in the Dáil in 1953. Much to his surprise, Archbishop McQuaid and the bishops publicly opposed the bill, despite their previous consent. De Valera's personal negotiations with Cardinal John D'Alton resulted in a compromise. The bill was amended to allow patients the choice of doctors and hospitals, and the proposed health inspections in the schools were deleted. The Health Act passed the Dáil in 1954 and increased eligibility for free or almost free health care from 30 percent to 85 percent of the population. Socialized medicine became a virtual reality for the Republic.

As it happened, de Valera had made some promises to Archbishop McQuaid and the Catholic League of Decency to gain their backing for the health bill. De Valera agreed to increase scrutiny of objectionable literature coming into Ireland. The government's Censorship Board banned 165 books in 1954, including those written by Irish authors such as Seán O'Faolain, Frank O'Connor, Seán O'Casey, and Liam O'Flaherty. As editor of Russell's *Irish Statesman* after the war, O'Faolain continued his assertion that Ireland did not reflect one culture but several with a distinctively English flavor. Always controversial, O'Casey's *The Bishop's Bonfire* produced riots at its 1955 Gaiety Theater performance. One cleric claimed that O'Casey approved of communism, atheism, and the repression of Catholics. Even with intensified censorship, Irish writers flourished in the 1950s, including some new faces such as Brendan Behan. Imprisoned in both England and Éire during World War II as an IRA agitator, Behan had a brief but meteoric career as a playwright. His best play, *The Quare Fellow* (1956), and a sequel, *The Hostage* (1958), were inspired by his prison experiences. Samuel Beckett also made a lasting mark on the Irish stage. Educated at Trinity College, Beckett spent two years in Paris with James Joyce and fought with the French Resistance during World War II. His most acclaimed play, *Waiting for Godot*, was presented first on a Paris stage in 1953 and later at Dublin's Pike Theater in 1956, where it played to sellout audiences for two years. In 1969,

Beckett joined Yeats and Shaw as the third Irish author to receive the Nobel Prize for literature.

The Fianna Fáil hold on government became more tenuous when by-elections reduced its majority, forcing a general election in May 1954. Buoyed by a 75 percent turnout, Fianna Fáil lost its majority, returning only sixty-five members of the Dáil, the party's worst performance in thirty years. Fine Gael rose to fifty seats, Labour won eighteen, Clann na Talmhan carried five contests, and Clann na Poblachta clung to three seats. Independents accounted for the remaining five seats. Fine Gael combined with Labour and Clann na Talmhan to form another coalition government. Costello was elected Taoiseach by a seventy-nine to sixty-six Dáil vote. Labour's William Norton became Tánaiste and minister of industry and commerce, and Liam Cosgrave, son of W. T. Cosgrave, who entered the Dáil in 1943, took over External Affairs. The coalition pledged to reduce taxes and prices while increasing welfare spending, not a realistic financial formula.

Minister of Health T. F. O'Higgins established the Voluntary Health Insurance Board to implement the 1954 Health Act and complete the socialization of health care in the Republic. The formerly close relationship between Costello and Archbishop McQuaid cooled. Costello showed more independence in making appointments to agencies such as the Censorship Board and by naming author Seán O'Faolain head (1956–1959) of the state Arts Council.

Economic problems continued to plague Republic governments. Unemployment rose to 10 percent in 1957, and the budget deficit remained at record highs despite tax increases. As Fianna Fáil continued to win most by-elections, Costello was forced to dissolve the Dáil and call an election in March 1957. The results gave Fianna Fáil seventy-eight seats, the best showing in more than a decade. Fine Gael dropped to forty members, and Labour was also reduced to eleven. The other coalition partner, Clann na Talmhan, salvaged just three seats, and Clann na Poblachta held only one seat as MacBride lost his reelection bid.

Eamon de Valera became Taoiseach for the last time at age seventy-five. Lemass resumed his post as Tánaiste and minister of industry and commerce. MacEntee moved from Finance to Health, and Ryan took over Finance. Fianna Fáil finally allowed some younger members into the cabinet led by Kevin Boland, the son of Gerry, as minister of defense. The cabinet changed again in 1959 when de Valera stepped down as Taoiseach in order to run for president at the retirement of Seán O'Kelly. De Valera won the presidency with a majority of 120,000 (56 percent), and Lemass became Taoiseach. A talented maverick, Lemass rather than de Valera had been called the true "dictator" of Fianna Fáil by McElligott back in 1948. Lemass's agnosticism also made him suspect to the Catholic hierarchy. Jack Lynch took Lemass's post at Industry and Commerce, and MacEntee became Tánaiste and minister of health and social welfare.

A concerted assault on proportional representation was underway by 1958. Many in Fianna Fáil thought the peculiar voting system restrained the quest for majority rule. The *Irish Independent* broke the news about the draft proposal and announced its opposition along with the *Irish Times*. The Labour party also quickly opposed the change, but Fine Gael hesitated since a single-constituency, direct-vote system appeared to favor larger parties such as theirs. Yet Liam Cosgrave soon led Fine Gael to oppose the change in proportional representation since the main beneficiary would be Fianna Fáil. Thus, Fine Gael's Cosgrave and Labour's Norton made the arguments that ending proportional representation would hurt minorities, was undemocratic, and would create an "unrepresentative" Dáil. The amendment passed the Dáil by a vote of seventy-six to fifty-eight, with two independents voting in the affirmative with Fianna Fáil. Although the Seanad voted against the proposal, it could only delay the inevitable outcome. The popular vote on the constitutional amendment coincided with the 1959 presidential election. The anti-amendment campaign featured strong press support and massive labor union backing. Despite having the advantage of de Valera running in the same election for president, Fianna Fáil lost the amendment vote by a narrow margin of 52 percent to 48 percent.

After the Republic of Ireland entered the United Nations in 1955, it became vigorous in promoting decolonization around the world. The first United Nations ambassador for the Republic, longtime secretary to the Department of External Affairs Frederick Henry Boland, was later elected president of the General Assembly in 1960. De Valera criticized the Republic of South Africa's apartheid policy and favored discussion of representation of Communist China, which incurred the wrath of the United States and the U.S. Catholic hierarchy. The Republic sent peace-keeping troops on seven United Nations missions before 1970. General Seán MacEoin served as commander in chief of U.N. forces in the Congo during 1960.

POLITICAL AND ECONOMIC CHANGE, 1959–1973

The 1960s was one of the best decades in the history of the nation for economic progress. An important bureaucratic shift in economic planning from Industry and Commerce to Finance occurred in the late 1950s.

Much of the credit was due to the efforts of Finance's secretary (1956–1969), Thomas Kenneth Whitaker, born in county Down and educated at the University of London. The framework for economic growth, a 1958 Finance Department white paper on economic development, was written by a committee chaired by Whitaker. The so-called five-year plan became known as the First Programme. It called for economic policy to shift from social aims to economic production targets by attracting foreign investment through incentives, free trade (i.e., reduced tariffs), and expanding exports through reduced taxes. The inducements to attract foreign investment included tax exemptions, land grants, financing for construction, and the prospect of cheap labor. Indeed, much of the white paper's philosophy was at odds with Taoiseach Lemass's previous Keynsian deficit-financing policies, which favored setting arbitrary employment targets and relying on tariff protection. Yet Lemass, like Whitaker, had come to question the old economic planning model. A reduction in tariffs in both 1963 and 1964 stimulated exports and helped encourage foreign investments; by 1969, 350 foreign companies had established operations in the Republic. Finance Minister Ryan reduced the income tax while increasing welfare benefits yet was able to eliminate the deficit for the fiscal 1960 budget.

Tourism also became a major component of the economic recovery in the 1960s through the efforts of the Tourist Board, second only to agriculture as a leader in the economy. Aer Lingus, the state airline that began North American flights in 1958, saw a growth in passengers of two-thirds from 1960 to 1961. By 1971, tourism revenue totaled £100 million, with most visitors arriving from Britain and the United States. An intended cornerstone of Fianna Fáil's economic recovery policy was membership in the European Economic Community (EEC), or Common Market; Ireland's application came in 1961. Unfortunately, the Republic's entry hinged on the admission of the United Kingdom, which had opted not to join in 1957 in order to preserve commonwealth ties. In the meantime, France's Charles de Gaulle had assumed leadership of the EEC and vetoed the British application. Thus, because the Republic's economic well-being depended on good trade relations with Britain, Ireland withdrew its application in 1963. Even without membership in the EEC, the Republic's economic growth averaged 4 percent per annum during the 1960s and living standards rose by 50 percent. Industrial employment rose from 257,000 in 1961 to 323,000 in 1977.

Another factor in the economic growth was a decline in emigration and the first noteworthy growth in population in the century. The census revealed a population increase from 2.82 million in 1961 to 2.98 million in 1971. Besides reduced emigration and a reverse immigration from the United States in the 1960s, there was a rise in the marriage rate, reflected in a decline of the average marriage age of men and women by two to three years. Declining emigration combined with increased immigration to place pressure on labor-management relations, so that the number of strikes increased in the early 1960s.

The election of 1961 was the first for Fianna Fáil without de Valera at the head of the ticket. The party held power behind Lemass with seventy seats, a decline of eight from 1957. Correspondingly, Fine Gael gained seven seats, for a total of forty-seven. The labor union split of 1945 was healed in 1959 with the merger of the Irish Trade Union Congress and the Congress of Irish Unions to create the Irish Congress of Trade Unions. The ITUC brought 250,000 members from sixty-four unions to unite with the CIU's 190,000 members in thirty unions. The labor union merger had the potential of helping the Labour party, but it won only fifteen seats in 1961. The 1961 contest witnessed the participation of a new party, the National Progressive Democrats, founded in 1958 by Noel Browne and Jack McQuillan, both former Clann na Poblachta members. With its socialist agenda, the NPD elected its two leaders to the Dáil, but merged into the Labour party in 1963. Lemass remained Taoiseach.

The Anglo-Irish Free Trade Agreement of 1965 became the capstone of economic stimulation. Taoiseach Lemass and British Labour Prime Minister Harold Wilson signed the agreement, which would cut import duties on British products entering the Republic by 10 percent each year, to culminate in free trade by 1975. It also eliminated most tariffs on Irish exports to Britain. Finally, the Republic came to realize the paramount importance of aligning their economy with that of the United Kingdom. Even before the 1965 agreement, the Finance Department unveiled the next stage of economic growth, called the Second Programme (1963–1964). Its main conclusion was that agriculture could not compete with trade and industry in promoting growth. Since much of the Second Programme's agenda depended on membership in the Common Market, the results were unimpressive. Irish banks organized into two consortiums by 1966. The Bank of Ireland Group consisted of the Bank of Ireland and the National and Hibernian banks, while the Allied Irish Banks Group included the Provincial, Munster and Leinster, and Royal banks.

Educational concerns rivaled economic policy for Lemass's attention. A 1966 white paper prepared by the Education Department produced revealing if unsurprising statistics. The high dropout rate resulted from one-third of students leaving school in the primary grades, another 36 percent departing during the postprimary (i.e., secondary) level, and 44 percent dropping out of vocational schools. The white paper also demonstrated social variations among students. Children of white-collar workers and farmers were four to five times more likely to remain in school through the secondary level than children of blue-collar families. Furthermore, 85 percent of university students came from middle- and upper-class families.

Minister of Education Patrick Hillery (1959–1965), launched a reform agenda in 1963. He stressed the need for increased educational opportunities, new comprehensive secondary schools, and improved technical training. Three comprehensive schools opened in 1966. A scholarship program initiated in 1961 allocated two-thirds of its funds for secondary students and one-third to university students. By 1966, the number of scholarships had tripled. The education budget increased from £25 million in 1963 to £144 million in 1973, much of it required to finance free secondary and postsecondary education authorized in 1966. The number of students in the secondary level increased from 121,000 in 1963 to 239,000 in 1974. Hillery's successor, Donal O'Malley, proposed in 1967 to merge Trinity College and University College, Dublin, while making University College in Cork and Galway independent. The bold idea was rejected by the Dáil, but a Higher Education Authority was created in 1968 to coordinate finances and curriculum in the universities.

Television played its first major role in Irish elections in 1965. Although a decade had passed since the first demonstration of television broadcasting in 1951, with the launching of the state-operated Radio Telefís Éireann (RTE) in 1961, television rapidly surpassed the print media and radio as the most influential medium. The RTE charter mirrored the British Broadcasting Company structure. As a state agency, RTE continued the policy of censorship already entrenched in the publishing realm. A veteran broadcaster, Eamonn Andrews, was named chairman of the RTE Authority. In 1963, there were 201,000 television licenses purchased compared with 337,000 radio licenses. By 1969, television licensing had passed radio by a margin of four to one.

Television may well have been a factor in the 75 percent election turnout in 1965, though the outcome changed the makeup of the Dáil very little. Campaigning on its record of economic achievement, Fianna Fáil increased their 1961 numbers by two seats to seventy-two. Seeking to shake up the electorate, Fine Gael's 1964 electoral manifesto, "The Just Society," was authored by Declan Costello, son of the former Taoiseach and TD since 1951. It called for increased social spending on welfare and education programs and suggested that a healthy tension between church and state would show the independence as well as involvement of both in improving Irish society. Costello found a kindred spirit in future Taoiseach Garret FitzGerald who agreed that Fine Gael needed to redefine itself. Fine Gael leaders calculated that the trend toward a three-party system required them to pull Labour away from Fianna Fáil by adopting more left-oriented policies. Despite the assumptions and policy shift, Fine Gael did not increase their 1961 total of forty-seven seats. On the other hand, Labour increased to twenty-one. Clann na Poblachta, with only one member, dissolved within months. Clann na Talmhan faded away with the death of Donnellan in 1964 and the retirement of Blowick in 1965.

In 1966, Lemass resigned as Taoiseach because of ill health. A tremendous struggle for his successor ensued, the first genuine contest for leadership since Fianna Fáil's founding. The challengers included the minister of agriculture, Charles J. Haughey, educated at University College, Dublin. A second contestant, the minister of industry and commerce, George Colley, like Haughey was a Dubliner educated at University College, Dublin, though he had been a TD only since 1961. Third was Donegal's Neil Blaney, minister of local government since 1958 representing rural constituencies. Blaney had created attention in 1963 with his Planning Act, which introduced town planning to regulate urban growth. The absence of a dominating force among the three led the parliamentary party to select a compromise candidate, Lemass's minister of finance, Jack Lynch, who was educated at University College, Cork, and first entered the Dáil in 1948. After nine years in civil service and a law practice, Lynch served as minister of education (1957–1959), and minister of industry and commerce (1959–1965) before taking over Finance. Haughey was given Lynch's post at Finance.

After the narrow 1959 defeat of a constitutional amendment to change the proportional representation system, there was a second attempt in 1968 pushed by Lynch. The combined fear of other parties about the potential domination of Fianna Fáil in a single constituency system again proved significant in the opposition led by all the major newspapers except Fianna Fáil's *Irish Press*. The amendment lost a second time, by 61 to 39 percent, a wider margin than the 1959 vote. Majorities in thirty-four of thirty-eight constituencies voted against the proposed amendment. It was the last time the issue of challenging proportional representation would appear in Republic politics.

The Dáil elections of 1969 produced a record 77 percent percent turnout. Fianna Fáil continued to remain stable with seventy-four seats. Fine Gael carried fifty, and Labour held eighteen seats; only one independent member was returned. Lynch remained Taoiseach, Erskine Childers, Jr., became Tánaiste, Minister of Health Patrick Hillery headed External Affairs, and Haughey remained at Finance. Lynch revived the Republic's application for EEC membership, in tandem with that of the United Kingdom, in 1972 following de Gaulle's death in 1970. Both nations were approved for entry in 1972 and took their seats on January 1, 1973.

Rapidly rising inflation prompted by oil price increases took a heavy toll on recently established foreign companies, which began to leave the Republic steadily by the end of the decade. Consumer price increases reached 8.2 percent in 1970 and rose again the next year to 8.9 percent. A rise in unemployment and increased emigration were the results of economic recession; unemployment grew from 6.7 percent in 1968 to 7.2 percent in 1971. Moreover, the Central Bank lacked the authority to control interest rates or the money supply, critical tools in an inflationary environment. The Central Bank Act of 1971 sought to remedy some deficiencies. The Central Bank became the regulator of commercial bank reserves previously placed in London, government accounts were transferred from the Bank of Ireland to the Central Bank, and the Central Bank could adjust the exchange rate. Although exports continued to increase in the late 1960s (47 percent for 1968–1971), imports grew at an equal pace (46 percent for 1968–1971) so that a negative balance of trade (£218 million for 1971) continued.

In addition to economic troubles reviving, problems in Northern Ireland after 1969 ended whatever prospects for reunification might have followed the détente of the 1960s. Upon hearing of military police repression of Catholics in the north, Lynch hinted at Republic intervention on their behalf. Sinn Féin split in 1970, with a majority adopting a socialist agenda and favoring participation in Republic politics at this auspicious moment, while a minority remained focused on reunification with Ulster. The result was a Provisional Sinn Féin and Provisional IRA being created by the minority. Both were committed to use violence to remove the British presence in Northern Ireland. In 1970, Taoiseach Lynch shocked the nation by dismissing two of his top ministers for possible involvement in shipping IRA arms from the United States to Northern Ireland. Minister of Finance Haughey and Minister of Agriculture Blaney were removed and soon indicted for participating in the arms shipments. Kevin Boland, minister of local government, resigned in protest to Haughey's and Blaney's dismissal. Ultimately Haughey and Blaney were acquitted in their trials, but Fianna Fáil faced serious internal divisions.

Boland led an unsuccessful 1971 challenge to Lynch at the Fianna Fáil *ard-fheis*. He then proceeded to form a new republican party, Aontacht Éireann (Irish Unity), to further his protest. Blaney's alienation from Lynch continued, but Haughey showed no bitterness and remained faithful to the party leadership. Following the lead of its chairman, Brendan Corish, who replaced Norton in 1960, the Labour party conference in 1970 decided to withdraw its support for Fianna Fáil and become independent again. Corish succeeded his father as TD for Wexford in 1945, served as minister of social welfare (1954–1957), and proclaimed Labour to be a socialist party when he took over in 1960. Corish participated in a fourteen-point joint election manifesto with Fine Gael, which focused on the ravages of inflation to the economy. With another 77 percent turnout, the 1973 election reduced Fianna Fáil to sixty-eight seats. Thus, Fine Gael with fifty-four members and Labour with nineteen formed a coalition government. Fine Gael's Liam Cosgrave became Taoiseach, and Labour's Corish was elected Tánaiste.

Cultural change was also evident in the Republic of the 1960s. The Ardmore Film Studios launched in 1958 brought motion picture productions to Ireland in increasing numbers, and the Cork Film Festival gained international acclaim. A rebuilt Abbey Theater opened in 1966 in Dublin, and Cork's opera house resumed performances in 1967. Renovations undertaken at the National Gallery were long overdue. Popular culture infiltrated Ireland from Britain with the invasion of the Beatles rock group performing at the Adelphi Theater in 1963. It set off a wave of 450 new music halls, accommodating rock bands attended by thousands of Irish youth.

A 1969 tax exemption brought many artists and writers to take permanent residence in Ireland rather than locating in other European nations, in sharp contrast to the traditional exodus of talent seeking opportunities abroad. Composer Seán Ó Riada wrote modern music including soundtracks for motion pictures. Robert Ballagh headlined a new generation of artists. Long Ireland's literary strength, playwrights continued to make their mark. Brian Friel's *Philadelphia, Here I Come* (1964) dealt humorously with subjects such as emigration and the generation gap. John B. Keane of Kerry criticized the Irish peasant obsession with the land in *The Field* (1964). Keane's *Sive* (1959) explored the problems that single women had in establishing a place of social respect in society.

Fiction continued to blend easily with nonfiction in the writers of the era. John McGahern's *The Dark* (1965) was banned because of sexual references in the adolescent coming-of-age saga. Edna O'Brien's several novels about the vicissitudes of girls growing into womanhood were also banned. James Plunkett's *Strumpet City* (1969) recounted labor-management struggles early in the century as well as slum living conditions for the working classes. Minister of Justice Brian Lenihan was persuaded in 1967 to sponsor a bill in the Dáil to limit banned books to twelve years. Its passage allowed hundreds of previously banned books to become available legally for the first time.

Although the role of the Catholic church in social policy such as censorship hardly lessened during the 1960s, developments in the papacy led to modifications of past stances. Papal encyclicals emanating from Vatican Councils I and II (1958–1965) stressed the church's social responsibility to help those with less material possessions. Irish bishops, led by Cardinal William Conway (elevated in 1963), were responsive to papal leadership. The church's documentary, *Radharc* (Look), broadcast on RTE, focused on social problems such as crime and poverty. The church faced problems by the 1960s of recruiting new clergy and keeping clerics from retiring to the secular world.

Members of the Dáil in all parties showed the impact of criticism of the role of the church in the Republic's constitution. Thus, with the consent of Cardinal Conway, Article 44 in the constitution citing the "special position" of the Catholic church was deleted in a 1972 amendment approved by 84 percent of the voters. Even with adjustments during the 1960s, fundamental doctrines of the church on social matters such as abortion and birth control did not change but were reaffirmed by the papacy. The previously silent growth of opposition to the contraception ban became more open by 1968 with the increased use of contraceptives no longer denied. In 1971, the women's movement protested the ban on imported contraceptives and staged some demonstrations to show that they were easily accessible. Assaults on the church's influence would increase as a younger generation was enticed by the world beyond Ireland.

NORTHERN IRELAND, 1939–1967

The long era of dominance by Lord Craigavon ended with his death in 1940. For some years prior to his passing, the Unionist leadership had become old and stale, a condition that did not change with Craigavon's replacement as prime minister. The minister of labor, sixty-nine-year-old John Andrews, succeeded as leader of the Unionist party and prime minister in November 1940. At the request of the Stormont government, Britain had not extended conscription to Northern Ireland at the beginning of World War II. Unlike World War I, there was little enthusiasm for the war effort in Ulster. Yet the war came to Northern Ireland, with four German air raids concentrating in the Belfast area during April and May 1941. About 1,100 people died in the raids and extensive property damage ensued. An estimated 200,000 residents of Belfast fled to the countryside.

The bombing damage was compounded by labor troubles, with strikes idling 10,000 workers by October 1942. A rebellion by Unionist backbenchers in January 1943 demanded new leadership. Although Andrews received backing from the Ulster Unionist Council, his parliamentary support did not follow, forcing him to resign in April. Agriculture Minister Sir Basil Brooke, a decorated World War I veteran and former commander of the Royal Ulster Constabulary, was tapped to become the Unionist party leader and prime minister in May. Much more competent than Andrews, Brooke saw the need for better public relations with the local population as well as with the British government.

Perhaps the most acute problem facing Stormont was a housing shortage, estimated to be in deficit by 100,000 units. A housing agency established in 1945 began the process of constructing new housing, which totaled 113,000 over the next two decades. Brooke also pledged to bring Northern Ireland's social benefits up to British levels. In the postwar election of 1945, the Unionist party held its thirty-three seats in the forty-eight-member Parliament. The Industrial Development Act (1945) provided incentives to attract new industry to Northern Ireland to supplement the traditional shipbuilding and linen industries. Northern Ireland's per capita income as a percentage of Great Britain's rose from 57 percent in 1938 to 68 percent in 1950, indicating modest postwar recovery. Still, unemployment remained between 5 and 10 percent for years after the war; the Catholic unemployment rate was almost three times the Protestant rate. Not surprisingly, Catholic emigration out of Northern Ireland was twice as great as Protestant emigration. The 1951 census showed a 7 percent population increase to 1.37 million.

Public services did improve in the postwar era. Welfare payments were brought in line with Britain's in 1946. The Health Act (1948) improved health care services, though it did not fund improvements at the main Catholic hospital in Belfast. The Education Act (1947) increased the financial aid for secondary and postsecondary students, Catholics and Protestants, and raised the compulsory school age to fifteen. Thanks in part to improved economic conditions and broader educational opportunities, a Catholic middle class grew in the postwar era. They proved less obeisant to either political nationalists or the Catholic hierarchy.

Continued anti-Catholic discrimination combined with Brooke's tendency to espouse Orange Order sentiments led to a revival of the IRA campaign in 1956. Although renewed IRA violence did not win wide support among Catholics or the Republic and was canceled in 1962, mounting economic troubles ended Brooke's tenure as prime minister in 1963. He was replaced by a more pragmatic Unionist, Terence O'Neill, Brooke's finance minister. O'Neill's plan for economic development took its cue from the program devised by T. K. Whitaker a few years earlier in the Republic. O'Neill established the Ministry of Economic Development and hired Ulster native and University of Glasgow economist Thomas Wilson to study the Northern Ireland economy and formulate policy. Wilson's 1965 report endorsed Whitaker's philosophy of attracting foreign investment through incentives (grants, tax allowances, etc.). An example was the American Goodyear tire company, which opened a factory in county Armagh in 1968. The gross domestic product of Northern Ireland rose at a higher rate than the United Kingdom in the later 1960s, with 40,000 new jobs created. Yet not all was as positive as it may have appeared at first. O'Neill angered many Protestant workers by recognizing the Northern Ireland branch of the Irish Congress of Trade Unions. Furthermore, there were employment layoffs in the shipbuilding and linen industries during the late 1950s and early 1960s. Thus, the net job gain was only 15,000, of which just 5,000 were in industry. Unemployment remained around 7 percent.

O'Neill also generated controversy among Protestants in 1965 by inviting the Republic's Taoiseach, Sean Lemass, to visit Belfast to confer with him. The next month, O'Neill paid a reciprocal visit to Dublin. Despite questions among Unionists about O'Neill's strategy, the party picked up three seats in the 1965 elections, while the Labour party lost two. After the election, O'Neill felt strong enough to declare the Protestant paramilitary Ulster Volunteer Force illegal in 1966. Although O'Neill won support from the small Catholic middle class, two of his policies alienated most Catholics in 1965. A publicly funded new industrial planned community was located in Protestant eastern Ulster rather than the Catholic western area. Also, the decision to place a new branch of Queen's University in Protestant-dominated Coleraine rather than

Catholic-majority Derry caused unrest. Moreover, there had been little substantive change in the political treatment of Catholics. Protestant control of 95 percent of the civil service had not been altered since the 1920s, and there was still only one Catholic cabinet member in the Stormont executive. In response, the Catholics began organizing for peaceful pressure, beginning with the Campaign for Social Justice, founded in 1964 to lobby for nondiscrimination in government housing policy. The stage was set for a massive civil rights campaign launched in 1968.

9

The Two Irelands, 1973–2000

By the 1970s, the Republic's political parties revolved around three major players: Fianna Fáil, Fine Gael, and Labour. Once Labour ceased being a consistent ally of Fianna Fáil, its independent strength allowed bargaining power with Fine Gael as well as Fianna Fáil, thereby increasing the frequency of coalition governments. Leadership in all three parties was claimed by the postrevolutionary generation. Therefore, differences between Fianna Fáil and Fine Gael, based on pragmatism rather than ideology, blurred their historical distinctions. After a fling with socialism, Labour became more moderate and practical in regard to policy positions and leadership.

Economic issues remained crucial but shared the spotlight with the Northern Ireland crisis. The years of inflationary damage to the economy in the 1970s and early 1980s finally subsided, allowing significant economic prosperity the 1990s. Trade and industry became more important, although agriculture continued to play a role. Steady export growth helped sustain a trade surplus after 1985. Membership in the EEC was not a panacea for the Republic's economic well-being as much as many thought. Ireland's integration into both the European and world economies left little room for national maneuvering.

The troubles emanating from Northern Ireland increased both tensions and cooperation between the Republic and United Kingdom governments, whether they were Labour or Conservative. The Republic's previous insistence on unification was modified to recognize majority rule in Northern Ireland regarding the question about its status. The Republic supported power-sharing schemes and cooperated in suppressing IRA violence.

POLITICS AND ECONOMICS, 1973–1982

The 1973 coalition government of Fine Gael and Labour (combined seventy-three seats in Dáil) was headed by Fine Gael's Liam Cosgrave as Taoiseach and Labour's Brendan Corish as Tánaiste and minister of health and social welfare. Coalition Finance Minister Richie Ryan was named chairman of both the International Monetary Fund and the World Bank in 1976. The parties' joint election manifesto in 1973 stressed their intent to deal with inflation, influenced mostly by oil prices, which increased tenfold from 1972 to 1973. Yet as other Western countries racked by inflation learned, government could do very little. Thus, the consumer price rise continued: 11 percent (1973), 17 percent (1974), 21 percent (1975). By 1976, the unemployment rate reached its highest levels since 1940, at 116,000. One area of improvement continued to be exports, which surpassed the £1 billion mark in November 1974. Taxes remained high; the standard income tax rate, set by the Income Tax Act (1967), was 35 percent. All intentions of balancing the budget after 1972 had to be shelved, so current budget deficits became commonplace. A current account deficit of £5 million in 1973 rose quickly to £259 million in 1975. Following a trend in all Western welfare states, the Republic's public spending as a percentage of the gross national product increased from 25 percent in 1956 to 40 percent in 1972.

Upon entrance to the EEC in January 1973, Fianna Fáil's Patrick Hillery became the Republic's commissioner. Fearing neglect of their interests by the government, the Irish Farmers Association (formed 1972) and the Confederation of Irish Industries established their own representatives at EEC headquarters in Brussels. The EEC transfer of £14 billion in benefits for 1973–1991 aided agriculture (£10 billion) in particular, which continued to lag industry in productivity. Farm income doubled from 1973 to 1978. Since government price supports for farmers had grown from 15 percent of agricultural income in 1957 to 50 percent in 1977, the EEC subsidies relieved budget pressures.

Although the office of president never received much prominence as a constitutional officer, several changes occurred in the office in the 1970s. In the May 1973 presidential election following de Valera's retirement, Fianna Fáil's Erskine Childers, Jr., a Protestant, defeated Fine Gael's Thomas F. O'Higgins; Childers died in November 1974, to be replaced by Cearbhall Ó Dálaigh. Then in October 1976 President Ó Dálaigh resigned over criticism—chiefly by Defense Minister Patrick Donegan—for submitting the Emergency Powers Bill, which allowed arbitrary detainment of criminal suspects for seven days, to the Supreme Court for an opinion before the Dáil passed it. Retiring European Community Commissioner Hillery was quickly elected without opposition to replace Ó Dálaigh and was reelected without opposition in 1983.

The general election of 1977 produced another 76 percent turnout and a major win for Fianna Fáil, which pummeled the coalition for the 100,000 unemployed. Fianna Fáil gained 16 seats for a total of 84 members, a solid majority out of 148 Dáil seats. Fine Gael lost 11 seats, down to 43, and Labour lost 2 seats, for a total of 17. Corish resigned the next month as Labour leader, succeeded by Frank Cluskey. Jack Lynch became Taoiseach again, and Colley was Tánaiste and minister of finance.

Yet there was little peace within Fianna Fáil regarding Lynch's leadership. Lynch faced criticism from within and without his party, mainly stemming from the 1970 removals of Blaney and Haughey and his Northern Ireland policy. Other factors causing damage to Lynch were a postal strike and a 20 percent increase in electric power rates. Fianna Fáil's weakness appeared in the inaugural elections to the European Parliament in June 1979. The Republic of Ireland was allotted fifteen seats and Northern Ireland three. Fianna Fáil won only five places, Fine Gael four, Labour four, and independents carried two seats. Taoiseach Lynch was criticized for Fianna Fáil's poor showing. He gained a temporary reprieve during a historic papal visit to Ireland in September by Pope John Paul II. The articulate pope made three public appearances, the largest in an open mass at Phoenix Park where 1 million Catholics attended. Despite the brief respite from the pope's visit, Lynch resigned as Taoiseach in December 1979.

A tense contest for Lynch's successor ensued between the leader of anti-Lynch forces, Charles Haughey, and George Colley, backed by the pro-Lynch faction. Nicknamed "The Boss," Haughey won the party leader's slot by a slim majority of six among Fianna Fáil Dáil members and became Taoiseach. Haughey's brusque style was often compared to that of disgraced former U.S. president Richard Nixon. Haughey replaced four members of the cabinet, with Michael O'Kennedy moving from Foreign Affairs to Colley's former post at Finance, and Brian Lenihan was named to head Foreign Affairs.

Although Fianna Fáil fulfilled its electoral promise in 1978 to repeal the Capital Gains (Wealth) Tax Act (1975), the lost revenue—an average of more than £5 million per annum—disrupted the budget. Furthermore, grievances about the tax code induced the government to create the Commission on Taxation (1980). The commission issued five reports (1980–1985) recommending structural reforms in the tax system. The changes included indexing based on inflation, reducing rates below 35 percent but closing all tax deductions other than personal exemptions, and a surcharge on excessively high incomes. Instead of following the commission's recommendations, the Dáil created four tax bands ranging from 25 percent to 60 percent, which remained in effect during the 1980s.

Labor problems, inflation, unemployment, and rising debt unleashed major blows to Fianna Fáil. The Republic experienced its first postal strike between February and June 1979. Annual consumer price increases went to historic highs of 18.2 percent in 1980 and 20.4 percent in 1981, while unemployment declined only slightly from the peak of 106,000 in 1977 to 90,000 (7.1 percent) in 1979. Even the population increase of 13 percent to 3.3 million in 1980 meant workers outstripped jobs. The Catholic church estimated that 20 percent of the population lived in poverty.

A sign of Ireland's movement away from its agricultural base was the growth of industrial employment from 164,000 in 1962 to 227,000 in 1980. Although industrial production from 1960 to 1973 at 6.5 percent per annum surpassed the 1950–1960 figure of 3.1 percent, growth had slowed to an averaged 5.1 percent between 1973 and 1979. The state subsidy of local government expenses increased from 46 percent in 1977 to 61 percent in 1979. Most alarming, because of recurring current budget deficits rising from £509 million (1979) to £988 million (1982), the national debt had skyrocketed from £4 million in 1977 to £10 million in 1981. Public borrowing totaled 20 percent of gross national product (the sum of all domestic production, not including foreign companies) in 1981, and GNP growth slowed to less than 1 percent by 1981, down from 3.5 percent in 1979. Economic problems thus defined Haughey's political dilemma and hastened elections in June 1981.

In April 1980, an appointed electoral commission recommended increasing the number of Dáil seats by 18 to 166, as well as increasing the number of five-member constituencies. These changes were in place by the 1981 election. The general election did not prove as damaging as Fianna Fáil feared, but the party still lost 6 seats in the Dáil to 78. As a result, Fine Gael's electoral promise to reduce the income tax led to a dramatic increase of 22 seats to 65. Although Labour lost 2 seats for a total of 15, it joined Fine Gael to form another coalition. Fine Gael's former foreign minister, Garret FitzGerald, became Taoiseach, and the new Labour leader, Michael O'Leary, became Tánaiste and minister for industry and energy. John Bruton of Fine Gael was named minister of finance. FitzGerald almost immediately made an enemy of the Catholic hierarchy by suggesting that the sectarian provisions of the constitution should be modified. Bruton's budget dealt with hyperinflation and budget deficits by freezing government hiring and salary increases, and hiking the value-added tax from 10 percent to 15 percent. Excise and other duties were raised as well. Haughey and Fianna Fáil assailed the government's fiscal policy as uncaring about people, setting the stage for another election in 1982.

The outcome of the general election of February 1982 was predictable. Although Fianna Fáil added only three seats to eighty-one and Fine Gael lost just two to sixty-three, it was enough to force FitzGerald's government from power when the three Marxist Workers' party (formerly Sinn Féin; new name adopted in 1977) members sided with Fianna Fáil. Labour kept its fifteen seats, and independents carried four contests. Haughey became Taoiseach for the second time; Ray MacSharry became Tánaiste and minister of finance. The dislike of Haughey among many Fianna Fáil members produced an October preelection fight for party leadership led by O'Malley and Martin O'Donoghue, who resigned from the cabinet, but Haughey beat back his rivals even while causing damage to party chances in the November election.

Fianna Fáil lost six seats in the November 1982 general election, reduced to seventy-five members, while Fine Gael added seven seats for a total of seventy; the Workers' party held two seats, along with three independents. With sixteen seats, Labour again aligned with Fine Gael to make FitzGerald Taoiseach for the second time. Because former Labour head Michael O'Leary joined Fine Gael, the new Labour leader, Dick Spring, won a three-way contest for O'Leary's successor and assumed the office of Tánaiste.

POLITICS OF COALITION, 1983–2000

The Fine Gael–Labour coalition government of 1982–1987 faced severe economic problems headed by inflation, which in 1986 remained unbearable at 17.4 percent. Unemployment reached an all-time high of 18.2

percent in 1985. The monetary union with Britain ended in 1979 when Ireland entered the European Monetary System, which had its own fixed exchange rates determined by comparing national rates to the average of the European Union. The Irish pound initially was overvalued, but it was expected to converge with the German mark. The Irish pound's real effective exchange rate (adjusted for inflation) rose by 21 percent from 1979 to 1986 and 44 percent versus the deutschemark. It was not until 1995 that the real effective exchange rate had reconverged with the nominal (actual) rate. Seeking to bring the Irish pound into line with Ireland's trading partners, in March 1983 the government devalued the currency by 5 percent and established a pattern of making government spending cuts. A property tax on home ownership was introduced in 1983.

Tensions mounted between Fine Gael and its Labour partner over economic policy in 1983. When Fine Gael proposed to refinance the nearly insolvent Dublin Gas Company at a cost of £126 million, Labour's Frank Cluskey, minister of trade, commerce, and tourism, resigned in December from the cabinet, protesting the use of public funds to bail out a private company. In October, the nation's largest motor vehicle insurance company, Private Motorist Protection Association, went into bankruptcy, forcing a government takeover of its operations. It was later acquired by Britain's Guardian Royal Exchange and most recently by France's AXA. On the positive side, construction of an aluminum plant on the Shannon was announced, the largest private capital investment project in the nation's history.

The Dáil voted to propose a prolife, antiabortion constitutional amendment in April 1983. The trend of increased abortions among Irish women raised alarm. Between 1980 and 1990, more than 41,000 Irish women had obtained abortions in Britain. The amendment proponents were led by Haughey's opposition Fianna Fáil party. Although FitzGerald had initially questioned the language of Haughey's amendment, he later took a positive view after the archbishop of Dublin, Dermot Ryan, announced support for the amendment. The difficulty of FitzGerald's position was evident in Labour's opposition to the measure from the beginning. The popular referendum gave the amendment a two-thirds majority in favor with a 55 percent voter turnout. Then in 1986, the existing constitutional ban on divorce was subjected to a referendum, which resulted in the public endorsement of the article. The Irish public remained conservative and continued to follow the direction of the Catholic hierarchy on such social matters.

In 1984, the postal service, An Post, and the telecommunications agency, Telecom Éireann, were made independent regulatory agencies and separated from the Department of Posts and Telegraph. Economic troubles and interparty coalition squabbles weakened FitzGerald's hold. Emigration had begun to rise again to 31,000 in 1985–1986. The number receiving public welfare reached 811,000 in 1986, further straining the budget. Civil service employees increased from 36,000 in 1968 to 60,000 in 1980. Public spending as a percentage of GDP, mostly on social programs, education, and government salaries, continued to rise from 40 percent in 1972 to 50 percent by 1980. The national debt in 1986 was one and a half times, the GNP, and the deficit accounted for 13 percent of GNP in 1987.

There remained very little social mobility in the Republic, and the tax structure was not redistributing wealth comparable to other welfare states. In 1985, the Republic's per capita GNP was only 59 percent of the European Community average. While large farmers, professionals, and commercial entrepreneurs remained prosperous, poor farmers and laborers were not keeping pace. A comparison of farm and industrial income showed progress for the large farmers. In 1971, family farm income was 75 percent of industrial income, but by 1977 it was 106 percent. Yet farm prices fell in the late 1970s during the rise in inflation, so that by 1980, farm income was only 53 percent of industrial income. The only bright spot in the economy was continued improvement of exports, with trade surpluses the rule after 1985. Republic exports to Europe increased from 17 percent to 42 percent between 1973 and 1991, while exports to Britain declined from 56 percent to 32 percent over the same period. The final economic blow was when unemployment reached 20 percent in 1987.

As the election of 1987 approached, some political shifts occurred. A 1985 split in Fianna Fáil over Haughey's opposition to the Anglo-Irish Agreement for Northern Ireland led Mary Harney to vote with the government in favor of the agreement. She was summarily expelled from Fianna Fáil by Haughey, causing Desmond O'Malley and two other Fianna Fáil TDs to form a new party, the Progressive Democrats. In the 1987 election, the Progressive Democrats won fourteen seats. Still, Fianna Fáil secured eighty-one seats and allied with independents to form a new government with Haughey as Taoiseach. Brian Lenihan became Tánaiste and foreign minister. Ray MacSharry served as minister of finance until he became European Community commissioner in November 1988. Haughey also named Mary O'Rourke (Lenihan's sister) to head education. Fine Gael's loss led to FitzGerald's resignation as party leader; he was replaced by economist Alan Dukes.

Seeking independent control for Fianna Fáil, the controversial Haughey called another general election in 1989, hoping that it would allow an end to the coalition. Instead, Fianna Fáil lost four seats, reducing its Dáil membership to seventy-seven, forcing Haughey to align with the Progressive Democrats, who also lost eight seats to control only six. Fine Gael gained four seats for a total of fifty-five, Labour added three seats for fifteen, the Workers' party increased three for a sum of seven, and six independents were elected. Having failed in his policy of constructive engagement with Fianna Fáil, Dukes was replaced as Fine Gael leader by John Bruton, former finance minister and deputy leader since 1987.

In the 1990 presidential election, with President Hillery retiring, Fianna Fáil nominated Tánaiste Lenihan. But party scandals took their toll, allowing Labour's Mary Robinson, a senator since the 1960s, to win the presidency, the first for a woman. Robinson was educated at Trinity College and Harvard Law School in the United States. She established a higher presidential profile than usual by supporting abortion and divorce rights. Robinson's personal popularity also helped boost Labour as a major party in the Republic.

At the end of January 1992, Taoiseach Haughey submitted his resignation because of allegations that he was aware of the tapping of some journalists' phones in 1982. Albert Reynolds was elected leader of Fianna Fáil and Taoiseach in early February, with sixty-one of the seventy-seven Dáil party members backing him. Reynolds did not possess a traditional political background. He became a successful businessman with a chain of dance halls in the 1960s and a pet food manufacturing firm in the 1970s. Reynolds was elected a Fianna Fáil TD in 1977. He quickly allied with Haughey against Taoiseach Lynch and gained a cabinet post in 1979. Reynolds was elected deputy leader of Fianna Fáil in 1983. He had served as minister of industry and commerce from 1987 until he replaced MacSharry at Finance in 1988. Reynolds dismissed most of Haughey's cabinet. Bertie Ahern remained as finance minister.

Reynolds became entangled in an abortion debate that related to the ratification of the European Community's Maastricht Treaty. When a fourteen-year-old girl became pregnant from a rape and desired an abortion, the 1983 constitutional ban (Amendment 8) put the case into the legal realm. The High Court initially blocked the abortion request, but the Supreme Court later allowed the abortion. Reynolds called for a modification of the constitution to cover such instances of abortions for pregnancies by rape. Haughey's government had attached an amendment to the Maastricht Treaty that recognized the constitutional ban on abortion, but the EC refused to allow the exception. Reynolds then proposed a referendum on the treaty, which effectively became a referendum on the abortion amendment. Abortion rights groups opposed the Irish amendment recognizing the ban on abortions, but the prolife anti-abortionists disliked Maastricht, claiming it would link Ireland too closely with European countries where abortions were permitted. Despite the fact that the abortion issue might overshadow the substantive economic aspects of the treaty, which Reynolds liked, 69 percent of participating voters approved the Maastricht Treaty in June.

The anticipated smooth transition into the European Monetary System was interrupted by currency crises in the 1990s. When Great Britain withdrew sterling from the European Union's exchange rate mechanism in September 1992, it resulted in a 15 percent decline in the exchange rate of the British currency. The Irish pound was thus overvalued, but the government seemed determined not to devalue. The resulting imbalance forced the Central Bank to buy back £5,000 million Irish pounds ($8 billion) to prop up the currency's value. Yet the very next year, the government surrendered to market pressures by devaluing the Irish pound by 10 percent, causing interest rates to decline. Combined with German financial problems stemming from national reunification in 1993, the European Union virtually abandoned its exchange rate mechanism.

To illustrate further how Ireland's economy was tied to international conditions, during the 1995 Mexican economic turmoil and international bailout, the Irish pound was devalued against the German mark rather than remaining tied to it. The plan for a European Monetary Union launched in 1989 had several stages intended to reach completion by 1999, but the outcome was delayed when some of the European Union nations (including especially the United Kingdom) objected to the terms of ending their own currency. Apart from the dilemma created by Britain's uncertain action, Ireland's large foreign debt of over £1.1 billion or $1.76 billion (1992), combined with high unemployment and an undeveloped infrastructure, could make participation in the European Monetary Union problematic, even though Irish governments have been committed to participation.

Meanwhile, Reynolds did not work well with coalition partner Progressive Democrats led by Desmond O'Malley. After a quarrel with O'Malley, Reynolds lost a vote of confidence in November and called for new elections. Fianna Fáil lost nine seats in the election, reducing their number to sixty-eight. Fortunately for Fianna Fáil, Fine Gael lost ten seats and with just forty-five lessened the likelihood they could form an anti–Fianna Fáil coalition. Labour was the big winner in 1992, adding seventeen seats for a total of thirty-three. Reynolds was able to form a coalition with Labour's Dick Spring, who became Tánaiste.

Reynolds became involved in another controversial issue, this one of a pedophile priest in 1994. Reynolds had appointed former attorney general Harry Whelehan as president of the High Court, but it was revealed that while attorney general, Whelehan had delayed the extradition to Northern Ireland of the child-molesting priest. When Reynolds refused to withdraw Whelehan's name for the High Court, Labour leader Dick Spring announced his party's withdrawal from the coalition. Reynolds was forced to resign as Taoiseach in November, and Ahern was unanimously elected as the new leader of Fianna Fáil. Ahern was unable to repair the Labour alliance, so that Fine Gael, with forty-seven seats, combined with Spring's thirty-two-member Labour party and six Progressive Democrats to form a coalition. Fine Gael's Bruton was elected Taoiseach, and Spring became Tánaiste and minister of foreign affairs. The Democratic Left, created in a 1992 split with the Workers' party, elected five TDs in 1994.

A native Dubliner, Bruton took a degree in economics at University College, Dublin, and received a law degree from King's Inn. He became the youngest TD when elected to the Dáil in 1969 for county Meath. Quickly Bruton became the Fine Gael spokesman for agricultural policy. His first cabinet post at Industry and Energy in 1983 was followed by promotion to Finance in 1986, where he orchestrated a 50 percent increase in the value-added tax.

American-style political scandal became a standard political feature of the 1990s. The headline scandal implicated former Taoiseach Haughey in 1997 for receiving, in exchange for political favors, a £1.3 million payoff from wealthy supermarket owner Ben Dunne. Haughey was indicted in 1999 for interfering in a judicial inquiry of the Dunne payments (bribes); his trial was scheduled to begin in 2000. In April 2000, Haughey agreed to pay £1 million in back taxes owed for the Dunne gifts. Other revelations suggested that Dunne had bribed Fine Gael and Labour party members as well. The following October, the Fianna Fáil minister for foreign affairs, Ray Burke, resigned because of charges he had received illegal payments regarding an urban development in county Dublin. The Flood Tribunal in 2000 revealed that real estate lobbyist Frank Dunlap in 1991–1992 bribed fifteen Dublin city and county councillors (including Fianna Fáil and Fine Gael party members) to rezone land for the Quarryvale shopping mall.

In response to corruption, the Dáil passed the Ethics in Public Office Act (1995), but it covered only government employees and not members of the Oireachtas or judges. TDs and judges were included in the Prevention of Corruption Act (2000), which made "corruption in public office" a crime. Calling for a purging of the corruption trend in a June 2000 speech at St. Patrick's cathedral, President Mary McAleese cited institutional failures in the civic community and the churches for allowing self-interest to override public service. Labour introduced a Dáil bill in 2000 to abolish corporate election contributions, but it was opposed by Fianna Fáil. Fine Gael favored a £3,000 cap on all contributions and full public disclosure.

Although income tax brackets were reduced in 1989 from four—ranging from 25 percent to 60 percent—to two (27 percent and 48 percent), the average marginal income tax rate rose from 39.5 percent in 1980 to 56 percent in 1994, making taxation a political issue. Both Fianna Fáil and Fine Gael promised to cut taxes as well as to reduce rising crime and unemployment. An economic recovery very likely saved Fianna Fáil from defeat. While revenues had grown from £8.6 billion in 1987 to £15.7 billion in 1996, the 1987 deficit of £192 million had been replaced by a £160 million surplus in 1996. Best of all for Fianna Fáil, the inflation rate had fallen to just 1.2 percent in 1997, lower than that of Britain. The GDP had risen 7.8 percent from 1993 to 1996, more than twice the British rate and four times the increase for Japan. The two largest sources of revenue, income taxes (32 percent of total) and sales (including value-added) taxes (40 percent), were both greater than EU averages (26 and 32 percent).

Thus, the June 1997 election returned Fianna Fáil to power with seventy-seven seats. Fine Gael gained eleven seats for a total of fifty-four. The big losers were Ruari Quinn's Labour party, which dropped fourteen down to a mere seventeen seats, and the Progressive Democrats, who fell from ten to four seats. Patricia Howard's Green Alliance party added one for a total of two; the Socialist party won its first seat; and Sinn Féin also won its first contest since 1922. There were six independents. Although the Democratic Left held its four seats in 1997, they decided to merge with the Labour party in February 1999. Fianna Fáil allied with the four Progressive Democrats and four independents to form a government with Ahern as Taoiseach. Progressive Democrat leader Mary Harney achieved the highest cabinet rank for a woman as Tánaiste and minister of employment and enterprise.

The economy's continued improvement offered the key strength to Ahern's government. Ireland's low investment taxes attracted additional foreign companies, which added needed jobs. Complementing the dramatic growth of the Irish computer software industry in the 1990s was the April 2000 announcement that American Home Products Corporation, a U.S. pharmaceutical giant, would spend $1 billion to build a 1 million square foot production facility near Dublin that would employ 1,200, the largest single industrial investment in Irish history. Also in 2000, another American firm, Lucent Technologies, announced an expansion of its facility outside Dublin. A 200,000 square foot building would be erected at a cost of $150 million, which would add 500 new jobs, for a total of 1,100 in Ireland. Also in April, a British clothing company, Morrison Outlets, announced the construction of an outlet mall in county Laois at a cost of £21 million (British sterling) or $31.5 million, which would create 400 jobs.

President Mary Robinson announced in September 1997 she would step down a couple of months before the end of her term in order to accept appointment as United Nations high commissioner for human rights. In the presidential election that followed in November, four women contested for the office. Fianna Fáil's Mary McAleese became the Republic's second woman president, defeating Fine Gael's Mary Banotti, a member of the European Parliament. A former resident of Northern Ireland who held dual British-Irish citizenship, McAleese had supported Sinn Féin but unlike Robinson had opposed legalizing abortion and divorce.

The Republic held the presidency of the European Union's executive council in 1975, 1979, 1984, and 1990, making a reputation for protecting small-state rights. Fianna Fáil did better in the European Parliament elections of 1994, adding two seats for a total of seven. But in the 1999 elections with a 50 percent turnout, they were reduced to six. Fine Gael retained its four seats, Labour held one seat and the Green party won two, the same as 1994. Environmental issues seemed more significant in the European Parliament than in the Dáil. A 1982 European Union study named Dublin the "most polluted" capital of the member states. A survey by the Department of Environment in 2000 showed an ambivalent attitude by most Irish toward environmental protection.

CULTURAL CHANGES IN THE REPUBLIC

One of the most notable cultural developments among the younger generation by the 1970s was the women's movement, which took its cue from feminist organizations in Europe and the United States. Republic membership in the European Community after 1973 at the least greatly stimulated change in women's issues. A December 1972 report by the Commission on the Status of Women made several significant proposals, which included an end to sex discrimination in hiring, equal pay for women, maternity and day care provisions for working women, and the availability of family planning advice. Women made up 27 percent of the nation's workforce by 1971. A state Council for the Status of Women was created as a result of the commission recommendations.

Gradually women acquired a greater role in a variety of areas in the Republic, but political parties did not assume a leadership position. In July 1973 the bar against married women serving in the civil service was terminated. Complementing the Nondiscriminatory Pay Act of 1974, the Employment Equality Act of 1977 set up an Employment Equality Agency with Sylvia Meehan as chair. Various firsts for women included ambassador for the Republic (1973), pilot for Aer Lingus flights (1979), justice on the High Court (1980), and chair of the Seanad (1982).

In elected political office, the gains were no faster. Only twenty-five women had been elected to the Seanad from 1922 to 1977, and only six women won seats in the Dáil in the 1977 election. However, things changed by the 1990s; the election of 1992 placed twenty women in the Dáil. The first woman cabinet member, Fianna Fáil's Maire Geoghagen-Quinn, was appointed in 1979, and the first senior cabinet post of health and social welfare was given to Labour's Eileen Desmond in 1981. The climax of women's gains was the election of Labour's Mary Robinson, member of the Seanad, as president in 1990. Mary McAleese became the second woman president in the election of 1997. Fianna Fáil pledged in 1991 to employ women in 40 percent of civil service posts, yet by mid-2000 had achieved only 27 percent.

Entwined with the women's movement were several legal-constitutional issues. An amendment to ban the importation of contraceptives (including birth control pills) had been enacted in 1935. Although contraceptives became available through the Family Planning Association after 1969, only a handful of family planning clinics existed by the 1970s in a few cities. However, polls reflected a decline in opposition to the availability of contraceptives from 63 percent in 1971 to 23 percent in 1977. Yet the Catholic hierarchy sustained its opposition to contraceptives. Following the rejection by the Dáil in 1974 of a bill to allow limited sale of contraceptives, the ban was challenged on constitutional grounds. In a landmark decision in 1977, the Supreme Court ruled that the government ban on the importation of contraceptives was unconstitutional. The next Dáil passed the limited sale measure (through pharmacies with prescriptions) in 1979, and in 1985 the Dáil permitted open sales of contraceptives.

Another issue that involved both women and the Catholic church was abortion, which was not banned in the 1922 or 1937 constitutions. Ireland's illegitimacy rate of less than 4 percent from the 1920s to the 1960s was the lowest in Europe. Yet the rate inched above 6 percent by the 1980s and peaked at 20 percent in 1995, a marked contrast to earlier eras. A referendum on a prolife, antiabortion constitutional amendment was approved by the Dáil in April 1983. The amendment passed by a two-to-one popular vote margin. The 1992 election included three proposed abortion amendments: one to broaden the grounds for abortion to cover events such as rapes, another to allow public information about abortions, and a third to allow Irish women to travel abroad to obtain abortions. The first abortion amendment to liberalize exceptions was defeated, but the other two, allowing publicity about abortions and travel outside the country for abortions, were approved. The denial of civil divorce was another concern raised by the women's movement. A referendum on a constitutional amendment to allow civil divorces was defeated in 1986, but a similar referendum narrowly passed in 1995 by 818,000 to 809,000.

By the mid-1980s, intellectuals such as Liam de Paor (*The Peoples of Ireland*) and Kevin O'Connor (*The Irish in Britain*) pointed to Ireland's youth as the main source of an identity crisis growing out of cultural pluralism. The younger generation sought to shed the old nationalist shibboleths—race, language, Catholicism—while remaining true to Ireland. The new ideology was called "pragmatism" by O'Connor, by which he meant a more flexible cultural-political attitude reflected by declining support for the Irish language and ambivalence about unification with Northern Ireland. Certainly the loosening of the Gaelic-language requirements, put in place during the Free State era, heralded a degree of cultural change. An end to the Gaelic language exam for a leaving certificate from the schools was approved in April 1973, though the compulsory instruction of Gaelic in primary and secondary schools remained. In November 1974, the government agreed to stop requiring civil servants to know Gaelic. A further social influence was materialism, which integrated Ireland's youth as never before with Western culture.

The diverse Anglo-Irish literary tradition of W. B. Yeats was carried forward by Seamus Heaney, who grew up Catholic in Protestant-dominated Ulster. Forced to come to grips with the social-political tensions of Northern Ireland, Heaney remembered his youth when Protestants and Catholics communed peacefully in the neighborhood. His interest in poetry, especially the romantics, grew while he was a student at Queen's University, Belfast. Like Yeats, Heaney appreciated both Irish and English literary contributions. After his first book of poems, *Death of a Naturalist*, was published in 1966, he spent several years teaching at Queen's. Beginning a series of visiting professorships in the United States in the early 1970s, Heaney broadened his perspective upon the interaction of politics and culture. While living in the Republic, Heaney published *North* (1975), which applied understanding rather than polemic to the full-blown Ulster crisis of the decade. In 1984, Heaney was named Boylston Professor of Rhetoric and Oratory at Harvard University, and in 1989 he was elected professor of poetry in Oxford University. He continued to publish widely noticed poetry and critical essays during the 1980s. Seamus Heaney was awarded the Nobel Prize for literature in 1995, completing the comparison with Yeats. In 1999, Heaney issued a magnificent new translation of *Beowulf*, hailed by critics and read by thousands in the English-speaking world.

Many poets and writers clung to Gaelic, determined that it would project traditions of the past into the future. Poets such as Máirtín Ó Direáin, who grew up in the Aran Islands, showed both a nostalgia for the past and attachment to Ireland's beautiful if sometimes harsh environment. The Gaeltacht area of western county Cork inspired native Seán Ó Riordáin long after he became a professor at University College, Cork. Ó Riordáin revered Irish devotion to family in his poems. Perhaps the most talented poet of the late twentieth century was the award-winning Medbh McGuckian, a Catholic native of Ulster who was educated at Queen's University, Belfast. Her lyrical poetry caused one critic to describe her as an "Irish Emily Dickinson." McGuckian imitated her mentor Heaney in weaving evocative images with real-life experiences. Most of her subjects related to domestic relations or nature. In works such as *The Flower Master* (1982) and *Venus and the Rain* (1984), McGuckian relied on haunting metaphors that span history from the classical era to the present to portray contemporary reality.

An even greater offbeat realism emerged in the writings of poet-novelist-playwright Dermot Bolger, who almost singlehandedly shredded Irish stereotypes popular in the United States and England. With no postsecondary education, eighteen-year-old Bolger founded the Raven Arts Press in the late 1970s and remained its editor until 1992. His 1986 poem, "The Lament for Arthur Cleary," reflected a female working-class cultural perspective set in the seedy quarters of Dublin, and was later adapted for the stage by Bolger. His 1987 novel, *The Woman's Daughter*, tells the story of a mother who abused and confined her daughter for seventeen years, leading the traumatized girl to fantasize about the outside world. In *The Journey Home* (1990), Bolger's teenage principal character relates the murderous consequences of opposition to corrupt politicians, a new and unfamiliar Irish phenomenon. In 1992's *Emily's Shoes*, the utter loneliness of an orphan reared by an aunt causes Emily to play with shoes.

Ireland's people and history gained major attention in the English-speaking world through the popularity of Irish-American Frank McCourt's *Angela's Ashes* (1996), which won the American Pulitzer Prize for literature in 1997. McCourt's nonjudgmental (mixing humor with pathos) recounting of a life of poverty and family struggles with his father's alcoholism focused on his mother, Angela, striving to beg, borrow, and employ thrift to keep the family going. The book became a motion picture in 2000.

NORTHERN IRELAND, 1967–2000

Responding to the failure of reform initiatives by Northern Ireland Prime Minister Terence O'Neill (1963–1969), the Northern Ireland Civil Rights Association (NICRA) was founded in February 1967 to promote change, including the principle of one man, one vote. The association was modeled after American civil rights organizations, which had carried several initiatives for minority rights in the United States. The idea was to avoid emphasis on the traditional nationalist goal of ending partition and instead seek equal opportunity for the Catholic minority under the existing government in the areas of jobs, education, housing, and voting rights. The association also called for the elimination of the police auxiliary B-specials and repeal of the Special Powers Act (1922) allowing arbitrary detainment of suspects. The association began public marches in Belfast and other cities during the summer of 1968, clashing with Protestant groups as well as the Royal Ulster Constabulary.

British Labour Prime Minister Harold Wilson admitted that problems existed for the Catholic minority and sought cooperation between Northern Ireland and the Republic. He urged O'Neill to move quickly in response to NICRA demands. O'Neill's five-point plan focused primarily on central government authority replacing that of local government councils, and also pledged to review the Special Powers Act. Whatever chance might have existed for progress disappeared when violence ensued by extremists on both sides. The Catholic civil rights leadership split over whether to pursue conciliation or further pressure. Hard-line unionists were spurred to resistance by the Presbyterian Reverend Ian Paisley, who exploited palpable Protestant fears of becoming a persecuted minority if Northern Ireland merged into the Republic. Paisley had founded the paramilitary Ulster Volunteer Force (UVF) in 1966.

Further clashes between the Catholic People's Democracy movement and Protestants in January 1969 raised questions about British intervention. When the February elections to Northern Ireland's Parliament revealed a unionist split, O'Neill submitted his resignation in April. The newly appointed prime minister, James Chichester-Clark, a former army officer, saw his primary task to restore order. As violence concentrated in Derry and Belfast continued during the summer, Britain was forced to take an increasingly larger role in Northern Ireland's affairs. Wilson's seven-point "Downing Street declaration" in August tried to address some of the Catholic concerns while at the same time assuring Protestants that any constitutional changes would be submitted to a popular vote.

Violence reached a peak in 1970 after the Provisional Irish Republican Army (PIRA), with Joe Cahill as its head, broke away from the official IRA. The Republic navy intercepted an IRA arms shipment in 1973 with Cahill on board; he was sentenced to three years in prison. Seamus Twomey assumed leadership of the PIRA in 1971, but he was also arrested and sentenced to prison by the Republic in 1973. The Provos were sustained by steady Irish American funding support, mainly through the Irish Northern Aid Committee (usually designated NORAID), founded by Michael Flannery in New York City in 1969. NORAID planted one hundred local chapters in northeastern United States cities and raised $5 million by 1987. In 1977, the U.S. government required NORAID to register as an agent of the Provisional IRA. Flannery was succeeded in 1988 by Martin Galvin as head of NORAID. Most of the monies collected by NORAID were used to purchase weapons for the Provisional IRA, a large portion of those weapons coming from Libya. The PIRA was soon joined by an even more radical republican group, the Irish National Liberation Army (1975).

Loyalist response to PIRA initiatives was to expand their own paramilitary organizations. The Ulster Defense Association (UDA), founded in 1971, joined Paisley's UVF. The most radical unionist group, concentrating on indiscriminate assassination of Catholics, was the Ulster Freedom Fighters (UFF), organized in 1973. Protestant paramilitaries received most of their arms and financing from unionist sympathizers in Great Britain.

The Royal Ulster Constabulary had to be placed under British authority and regular British army troops brought in to separate the two sides. Britain ordered the disbanding of the B-specials in 1970, replaced by the Ulster Defence Regiment, a branch of the British army. In part because of its Protestant makeup, the UDR was disbanded in 1992. Meanwhile, armed clashes continued unabated. Although government leaders changed—Conservative Edward Heath succeeded Wilson as Britain's prime minister and Brian Faulkner (1971–1972) took Chichester-Clark's spot in Northern Ireland—little changed in Ulster. In August 1971, Britain inaugurated a controversial internment policy, something that the Republic itself had used at times against the IRA. When British troops killed thirteen Catholic demonstrators in Derry's infamous "Bloody Sunday" (1972), bringing the number of deaths from violent clashes and bombings to 467, Britain suspended the Northern Ireland government and initiated direct British rule. William Whitelaw was named secretary of state for Northern Ireland with cabinet rank.

Meanwhile, two moderate parties made their appearance in 1970. Succeeding the old Nationalist party, the Catholic Social Democratic and Labour party (SDLP), headed by John Hume, focused on economic reforms and advocated a peaceful union with the Republic. Born in Derry and educated at Queen's University, Belfast, Hume had been both a teacher and a businessman before becoming involved in politics as a member of the NICRA. In the spirit of Parnell and Redmond, Hume revived the tradition of constitutional nationalism. The Alliance party appealed to liberal Protestants and Catholics, as well as women, to seek a middle ground on all issues. The injection of moderation was at best premature in the emotionally charged environment. Obviously, Britain hoped external governance would be short-lived, but restoration of local rule depended on cooperation among various unionist-nationalist elements, some of which had declared war against each other.

Britain's March 1973 white paper proposed a power-sharing executive and assembly once again based on proportional representation. The British Parliament authorized the creation of an eighty-seat assembly and a plural executive. Although unionist parties were predominant in the June elections, SDLP won nineteen seats and Alliance eight. Heath's government cultivated moderate nationalist and unionist sentiment in the

1973 Sunningdale Agreement wherein Taoiseach Liam Cosgrave agreed that the Republic would respect the wishes of the majority in Northern Ireland regarding partition. The Ulster Unionist, Alliance, and SDLP parties also initialed the agreement. The Republic agreed to accommodate the majority-rule policy, though constitution Articles 2 and 3 referring to Northern Ireland as part of the Republic were deemed intact by the Supreme Court of the Republic. In return for Cosgrave's concessions, Heath promised to reestablish the Council of Ireland with representatives from the Republic and Britain as well as Northern Ireland to discuss the cause of peace and cooperation.

The creation of a local government and the Sunningdale declaration were not greeted favorably by Paisley's radical unionists concerned about security issues. In May 1974, the Protestant Ulster Workers Council authorized a successful strike backed by Paisley's Democratic Unionist party (created in 1971). The strike forced Faulkner to suspend the assembly, and direct British rule was resumed. In July 1974, Britain's Parliament enacted recommendations of a white paper calling for a constitutional convention to be elected by proportional representation. The convention met from May 1975 to March 1976 chaired by Sir Robert Lowry, but delegates could not agree on the appropriate form of government, voting forty-two to thirty-one against a power-sharing executive. Political failure invited more violence; the PIRA exploded fifty bombs in Northern Ireland and Britain during late 1978. Prime Minister Margaret Thatcher's Conservative party government proposed yet another power-sharing assembly in 1982, but Hume's SDLP members refused to take their seats, leaving only Unionists as participants. Thatcher met with Unionist leaders Paisley (DUP) and James Molyneaux (Ulster Unionist party) along with Hume in 1986, seeking to resolve the differences. Hume seemed amenable to Thatcher's suggestions, prompting the radical unionists to stage another strike, forcing the dissolution of the assembly in June.

British Labour's Fair Employment Act (1976) intended to end Northern Ireland job discrimination, but it contained important loopholes and did not end concerns among Catholics about fair treatment. Thatcher pushed for the enactment of a 1989 fair employment law to close loopholes in the 1976 measure by establishing a Fair Employment Commission. Meanwhile, the cost to British taxpayers of direct rule mushroomed. The British subvention (subsidy) for Northern Ireland rose from £74 million in 1968–1969 to £620 million in 1976–1977 and continued to escalate to £1.5

billion in 1987–1988. By 1982–1983, the per capita public expenditure in Northern Ireland had surpassed other United Kingdom regions (England, Scotland, Wales).

British efforts to curb violence by extremists led to the adoption of some dubious measures. Although in 1973 Britain repealed Stormont's infamous Special Powers Act, which had allowed repression of disloyal Catholics, its replacement, the Emergency Provisions Act (1973), created the equally controversial Diplock courts, allowing trial of suspected terrorists without a jury. The suspension of jury trials was deemed necessary because of threats of violence by the PIRA upon jurors. Law-abiding Catholics decried the British system as a denial of constitutional protections. Ten PIRA prisoners held at Maze Prison in Belfast participating in a hunger strike in 1981 died, with international media reporting the events.

Meanwhile, Thatcher's government resumed discussions at Hillsborough Castle with Taoiseach Garret FitzGerald over north-south relations, leading to the Anglo-Irish Agreement of 1985. The pact called for establishment of an Anglo-Irish Intergovernmental Conference, co-chaired by the British secretary of state for Northern Ireland and the Republic's foreign minister. Regular meetings thereafter touched on issues such as border security, improving Catholic rights in Ulster, and expanding the economy in north and south through an international fund to stimulate foreign investment. Although the SDLP applauded British cooperation with the Republic, the unionist response was negative again with resignations of MPs from Parliament.

In the spring of 1991, the Unionist parties, along with Alliance and SDLP, agreed to new talks, and the Protestant paramilitaries announced a cease-fire during those negotiations led by Northern Ireland Secretary Peter Brooke (1989–1992). After disputes about the location of talks between Northern Ireland and the Republic impeded progress, the Protestant paramilitaries and PIRA resumed their militancy in May. Despite further Northern Ireland intraparty meetings in 1992, the Unionists withdrew from discussions in November.

Another Anglo-Irish initiative in December 1993 resulted in a pact between British Prime Minister John Major and the Republic Taoiseach Reynolds. The so-called Downing Street Declaration offered to pursue a fully representative, devolved government for Northern Ireland if the PIRA would agree to a cease-fire. Such a cease-fire was announced by the PIRA in August 1994 followed by similar Protestant paramilitary pledges in October. Negotiations were soon underway led by Britain and the Republic using the intermediary of a U.S. envoy, George Mitchell. Intense pressure was brought to bear on the warring parties in Northern Ireland to compromise their positions. Nonetheless, the Provos returned to bombings in February 1996, ending the cease-fire.

The crafting of yet another agreement to replace British direct rule with an elected multiparty government for Northern Ireland accompanied by an end to the violence was part of the so-called Good Friday Agreement in April 1998. The proposal included an elected assembly with proportional representation similar to that used in the Republic since 1922. A collective executive made up of ten ministers would represent the four main political parties: the SDLP headed by Hume and Sean Mallon, the Ulster Unionist party presided over by William David Trimble, Paisley's Democratic Unionist party, and Sinn Féin led by Gerry Adams, Martin Maguiness, and Pat Doherty. Unionists insisted that a key precondition to the formation of the executive would be the beginnings of disarmament by the PIRA, which supposedly could be achieved through Sinn Féin influence. Republicans gained the concession of a reform of the Royal Ulster Constabulary to make it more representative (only 8 percent of members were Catholic).

Although elections to the assembly proceeded on schedule, Unionists set a mid-1999 deadline for PIRA compliance with disarmament provisions. When a PIRA pledge was not forthcoming, Unionists announced they would not participate in the creation of the executive committee. The Good Friday bargain was on the verge of collapse and Mitchell was brought back to prop up the discussions. Pressure mounted on the PIRA to comply, and they finally agreed in late 1999. The formation of the multiparty executive went forward in December. Trimble became first minister in the cabinet, and SDLP's Mallon was named deputy head. Sinn Féin's two seats in the executive went to Adams and Maguiness. The Republic of Ireland fulfilled its obligations under the Good Friday Agreement to recognize Northern Ireland's existence by suspending Articles 2 and 3 in its constitution. David Trimble and John Hume received the 1998 Nobel Peace Prize for their leading roles in crafting the peace plan.

The new government's permanence depended on PIRA compliance to begin disarming within two months. General John de Chastelain headed a separate decommissioning agency charged with producing a detailed agenda for disarmament. When the PIRA commitment remained unfulfilled, the British minister, Peter Mandelson, threatened to terminate the new government and resume direct British control. Despite tremendous diplomatic pressures from British Prime Minister Tony Blair and Republic Taoiseach Bertie Ahern, Sinn Féin could not deliver an PIRA pledge, and the short-lived Northern Ireland government was suspended by Mandelson in February 2000. The deadline for progress on arms decommissioning was set for May, although Taoiseach Ahern and Prime Minister Blair sought to delink the resumption of devolved government with the decommissioning process. The return of direct British rule was followed by a challenge to David Trimble's leadership of the Ulster Unionist party. At a party convocation in March 2000, only 57 percent of the delegates supported Trimble, and the party passed a resolution rejecting the Good Friday peace clause changing the name of the Royal Ulster Constabulary.

A new breakthrough came in late May 2000 when the Ulster Unionist party council voted narrowly to return to power sharing with the other parties based merely on an PIRA pledge to allow the de Chastelain commission to inspect arms caches by early summer. The Northern Ireland executive reconvened in early June, but without participation of the two Democratic Unionist party councillors. Trimble (UUP) again became first minister, and SDLP's Mallon held the deputy first minister post. The representative assembly also began deliberations, raising hopes for cooperation to resolve historic differences in the Northern Ireland community. Meanwhile, the United Kingdom Parliament enacted a police bill that changed the name from the Royal Ulster Constabulary to the Police Service of Northern Ireland, required police recruitment on a fifty-fifty Protestant-Catholic ratio, and established a supervisory police board composed of political appointees.

The Irish are indeed a diverse people who have a rich history. Much of their history involved a struggle for freedom from occupying peoples. Since that objective was achieved finally in the separation from Great Britain in the twentieth century, Irish attention has focused upon building a nation-state. The achievement of that goal continues to be complicated by the division between north and south. Nonetheless, signs of cooperation have appeared with the lessening of anti-British feeling in the south and anti-Irish attitudes among the Protestant north. The growth of the economy has created new opportunities for Ireland's youth to merge into the material culture of Europe. Ireland's ability to maintain its distinctive cultural identity undoubtedly will be affected by its participation in the European Union. Yet, overall prospects for peace and prosperity for all Ireland are greater than ever before in its history.

Notable Persons in Irish History

Samuel Barclay Beckett (1906–1989), novelist and playwright; lived most of his career in Paris; most notable play *Waiting for Godot* (1953); won Nobel Prize for literature (1969).

George Berkeley (1685–1753), bishop of Coyne and philosopher; fellow of Trinity College; best work *A Treatise Concerning Principles of Human Knowledge* (1710).

Brian Boru (c.941–1014), "king of Ireland"; from Munster; came close to unifying Ireland; defeated Danes at Battle of Clontarf (1014) but was killed.

Edmund Burke (1729–1797), political philosopher and Whig party leader in British Parliament; championed cause of Irish Catholics in *A Tract on the Popery Laws* (1761).

James Butler (1610–1688), duke of Ormond and Charles II's lord lieutenant; pleaded for fair treatment of Catholics.

Michael Collins (1890–1922), republican revolutionary leader of Irish Republican Army; first commander of Irish Free State military.

Paul Cullen (1803–1878), conservative Catholic cleric and cardinal (1866); archbishop of Armagh (1850) and Dublin (1852); opposed Young Ireland and Irish Republican Brotherhood.

Thomas Osborne Davis (1814–1845), nationalist poet and cofounder of *Nation* (1842).

Eamon de Valera (1882–1975), leader of Sinn Féin and founder of Fianna Fáil party; chief executive under Irish Free State; Taoiseach and president in the Republic.

John Dillon (1851–1927), moderate nationalist head of parliamentary party; advocate of home rule and land reform.

Henry Grattan (1746–1820), Protestant political leader of Irish Parliament during legislative independence; supported Catholic emancipation.

Seamus Heaney (1939–   ), leading literary figure of late twentieth century; won Nobel Prize for literature in 1995.

James Joyce (1882–1941), expatriate novelist, author of *Dubliners* (1914) and *Portrait of the Artist as a Young Man* (1916).

Sean Lemass (1899–1971), leading Fianna Fáil economic adviser as minister of industry and commerce; succeeded Eamon de Valera as Taoiseach in 1959.

Diarmait MacMurrough (1110–1171), king of Leinster; invited Normans to Ireland.

Daniel O'Connell (1775–1847), nationalist "Liberator" who led Catholic emancipation campaign and opposition to Union before famine.

Rory O'Connor (?1116–1198), Irish king whose clash with Diarmait MacMurrough led to Anglo-Norman invasion and recognition of Henry II as king of Ireland.

Hugh O'Neill (1550–1616), earl of Tyrone; last Irish chieftain in Ulster to challenge English rule; exile opened way for colonization of Ulster.

Charles Stewart Parnell (1846–1891), key home rule leader of Irish parliamentary party; tainted with scandal involving Mrs. O'Shea.

Patrick (c.415–c.453), British missionary credited with first successful expansion of Christianity across Ireland.

Patrick Pearse (1879–1916), literary nationalist named president of the Republic at Easter Rebellion; executed thereafter.

John Redmond (1856–1918), moderate nationalist leader who succeeded Charles Parnell in promoting home rule bill.

Mary Robinson (1944–   ), first woman president of the Republic (1990–1997); United Nations high commissioner for human rights (1997–   ).

George Bernard Shaw (1856–1950), expatriate Irish playwright who won Nobel Prize for literature in 1926; best known in Ireland for *John Bull's Other Island* (1904).

Jonathan Swift (1667–1745), dean of St. Patrick's Cathedral; Anglo-Irish author of *Modest Proposal* (1729) and *Drapier's Letters* (1724), which criticized British policy in Ireland.

John Myllington Synge (1871–1909), playwright; wrote controversial comedy *Playboy of the Western World* (1907).

Theobald Wolfe Tone (1763–1798), republican leader of United Irishmen; committed suicide after failed rebellion of 1798.

Oscar Wilde (1854–1900), novelist; wrote *Picture of Dorian Gray* (1891) and *The Importance of Being Earnest* (1895).

William Butler Yeats (1865–1939), poet and playwright; poems include *The Tower* (1928) and *The Winding Stair* (1933); won Noble Prize for literature (1923).

Bibliographic Essay

Bibliographies of Irish history can be found in *Irish Historiography, 1936–1970*, edited by T. W. Moody (Dublin: Irish Committee of Historical Sciences, 1971), and *Irish Historiography, 1970–79*, edited by J. J. Lee (Cork: Cork University Press, 1981). The annual bibliography of British and Irish history has been published by the Royal Historical Society since 1976. There are also annual bibliographies in the professional journal *Irish Historical Studies*, published since 1936.

The most important ongoing scholarly project, sponsored by the Royal Irish Academy, is the multiauthor *New History of Ireland* published by Oxford University Press. Most of the planned volumes have been published: volume 2, *Medieval Ireland, 1169–1534*, edited by Art Cosgrove (1993); volume 3, *Early Modern Ireland, 1534–1691*, edited by T. W. Moody, F. X. Martin, and E. J. Byrne (1976); volume 4, *Eighteenth-Century Ireland, 1691–1800*, edited by T. W. Moody and W. E. Vaughan (1986); volume 5, *Ireland under the Union I, 1801–1870*, edited by W. E. Vaughan (1989); volume 6, *Ireland under the Union II, 1870–1921*, edited by W. E. Vaughan (1996); volume 8, *Chronology of Irish History to 1976* (1982); and volume 9, *Maps, Genealogies, Lists* (1983). The Longman Group has also embarked on an excellent history of Ireland series with Steven G. Ellis as series editor. Volumes published thus far in the series include Dáibhí

Ó Cróinin, *Early Medieval Ireland, 400–1200* (1995) and Steven G. Ellis, *Ireland in the Age of the Tudors, 1447–1603* (1998). Forthcoming volumes will be written by Robin Frame (1200–1447), David Hayton (1603–1735), Tom Bartlett and Kevin Whelan (1735–1870), and Mary Harris (1870–present).

Other period histories offering considerable detail include Michael J. O'Kelly, *Early Ireland: An Introduction to Irish Prehistory* (New York: Cambridge University Press, 1989), Goddard Henry Orpen, *Ireland under the Normans, 1169–1333* (4 vols.; Oxford: Clarendon Press, 1911–20), A. J. Otway-Ruthven, *A History of Medieval Ireland*, 2nd ed. (New York: St. Martin's Press, 1980), Edmund Curtis, *History of Medieval Ireland from 1086 to 1513*, 2nd ed. (London: Methuen, 1938), Richard Bagwell, *Ireland under the Tudors*, 3 vols. (London: Longmans, Green, 1885–1890), Richard Bagwell, *Ireland under the Stuarts*, 3 vols. (London: Longmans & Co., 1909–1916), Robert Brendan McDowell, *Ireland in the Age of Imperialism and Revolution, 1760–1801* (Oxford: Clarendon Press, 1979), and Alvin Jackson, *Ireland, 1798–1998* (Oxford: Blackwell, 1999).

Originally composed for a Radio Telefís Éireann series, the essays in T. W. Moody and F. X. Martin, *The Course of Irish History* (New York: Weybright and Talley, 1967), offer penetrating insights into many aspects of Irish history. The importance of religion in shaping early Ireland is revealed in Kathleen Hughes, *The Church in Early Irish Society* (Ithaca, N.Y.: Cornell University Press, 1966). The impact of early nineteenth-century nationalism on Irish culture is treated in R. B. McDowell, *Public Opinion and Government Policy, 1801–1846* (London: Faber & Faber, 1952). Among many good works on the Great Famine, the most comprehensive is Cormac Ó Gráda's *Black '47 and Beyond: The Great Irish Famine in History, Economy and Memory* (Princeton, N.J.: Princeton University Press, 1999). A comprehensive study of the home rule era is Alan O'Day, *Irish Home Rule, 1867–1921* (Manchester: Manchester University Press, 1998). Thomas Hennessey, *Dividing Ireland: World War I and Partition* (New York: Routledge, 1998), covers events such as the home rule bill, the Easter Rebellion, and the Irish Convention. A provocative personal interpretation of the twentieth century is Joseph Lee's *Ireland, 1912–1985* (New York: Cambridge University Press, 1989). Several works by Maria Luddy recount women's roles in Irish history. The best anthology of Irish literature is Maureen O'Rourke Murphy and James MacKillop, *Irish Literature: A Reader* (Syracuse, N.Y.: Syracuse University Press, 1987). For cultural history, see Terence Brown, *Ireland: A Social and Cultural History, 1922 to the Present* (Ithaca, N.Y.: Cornell University Press, 1985). An excellent explanation of modern economic history for nonspecialists is Cormac Ó Gráda, *A Rocky Road: The Irish Economy since the 1920s* (Manchester: Manchester University Press, 1997).

Among the profuse literature on Northern Ireland, see especially Paul Bew, Peter Gibbon, and Henry Patterson, *Northern Ireland, 1921–94: Political Forces and Social Classes* (London: Serif, 1995), and Tom Wilson, *Ulster: Conflict and Consent* (Oxford: Basil Blackwell, 1989).

Index

About the Author

DANIEL WEBSTER HOLLIS, III, is professor of history at Jacksonville State University, in Alabama, where he has taught for thirty years. He is the author of four books, the most recent being *The ABC-CLIO World History Companion to Utopian Movements* (1998). He has taught Irish history and published articles and delivered papers on Northern Ireland.